Calila

Campos Ibéricos
Bucknell Studies in Iberian Literatures and Cultures

General Editors:
Isabel Cuñado, Bucknell University
Jason McCloskey, Bucknell University

Campos Ibéricos is a series of monographs and edited volumes that focuses on the literary and cultural traditions of Spain in all of its rich historical, social, and linguistic diversity. The series provides a space for interdisciplinary and theoretical scholarship exploring the intersections between literature, culture, the arts, and media from medieval to contemporary Iberia. Studies on all authors, texts, and cultural phenomena are welcome and works on understudied writers and genres are specially sought.

Titles in the Series

Joan L. Brown, *Calila: The Later Novels of Carmen Martín Gaite*

Andrés Lema-Hincapié and Conxita Domènech, eds., *Indiscreet Fantasies: Iberian Queer Cinema*

Katie J. Vater, *Between Market and Myth: The Spanish Artist Novel in the Post-Transition, 1992–2014*

Perdona el tono de mi carta, pero a veces me gustaría retirarme a una isla desierta o volver a tener mi antiguo poder para soñar con ella. Parece, y todos lo vaticinan, que la época de las máquinas acabará aplastando por completo a la buena literatura. Yo, por si acaso, ya he alquilado un huerto en una ciudad imaginaria. Todavía no sé cómo se llama. Tal vez no tenga nombre.

Me encantó ver a Alex y Sarah con sus respectivos animales y su dulce e ingenua mirada. ¡Qué suerte tienes de poder convivir con una familia tan encantadora! Les deseo a esos niños lo mejor en la vida, como un hada anacrónica. Porque en mis deseos va incluido el de que no renuncien a sus sueños, fantasías e idealismo. Ni al riesgo.

Os quiere mucho vuestra Calila

Frontispiece: Letter from Carmen Martín Gaite to Joan L. Brown, 14 July 1997 (excerpt).
Source: Letter, gray paper with black ink, 8 × 8 ¼ in.

Frontispiece Transcription

Perdona el tono de mi carta, pero a veces me gustaría retirarme a una isla desierta o volver a tener mi antiguo poder para soñar con ella. Parece, y todos lo vaticinan, que la época de las máquinas acabará aplastando por completo a la buena literatura. Yo, por si acaso, ya he alquilado un huerto en una ciudad imaginaria. Todavía no sé cómo se llama. Tal vez no tenga nombre.

Me encantó ver a Alex y Sarah con sus respectivos animales y su dulce e ingenua mirada. ¡Qué suerte tienes de poder convivir con una familia tan encantadora! Les deseo a esos niños lo mejor en la vida, como un hada anacrónica. Porque en mis deseos va incluido el de que no renuncien a sus sueños, fantasías e idealismo. Ni al riesgo.

Os quiere mucho vuestra Calila

———

[Forgive the tone of my letter, but sometimes I'd like to retreat to a desert island or go back to having my old power to conjure one up. It appears, and everyone predicts, that the age of technology will ultimately overwhelm good literature completely. Just in case, I have leased a garden in an imaginary city. I don't know yet what it's called. Maybe it has no name.

I was delighted to see Alex and Sarah with their respective animals and their sweet and trusting faces. You are so lucky to be able to live with such a charming family! I wish those children the best in life, like a timeless fairy godmother. Because among my wishes are that they never give up their dreams, fantasies, and idealism. And that they never shy away from risk.

You are much loved by your Calila]

Calila

The Later Novels of Carmen Martín Gaite

JOAN L. BROWN

Bucknell | UNIVERSITY
UNIVERSITY | PRESS

LEWISBURG, PENNSYLVANIA

Names: Brown, Joan Lipman, author.
Title: Calila : the later novels of Carmen Martín Gaite / Joan L. Brown.
Description: Lewisburg, Pennsylvania : Bucknell University Press, [2021] |
    Includes bibliographical references and index.
Identifiers: LCCN 2020027830 | ISBN 9781684483051 (paperback ; alk. paper) |
    ISBN 9781684483068 (cloth ; alk. paper) | ISBN 9781684483075 (epub) |
    ISBN 9781684483082 (mobi) | ISBN 9781684483099 (pdf)
Subjects: LCSH: Martín Gaite, Carmen—Criticism and interpretation.
Classification: LCC PQ6623.A7657 Z58 2021 | DDC 863/.64—dc23
LC record available at https://lccn.loc.gov/2020027830

A British Cataloging-in-Publication record for this book is available from the
British Library.

⊖ The paper used in this publication meets the requirements of the American National
Standard for Information Sciences—Permanence of Paper for Printed Library Materials,
ANSI Z39.48-1992.

www.bucknelluniversitypress.org

Distributed worldwide by Rutgers University Press

Manufactured in the United States of America

To Mark and our cherished friend Calila

Contents

Illustrations

Calila

Introduction

CALILA AND HER LATER NOVELS

Carmen Martín Gaite (1925–2000) was my dear friend for a quarter of a century (figure I.1). I first met her in the mid-seventies when I was a graduate student in Spanish at the University of Pennsylvania. Disappointed by the absence of women on our reading lists, I asked the eminent professor Gonzalo Sobejano the question that would shape my future: Were there any great contemporary woman writers from Spain that I had not heard of? He sent me to the library with a list of several women authors. The works of the first two were unremarkable, and today no one remembers their names. But the third author was wonderful and amazing: Carmen Martín Gaite. When I read her novels (at that time she had written only three) I was enthralled. Oblivious of the fact that no one at Penn had ever written a dissertation on a living writer—much less a woman author—I chose Martín Gaite's literature as my dissertation topic, with Gonzalo Sobejano as my director. When I had finished the dissertation I traveled from Philadelphia to Madrid for a single appointment with Carmen Martín Gaite. From that day in 1976 when she opened the door of her apartment to greet me, we became friends. I was just a few years older than her daughter Marta and was welcomed warmly by both. Gradually I got to know her family, and she got to know mine. We shared milestones in each other's lives. When I went to Madrid I stayed in her home, and when she came to Philadelphia she stayed with us. After a couple of years, she asked me to call her by the name that her closest friends and daughter used: Calila.[1]

Our professional relationship was mutually supportive. She insisted on writing what would be her only autobiography for my 1987 book on her fiction, *Secrets from the Back Room: The Fiction of Carmen Martín Gaite*, and that book in turn helped spread her fame. (Some of our experiences in both Spain and the United States are documented in her posthumously published *Cuadernos de todo* [Notebooks about everything] and *Visión de Nueva York* [Vision of New York].) By the time she began writing her novels of the 1990s, I was more friend than critic.

Figure I.1. Joan L. Brown and Carmen Martin Gaite at the University of
Delaware, 1979

She would ruminate about the novels in her letters, and when I visited her in
Madrid she would read aloud passages of her current novel-in-progress from one
of her notebooks. During this period we became collaborators on our own project:
an "action-learning" conversational Spanish textbook for North American students that we called *Conversaciones creadoras* [Creative conversations], for
which she wrote original unfinished vignettes in dialogue form; the book is now
in its fourth edition. My trips to Spain were nearly always in the late spring or
early summer. She loved the Feria del Libro de Madrid [Madrid Book Fair] and
often invited me to accompany her in late May when it opened, so some years I
was able to get hot-off-the-press copies of her latest novel as it was introduced
there. I vividly recall the experience of the two of us being trailed by television
crews as she strolled past the line of bookstore stalls in Retiro Park, every inch
the reigning monarch: La Reina de la Feria del Libro [Queen of the Book Fair].
Sometimes fans gave her flowers. One book inscription (in a novel by Mexican
author Elena Poniatowska) reads: "Recuerdo de nuestra visita a la Feria del Libro,
en el día de su inauguración, 25 de mayo de 1990, yo de rojo y negro, y tú de seda
azul, las dos con claveles blancos en la mano. Calila" [Souvenir of our visit to
the Book Fair, the day of its inauguration, 25 May 1990. I was dressed in red and
black and you in blue silk, both of us holding white carnations] (Book dedication to Brown, *La "Flor de Lis"* [The "fleur de lys"]). Some of her novels of the
nineties arrived by mail, usually sent by her though occasionally shipped directly

from the publisher. When each book arrived I read it avidly, beginning with her handwritten dedication, often decorated with drawings and stickers. But I felt too close to the novels, and to her, to write about them dispassionately. Instead I turned my research to the larger issue of why she and other brilliant women writers had been largely excluded from the Hispanic literary canon, an investigation that led to a broader study of the Spanish and Spanish-American literary canon in the twenty-first century (*Confronting Our Canons*).

It has now been many years since I heard her voice, and her last letter carries a date from the previous century. My critical perspective on the works of Carmen Martín Gaite has recovered its objectivity. In this book, as in any scholarly study, she will be referred to as "Martín Gaite" or "the author." Nevertheless, my friend Calila contributed to these chapters, with insights from our conversations and correspondence over more than two decades. Except for one early letter that I shared in her *Obras completas* [Complete works] ("Carta"), none of our correspondence has been published. The author's sister and heir, Ana María (Anita) Martín Gaite (1924–2019), who was my friend for even longer than the author, trusted me to publish or quote from her sister's letters. She knew that the author considered me her "amiga, exégeta y albacea testamentaria de mis escritos" [friend, exegete and designated executor of my writings] as she wrote in 1983 (Book dedication to Brown, *El cuento de nunca acabar* [The never-ending story]). But Anita did not trust everyone. As is by now well known, she destroyed most of her sister's personal correspondence immediately after her death, motivated by a desire to protect her privacy. Anita did share a trove with the world, however, placing the Carmen Martín Gaite archive with a private foundation that promised to make it accessible to scholars. Her papers and photographs are now housed in a library in Valladolid and in an indexed collection online (Archivo Carmen Martín Gaite). The author's country home in El Boalo has also been made into a "casa-museo" [house-museum] thanks to Anita's efforts.

My aim with this book is to call attention to the fascinating novels that Martín Gaite wrote during the most prolific decade of her career. A reward for delaying my study of these works is that scholars have by now contributed important insights into each of them—criticism that is incorporated into the chapters to come. Each core chapter is devoted to a single novel. The novels are presented in the order in which they were published to highlight the author's trajectory, but chapters also can be read independently.[2] Every chapter has an overview of the work including relevant history (her own and Spain's), followed by original analysis supported by appropriate secondary sources. Chapter 1 supplies background on Martín Gaite's life and literature. Chapter 2 is devoted to *Caperucita en Manhattan* [Red Riding Hood in Manhattan] (1990). This fantastic young adult novel set in New York City—ahead of its time in Spain and beloved around the world—enabled Martín Gaite to return to fiction writing after a long absence. Chapter 3 features the second-most-studied work in the author's oeuvre, after her National Prize–winning *El cuarto de atrás* (1978) [*The Back Room* 1983]. *Nubosidad variable* (1992) [*Variable Cloud* 1995] is an epistolary novel that invokes third-wave feminism, narrated by two fascinating women in post-Transition Spain. Chapter 4 examines *La Reina de las Nieves* (1994) [*The Farewell Angel* 1999], a collage-like novel with a twentysomething male protagonist. This novel uses conventions of fairy tales and detective fiction to recover Spain's "lost generation" (lost to heroin and AIDS during the transition to democracy). Chapter 5 analyzes *Lo raro es vivir* (1996) [*Living's the Strange Thing* 2004], a Proustian memoir of maternal-filial love and an exploration of existential doubts in precarious times. Chapter 6 addresses *Irse de casa* [Leaving home] (1998), a tapestry of interrelated stories surrounding a successful woman's quest for fulfillment in the provincial Spanish town of her youth. Chapter 7 examines *Los parentescos* [Family relations] (2001), the posthumously published, nearly finished metaliterary bildungsroman or novel of development about a gifted young man who tries to decipher family secrets. Though techniques vary, these novels are unified by an enduring theme: the search for identity and meaning through examination of the past, in order to attain a brighter future.

My hope is that others will discover that the "second half" of Martín Gaite's novelistic production, comprising her six novels from the 1990s, is as compelling as her previous five novels from the 1950s to 1981 (the period covered in *Secrets from the Back Room*). These later novels are fascinating as a record of the author's personal journey, as she recovered from the death of her only child, and as chronicle of Spain's evolution after Franco, who rose to power in the Civil War of 1936–1939 and dominated the country until 1975. All but the first novel (set in New York City) offer a window into the realities of contemporary Spain. They elucidate the transition to democratic rule from the mid-1970s to the mid-1980s, the post-Transition expansion that encompassed Spain's triumphalist year of 1992, and the changeover to a conservative government (with its fascist contingent) that began in 1996. Issues explored in these late-twentieth-century novels continue to resonate today, from women's self-actualization to the state of the earth's environment to the vicissitudes of the modern family to uncontrolled plagues to the recovery of historical memory. Readers will find another reason to appreciate Martín Gaite's later novels: they offer immense reading pleasure. All of them display her virtuosity as a novelist. Characters and plots are developed in language that is at once precise and lyrical, with original metaphors, sharp dialogues, pithy observations, and unexpected plot twists. All six novels demonstrate the power of a mature author who knows how to capture—and hold—the reader's attention. This is not surprising, since Martín Gaite cared most of all about her readers, describing her fiction as a "bridge" to others that would not serve unless it was both "firm" and "well-made" ("The Virtues of Reading" 351).

English translations are supplied here for all Spanish citations, to make this bridge accessible to all who are interested in European literature by women, the contemporary novel, and Spain's recent past. Published translations are used whenever available. When no English version exists (or when the English version needs clarification) I have provided my own translations from the original Spanish source. Any discrepancies in these translations are wholly my responsibility. Unlike other translators of Martín Gaite novels who had the benefit of her counsel, I did not have the option of asking my friend Calila for guidance, much as I longed to do so.

CHAPTER 1

Backstory

CARMEN MARTÍN GAITE'S EARLIER
LIFE AND LITERATURE

The later stage of Martín Gaite's career is best appreciated in the context of her earlier life and works, up to and including the publication of her most famous novel. Carmen Martín Gaite's life story is as intriguing as her literature.[1] She was the brilliant, beautiful girl from the provinces of Spain who grew up to become a world-renowned author. Of all Spanish writers, she is the only one to publish continuously over half a century, chronicling the most tumultuous era in the country's modern history. The list of superlatives associated with her name is long. She was the first woman to win Spain's Premio Nacional de Literatura [National Prize for Literature], and the only person to win it twice—the second time for lifetime achievement (the Premio Nacional de las Letras Españolas [National Prize for Spanish Literature]). Martín Gaite earned many other major literary prizes, both for individual works (such as the Premio Nadal [Nadal Prize]) and for her contributions over a lifetime, including the Premio Príncipe de Asturias [Prince of Asturias Prize], awarded by the man who is now king of Spain, Felipe VI. On the international stage, she was the first Spanish woman to be named an honorary fellow of the Modern Language Association, joining an elite set of the world's most esteemed contemporary authors—a group that had only three Spaniards when she was inducted.

Martín Gaite is her country's most-studied contemporary woman author, according to the *MLA International Bibliography*. Her status as a subject of academic study reflects scholars' appreciation of her writing, and this enjoyment extends to the reading public. Her books have been translated into English and more than a half-dozen other languages, winning prizes for literature in translation in France and Italy. Her novels have remained in print from the time they appeared, engaging new readers with their riveting stories, masterful prose, inventive forms, and astute depictions of society. Though she is best known as a novelist, Martín Gaite contributed to nearly every literary genre, from novellas and short stories to essays, reviews, literary theory, screenplays, poetry, dramas, children's stories, and television miniseries. She held a doctorate in literary and cultural studies from the University of Madrid and published acclaimed books on Spanish literature and culture in the eighteenth and twentieth centuries. She also kept a series of journals, delivered lectures, and created collages, all of which were published posthumously as extensions of her legacy. Her literary inheritance also has been transmitted through the works of other Spanish writers—men and women whom she generously mentored over the years.

CHILDHOOD THROUGH UNIVERSITY: SALAMANCA, 1925–1949

Carmen Martín Gaite's life defined her literature, and vice versa. Her worldview was shaped by a set of unusual circumstances that began at birth. She was, as she always said, a girl from the provinces. But her upbringing was by no means traditional, and it had a paradoxical effect: she grew into an adult who was anything but provincial. María del Carmen de la Concepción (the name on her birth certificate) was born on 8 December 1925, at her family's home on a placid square in Salamanca, the Plaza de los Bandos.[2] She described her family as belonging to the "clase burguesa acomodada" [comfortable bourgeoisie] (Interview). Her father, José López Martín (1885–1978), was a highly respected notary (a cross between an attorney and a judge in Spain) from Valladolid, near Salamanca. He was a liberal thinker who believed in—and published on—women's rights. He was also a friend of Miguel de Unamuno, who until the Civil War headed the venerable University of Salamanca and who was a frequent visitor in their home. The author's mother, María Gaite Veloso (1894–1978), was a lovely, wise, and generous professor's daughter who had come to Salamanca when two of her brothers studied at the university there. The couple had two children: Ana María (Anita), born in 1924, and Carmen nearly two years later. The two siblings got along well, even though they were "muy diferentes de carácter" [by nature very different] (Interview).

   The sisters were educated by subject tutors at home—the only alternative to the "finishing school" orientation of the religious private schools for girls in Salamanca. Their father also inspired a love of learning in his daughters, sharing his passion for literature, history, and art, as well as his extensive library. Martín Gaite was eternally grateful that she had not been forced to go to a "colegio de monjas" [school run by nuns], because she felt that this experience marked a person for life: "Las que han asistido se han resignado—hay que aceptar lo que Dios mande—o han rebelado de mayores, también de una manera exagerada" [The women who attended either resigned themselves to it—accepting it as God's will—or they rebelled when they were older, in both cases going overboard] (Interview). Martín Gaite did not follow either of those two paths. She did not conform, and she did not rebel, since her family supported her lifelong quest for freedom. Her first taste of liberty came during summers in Galicia, where the family spent two or three months each year in the village of San Lorenzo de Piñor, outside her mother's birthplace of Ourense. During those youthful summers she climbed trees, helped herself to fruit from neighboring orchards, rode in wagons pulled by oxen, and became, in her words, "indómita y poco melindrosa" ("Bosquejo autobiográfico" 227) ["headstrong and something of a tomboy"] ("Autobiographical Sketch" 237). These experiences led her to consider herself Galician, at least in terms of what she called "mis raíces sentimentales, de mentalidad" [my emotional roots, my mentality] (Interview). The popular notion of Galicia associates this northern region with mystery and longing; psychiatrists have also identified unusual resilience among Galicians, which they ascribe to inherent optimism and strong family ties (described by Ana Ramil).

The author spent her early childhood in a less frenzied era, before television or traffic, and this serenity fostered her imagination. It also promoted her skills of observation. Her life was lived in the confines of the strictly traditional city into which she was born, presided over by a cathedral clock that she memorably described in her first novel *Entre visillos* as a watchful "ojo gigantesco" (24) ["gigantic eye"] (*Behind the Curtains* 18). This was a town in which behavior followed traditional protocols. For example, each evening the young women strolled around the Plaza Mayor, or town square, in a clockwise direction, while the young men strolled counterclockwise. Anita Martín Gaite enjoyed recalling that her sister used to flaunt this convention; if she and a young man became engrossed in conversation, she would walk alongside him as they talked, leaving the girls' contingent almost without realizing it. Rejection of the strict rules of Salamanca was inevitable, and both the author and her sister would leave the town after growing up, searching for new experiences elsewhere. Her sister was the first to depart Salamanca: in 1935 she went to Madrid to attend the prestigious, liberal Institución Libre de Enseñanza [Free Institute of Education]. But her time there would last only until her first summer vacation.

For Martín Gaite's generation of Spaniards, collective history shaped personal destiny. Born under the dictatorship of Miguel Primo de Rivera, which lasted from 1923 to 1930, Martín Gaite lived through the liberal Second Republic, inaugurated in 1931. She was eleven years old when the Spanish Civil War began in July 1936, making her one of the "niños de la guerra" or "children of the war." This generation would remember the war as they experienced it, from a child's perspective. As Martín Gaite recalled, the outbreak of war shattered her family's plans, along with so many others' ("Bosquejo" 228; "Sketch" 238). Although she was supposed to follow her sister to the progressive school in Madrid, that was not to be. Instead she attended school locally after the war started, at the Instituto Femenino, or public girls' high school, that included girls of various social classes—an experience she would later depict in *Entre visillos*. As Martín Gaite recollected: "Yo allí por primera vez comprendí cómo era enfrentarme con niñas de condiciones distintas" [It was there that I learned what it was like to encounter girls from different backgrounds], including her best friend whose mother and father were teachers—both jailed for being "reds" (Interview). An unexpected development was that the Civil War left several outstanding professors stranded in Salamanca, and she had the benefit of their instruction at her school, something that she later credited with inspiring her future vocation. The Martín Gaite family spent the Civil War of 1936–1939 in Salamanca, where General Francisco Franco had his headquarters. The family lived in fear due to their liberal leanings, though neither parent belonged to a political party (Interview). The author's favorite uncle, Joaquín Gaite, was not so fortunate; he was shot by Franco's Nationalists for being a card-carrying member of the Socialist Party, as the author would reveal after censorship ended in *El cuarto de atrás* (1978) [*The Back Room* 1983].

After high school, in 1943, Martín Gaite entered the University of Salamanca to study Romance philology (language and literature). The program consisted of five years of study: two years of "estudios comunes" [general requirements] and three of courses in her specialization (which included courses in French, Portuguese, Italian, and Romanian). Her entering class was small: four men and seven women. One of the young men was Ignacio Aldecoa, a superbly gifted writer from northern Spain who would become a dear friend. Most of her contemporaries were uninterested in their studies, but she was fascinated by what she was learning (Interview). At the University of Salamanca she participated in student theater—even toying with the idea of becoming a professional actress—and was a contributor of prose and poetry to the literary magazine *Trabajos y días* [Works and days], later publishing a few of the same poems in her anthology *A rachas* [In a gust of wind] (1976). Two summer programs were decisive for her development. In 1946 she spent one-and-a-half months in Coimbra, Portugal, and in the summer of 1948—after finishing her university degree—she got a scholarship for summer school at the University of Cannes, France. These experiences allowed her to see far beyond the Spanish provincial capital where she was born.[3] When she returned from Cannes she told her parents that she wanted to leave Salamanca to pursue a doctorate in Madrid. With their support, she moved to Madrid in 1949. Her father requested a transfer and the family joined her in the Spanish capital the following year. Her parents lived in a large, elegant apartment at Calle de Alcalá 35 for the rest of their lives; Martín Gaite also lived there until she married.

BECOMING A WRITER IN THE FRANCO ERA: MADRID, 1949–1975

For the first year after she moved to Madrid, Martín Gaite stayed in a small apartment that her father had bought for two retired family maids. Former classmate Ignacio Aldecoa was already living and studying in the capital. He would become her conduit to a group of friends who would alter her life forever: Jesús Fernández Santos, Alfonso Sastre, Rafael Sánchez Ferlosio (whom she would marry), and Josefina Rodríguez (Aldecoa's future wife), among others. With the exception of Josefina Rodríguez, none was a committed student; all were excellent writers destined for fame. These friends soon became Martín Gaite's peer group. As Josefina Rodríguez de Aldecoa recalled: "formábamos un bloque de amistad y camaradería absolutamente ebrio de literatura" [together we formed a unit based on friendship and camaraderie, completely intoxicated by literature] ("Notas biográficas" [Biographical notes] 19). Martín Gaite characterized their affinity for literature in even stronger terms: "todos llevaban en la sangre el virus de la literatura" ("Bosquejo" 230) ["all carried the virus of literature in their blood"] ("Sketch" 240). These young writers would become known in literary history as the "generación del medio siglo" [midcentury generation].[4] This cohort had grown up surrounded by war and deprivation: first Spain's Civil War and then the Second World War from 1939 to 1945 (years that in Spain comprised the harsh period known as "la primera posguerra" [the first postwar era]). Unlike their parents, this generation had never known a freer time. Censorship and privation extended throughout the educational system, up to and including Spain's universities. This meant that the youthful friends relied entirely on one another for intellectual stimulation and support. They exchanged books among themselves as they shared bottles of wine, discussing literature while moving from tavern to tavern. In the company of these friends Martín Gaite began writing articles and short stories and publishing them in literary magazines. She gradually stopped working on her dissertation on medieval Galician-Portuguese songbooks, in part because her apathetic dissertation director did nothing to encourage her research.

Although they were a heterogeneous group, members of this generation were unified by shared circumstances. For all of them, censorship became an incentive or spur to honestly depict the world around them, through a type of literature that would be called social realism or neorealism (influenced by the aesthetic of Italian neorealist cinema after the Second World War). In the absence of a free press, truths had to be communicated obliquely, through art.[5] Martín Gaite began writing fiction that fit well within this movement, often providing a window into the lives of those who seemed invisible (for example, adolescent girls who left the provinces to work as maids in the city). Throughout her life, she also cultivated another creative strand: fantastic literature. Influenced by Italo Svevo (who knew and studied English with James Joyce), Franz Kafka, William Faulkner, and others, she was tantalized by the innovative possibilities of the fantastic. As she noted in a perceptive journal entry years later: "Toda mi literatura oscila entre lo excepcional soñado desde lo cotidiano y al revés" [All of my literature veers between the extraordinary conjured up from a realistic perspective and vice versa] (*Cuadernos de todo* [Notebooks about everything] 572).

Her first attempt at fantastic literature was the result of a health emergency that brought on delirious fevers. In 1949, before final exams after her first year at the University of Madrid, she became seriously ill with typhus (at a time when penicillin had not yet arrived in Spain). She was taken home to Salamanca by ambulance to recover. When she was better, she wrote a disjointed short novel with surrealist overtones that she called *El libro de la fiebre* [The book of fever]. She published only a few fragments during her lifetime, but saved the manuscript, which was published posthumously in 2007.

In 1949 and 1950 she began seeing Rafael Sánchez Ferlosio (1927–2019) as part of a group; soon their relationship became exclusive and in 1950 the couple decided to marry. The wedding took place in Madrid in October 1953, after he finished his military service. The two moved into a top-floor apartment at Calle del Doctor Esquerdo 43—a wedding present from her father. The apartment, with its checkerboard hallway tiles and expansive terrace, was immortalized in *El cuarto de atrás*; she would live there for the rest of her life. (An exterior plaque now commemorates the building's most illustrious resident.) Although they had very different personalities—he was "más crítico que yo, más inadaptado y menos sociable" ("Bosquejo" 232) ["more critical than I, more maladjusted and less sociable"] ("Sketch" 242)—the two shared a fervent desire to write. Together with Ignacio Aldecoa and Alfonso Sastre, he had just founded the short-lived but influential literary journal *Revista española* [Spanish journal].[6] After their wedding the couple spent two months in Italy, where Sánchez Ferlosio's mother's family lived. Martín Gaite found that Italian translations of world literature were excellent, and she devoured works by Dostoevsky, Tolstoy (notably *War and Peace*), Melville, and Balzac. She also read novels by Italian authors led by Italo Svevo and including Italo Calvino, Cesare Pavese, Alberto Moravia, and Natalia Ginzburg. They returned to Italy each year, sometimes going more than once a year, until her husband's maternal grandparents died in 1960 (Interview).

Martín Gaite's first recognition for her fiction came in 1954, when her short novel *El balneario* [The spa] (1955) won the Premio Café Gijón, a prize awarded by an elite circle of literary critics who met regularly at the venerable Madrid café. (Literary prizes were commonly awarded at the end of the year in which a work was completed, with publication early the next year.) The novella takes up the strand of the fantastic when a couple's arrival at a rural spa transforms into a series of freakish adventures, culminating in a surprise revelation. Also in 1955, the author and her husband experienced personal tragedy. Their son Miguel, born in October 1954, died of meningitis the following May. On 22 May 1956 Martín Gaite gave birth to a daughter, Marta Sánchez Martín. When she was in her crib Marta used to twist herself in her sheets, leading to a lifelong nickname used exclusively by her parents: "La Torci" [The Twister]. Marta returned the favor, giving her mother a nickname that would be shared more widely. When Marta was learning to talk, she mispronounced the name "Carmen," instead saying

"Calila." This name delighted her mother, who used it with close friends for the rest of her life.

Her career was definitively launched the next year, when she won what was then Spain's most prestigious literary prize. Martín Gaite won the Premio Nadal of 1957 with her first full-length novel, *Entre visillos* (1958) [*Behind the Curtains* 1990]. Written in the social-realist mode that predominated at midcentury, the novel is a cinematic, minutely observed story of a decisive year in the life of a nonconformist female protagonist. Set in an unnamed town that is clearly identifiable as Salamanca, the novel immerses the reader in the claustrophobic environment of a provincial capital in postwar Spain, inspiring hope that the bright young heroine will eventually escape this confining world. The novel's expertly crafted prose, mesmerizing scenes, wise observations, and pitch-perfect dialogues would become hallmarks of the author's fiction. Martín Gaite's next work, a novella entitled *Las ataduras* [Binding ties] (1960), follows a gifted young woman from a town in Galicia who looks back at rural life in Spain from her present home in Paris. (Each of the author's novellas was published in an eponymous volume with additional short stories, most of which continued in the neorealist mode.) A few years later, for her thirty-sixth birthday in 1961, Martín Gaite's five-year-old daughter gave her a gift that would have lifelong importance: a spiral notebook labeled "Cuaderno de todo" [Notebook about everything]. She would eventually fill more than one hundred of these all-purpose notebooks; selections from some of them were published posthumously in 2002 as *Cuadernos de todo*.

In 1962 Martín Gaite broke with the prevailing social-realist aesthetic in Spain to publish a new type of psychological novel. Influenced by Italo Svevo and especially his retrospective novel *La coscienza di Zeno* [*Zeno's Conscience*], with its emphasis on "la instrospección de los comportamientos" [self-analysis to understand behaviors] (Interview), *Ritmo lento* [A slower rhythm] (1963) was a landmark novel that was underappreciated in its day, as critics have subsequently noted (Brown "*Tiempo de silencio*" and *Secrets* 87–104; Teruel "*Ritmo lento*"). The work (which did not appear in bookstores until 1963) is a fragmented portrait of a gifted, hyperrational young man who cannot adapt to the hypocrisies of the world around him. Narrated by the protagonist from an upscale mental institution outside Madrid, its first-person reminiscences are framed by objective bookends: a prologue and an epilogue in the third person. The reader must assemble the main character's life, since his flashbacks are not presented in chronological order. The plot of the novel is essentially a quest for meaning, to understand his development. Despite its achievements, the book's reception was disappointing, with few reviews—something that the author said she never understood (Interview with Brown, 23 April 1979). *Ritmo lento* was runner-up for the prestigious Premio Biblioteca Breve in 1962, the first time it was awarded to a work from Latin America: Peruvian Mario Vargas Llosa's *La ciudad y los perros* [*The Time of the Hero* 1963]. And in the annals of literary history, a novel by the author's friend Luis Martín-Santos, *Tiempo de silencio* (1962) [*Time of Silence* 1964]— which also moved beyond social realism to psychological analysis—was credited with renovation of the Spanish novel, even though it, too, had been ignored by critics in Spain when it appeared.[7]

In the ensuing decade Martín Gaite took a break from fiction, beginning what she called "un paréntesis de estudio que se traduce en . . . dos libros" [a pause for research that translated into . . . two books] (Interview). She explained that when she finished *Ritmo lento* she was tired of novel writing—tired of continually delving into her own psyche (Interview). She would later describe herself as having been "bastante desilusionada con respecto al género" [rather disillusioned with the genre] (Brown, *Secrets* 105). Scholarship was Martín Gaite's second passion, and she avidly turned to research. Her first subject of investigation (and first book from this period) involved a fascinating eighteenth-century diplomat named don Melchor de Macanaz, a brilliant and complex figure who was pursued by the Inquisition. With the support of a research grant, she traveled to archives in Spain and France to piece together the mystery of his life; her biography *El proceso de Macanaz* [Macanaz's trial] was published in 1970. In this same year, she and Sánchez Ferlosio separated. (Divorce was illegal during the Franco dictatorship and the formal dissolution of their marriage came much later.) The two remained on friendly terms after he moved out, co-parenting their daughter over the years.

As she was following the trail of Macanaz, whom she fondly called "mi muerto" [my dead man], Martín Gaite became interested in love and courtship customs in Spain in the eighteenth century. Her research on the mores of the period, and especially the custom whereby affluent married women could enjoy the attention of a male escort, led to two important publications. The first was a dissertation that allowed her to complete her PhD, with honors, in 1972. Her revised dissertation was published later that year as *Usos amorosos del dieciocho en España* [*Love Customs in Eighteenth-Century Spain* 1991]. A third nonfiction publication from this period was a 1973 collection of essays entitled *La búsqueda de interlocutor y otras búsquedas* [The search for a conversational partner and other searches], which explored questions such as the characteristics of an ideal conversational partner and the effects of advertising on women's self-esteem. Martín Gaite's "return" to fiction came twelve years after her previous novel, in 1974, with the publication of *Retahílas* [Yarns]. In fact, she had been taking notes for the novel for eight years, even as she worked in archives.[8] The novel is set in a country manor in Galicia, where the family matriarch is dying. It tells the story of a night-long conversation between two relatives who have returned to the ancestral home: a sophisticated fortysomething aunt and her admiring nephew in his twenties. Their dialogue comprises alternating monologues that can be described as "verbal missives" (Brown, *Secrets* 113). The two explore the passions, memories, loves, and longings of two generations, ending only when they are interrupted at dawn. While the novel's technique is new, the overarching theme is a recurring one in Martín Gaite's oeuvre: the need for communication, and especially for a conversational partner.

History and Memory after Dictatorship: Madrid 1975–1978

Franco's death in 1975 marked the beginning of what would become today's Spain. After nearly forty years of censorship and repression, the country began transitioning to democratic rule. The national task of retrieving historical memories started on the day Franco died; this was the day Martín Gaite began taking notes for her most celebrated work of literature, the novelistic memoir *El cuarto de atrás*. That would not be her first post-Franco novel; the distinction goes to *Fragmentos de interior* [Inner fragments] (1976), a fast-paced story of a fractured Madrid family, including its household retinue, during a time of social upheaval. Also in 1976 she published her poetry collection *A rachas*, which would go through two subsequent iterations in 1993 and 2000, and the commissioned biography of an early twentieth-century engineer, *El conde de Guadalhorce* [The Count of Guadalhorce]. That same year she began a job as weekly book reviewer for the newly inaugurated newspaper *Diario 16* [Daily 16], a position she kept until 1980. As she observed in her "Autobiographical Sketch," those years as a book critic broadened her exposure to literature and literary theory. She reviewed some of the tide of international literature that was now surging into Spain, along with new works from Spain and Latin America.[9] The opinions that she formulated for her weekly book reviews also found their way into her book-in-progress on the theory of narrative, entitled *El cuento de nunca acabar* [The never-ending story]—a book that she used to joke was too true to its name. As she worked on her own projects (and she always had several in development at the same time) Martín Gaite also translated the works of others for publication in Spanish. Over the years she translated books from Italian (by authors such as Natalia Ginzburg, Italo Svevo, and Primo Levi), French (Charles Perrault, Antoine de Saint-Exupéry), German (Rainer Maria Rilke), and English (Emily Brontë, George MacDonald, William Carlos Williams, and Virginia Woolf).

Martín Gaite's next novel is her most acclaimed. From the time it appeared in 1978, *El cuarto de atrás* has enthralled readers and critics, winning the Premio Nacional de Literatura and securing Martín Gaite's place in world literature. The novel tells the story of a nocturnal visit by a mysterious man in black, who may or may not exist, to a character who unequivocally represents the author. The visitor comes to interview her on a stormy night when she is suffering from insomnia; although she has no recollection of making an appointment, she allows him into her home. A sharp literary critic, the man in black deploys an array of resources—including colored pills that loosen the memory—to elicit long-suppressed memories of the Civil War and its aftermath. As the two speak, a pile of pages grows next to her typewriter; eventually the reader finds that these pages comprise the novel. At a time when the government had just opted for reconciliation over reckoning with the past, granting amnesty to all political crimes prior to 1977, Martín Gaite was one of the first to confront the reality that historical memory could not be denied. She also recognized that painful memories from the back room could not be summoned up at will. A fantastic visitor is the perfect companion for a trip back in time to an era that was both frightening and bizarre, especially for those who experienced it as children. Mindful of Todorov's taxonomy of the fantastic (she literally stumbles over his book on fantastic literature in the first chapter), *El cuarto de atrás* is a fantastic novel that draws attention to the process of its creation. These features anticipate the three major strands of the Spanish novel today: historical memory, metafiction, and the fantastic.

The author was aware of the special nature of this hybrid creation, which is at once a fantastic novel and a realistic memoir of growing up in Franco's Spain (Brown "Fantastic Memoir"). As she explained while she was writing it, in a letter from Madrid dated 9 January 1978:

> Estoy consiguiendo un clima bastante mágico y original y me da la impresión de que será uno de mis libros más insólitos y difíciles de clasificar. ¿Memorias? ¿Relato fantástico? ¿Reflexión sobre la tarea del escritor? No sé, de todo un poco. Seguramente desconcertará a los críticos, pero a mí me gusta, precisamente por lo raro.

> [I'm managing to create a magical and unique atmosphere and I sense that this will be one of my most unusual books, not easy to classify. Memoir? Fantastic tale? Meditation on the role of the author? I don't know, a little of everything. It will probably fluster critics, but I like it, precisely because of its strangeness.] ("Carta a Joan L. Brown" 1152)

She also sensed that this novel was her most accomplished to date. After delivering the manuscript to her publisher (Destino) in Barcelona—in time for the novel to appear at the Madrid Book Fair—she wrote exultantly that this was her best novel ever. Between January and April of 1978 she had spent eight hours a day writing, "en estado total de trance" [in a total trance], as she finished the novel. Now she felt as though the man in black was almost a coauthor: "La releo y no me parece mía, él me ha inspirado. . . . Ha sido una visita mágica, de cuyo rastro irreal vivo todavía, como después de un sueño maravilloso. La única pena es que ya haya desaparecido, se esfumó al amanecer." [I reread it and it doesn't seem to be mine, he inspired me. . . . It was a magical visit, whose unreal traces are still with me, like after a marvelous dream. The only sad thing is that he had to disappear—he vanished at dawn] (Letter to Brown, Madrid, 11 April 1978).

Soon after the publication of *El cuarto de atrás*, Martín Gaite suffered a terrible blow: the loss of both her parents. Her father died in October 1978 and her mother in December of that year. By ten days, her mother missed learning that the novel of her daughter's that had been her favorite had won the country's highest literary honor. The winter of 1978 was exceptionally difficult; not only did Martín Gaite lose her parents but her sister Anita subsequently became ill and moved in with the author and her daughter. Renewal would come in the spring. In April 1979, Martín Gaite would visit the United States for the first time, as a guest of honor at a conference on the contemporary Spanish novel at Yale. We planned for her to stay in Philadelphia before she and I went to the conference, to rest and acclimate after traveling so far. She described her feelings in a letter before her arrival, setting out the resilient philosophy that would guide her in the future:

> Me vendrá muy bien este descanso inicial. Cuando empezaba a reponerme un poco de la muerte de mi madre, mi hermana se puso enferma y se vino aquí a que yo la cuidara y lleva con nosotras un mes. Te confieso que estoy agobiada de problemas relacionados con la enfermedad y que ya no puedo más. De verdad que tengo unas ganas de irme a bailar que no te imaginas, no se puede uno dejar cercar así por la desgracia, te vuelves apocada y parece que acaba doliéndote todo el cuerpo o que también tú tienes la muerte cerca. Así que por todo esto mi idea es empezar el viaje descansando en tu casa.

> [That initial rest period will be good for me. Just when I was starting to pull myself together after my mother's death, my sister got sick and came here for me to take care of her; she's been with us for a month. I confess that I'm overwhelmed with illness-related problems and I've reached my limit. Honestly, you can't believe how much I want to go out dancing; you can't let yourself be trapped that way when something bad happens, you become fearful and you end up feeling that your whole body aches or that you, too, see death approaching. So with all this in mind my plan is to begin my trip with a rest at your house.] (Letter to Brown, Madrid, 5 March 1979)

This first visit to the United States would mark a new step in the author's journey, bringing her closer to the most prolific period in her career. But much would happen before the publication of her next novel, *Caperucita en Manhattan* [Red Riding Hood in Manhattan], in 1990. An account of that novel begins with the second gap in Martín Gaite's literary production—one that would also endure for a dozen years.

CHAPTER 2

Caperucita en Manhattan

A YOUNG ADULT NOVEL OF RECOVERY

Carmen Martín Gaite's first novel of the 1990s is the most crucial one, as well as the most misunderstood. Though it was written for a Spanish audience, it is not about Spain. As its title announces, *Caperucita en Manhattan* [Red Riding Hood in Manhattan] (1990) is set in the United States—specifically, in New York City. That is only one of the anomalies associated with this remarkable work. *Caperucita en Manhattan* has been denied its rightful place in the Martín Gaite novel canon because it was ahead of its time. It is a captivating young adult (YA) novel for all ages. Unfortunately, the category of YA fiction did not exist in Spain when it appeared, so critics have lumped it with the author's two children's books—when they studied it at all. Despite critical neglect, readers have made this Martín Gaite's most beloved work of fiction, treasured around the world. It has been translated into Catalan, Danish, Dutch, French, German, Greek, Italian, Japanese, Korean, Latvian, Norwegian, Polish, Portuguese, Swedish, and even Esperanto. The novel's charms are compelling and transcendent. In beautifully flowing prose, Martín Gaite spins a modern-day adventure of female empowerment, engaging readers in an exciting adventure. This story has all of the defining characteristics of Martín Gaite's fiction: astute character development, cinematic scenes, pitch-perfect dialogue, sharp social criticism, abundant cultural information, surprising plot twists, and humor that here ranges from subtle to hilarious. It also invokes the fantastic, with a magical character who seems completely real. In addition to its literary attainment, the novel has a key place in the author's biography, making the novel as decisive for life as it is for her literary canon. *Caperucita en Manhattan* enabled Martín Gaite's revival and return to novel writing after an absence of over a decade—a period that threatened to stretch on interminably.

Public Success and Personal Loss

After the triumph of her National Prize–winning 1978 novel *El cuarto de atrás* Martín Gaite abandoned fiction writing for the second time in her career.[1] During this period she got to know the United States. She crossed the Atlantic for the first time in April 1979 for a conference on the contemporary Spanish novel at Yale University, where she and fellow novelist (and friend) Juan Benet were the guests of honor. Benet was bristly and stand-offish, telling the audience that he didn't know what he was doing there and that he felt like a cactus on display; Martín Gaite was so charming and approachable that she made up for his rudeness. As always, when she agreed to do something, she made an effort to do it well. We sat next to each other during the conference and passed notes back and forth, which she likened to two schoolgirls in class. After a series of uninspiring talks she wrote: "Me animo porque ahora me parece que lo que yo voy a leer es más divertido, y eso me ayudará a leerlo con seguridad, lentitud y buena entonación, do you think so?" [This is encouraging because I think that what I'm going to read is more entertaining, and that will help me read it confidently, slowly, and clearly. . . .] (Note to Brown, New Haven, 21 April 1979).[2]

After spending three days in New Haven, she discovered New York City, which she called "la ciudad más fascinante del mundo" ("Bosquejo" 235) ["the most fascinating city in the world"] ("Sketch" 245). Invitations to return to the United States soon began to arrive. As she recalled in a posthumously published talk about *Caperucita en Manhattan* entitled "La libertad como símbolo" [Liberty as a symbol], the Yale conference was "la chispa que encendió una serie posterior de ofrecimientos de trabajo" [the spark that ignited a subsequent series of job offers] ("La libertad" 139) in the United States. Months later, in the fall of 1980, she returned to New York City as a visiting professor at Barnard College—a semester that would leave an indelible mark. A photograph taken in Morningside Heights shows her on the Columbia University campus, not far from her apartment in Butler Hall (figure 2.1).

Writing shortly before she left Madrid for New York, Martín Gaite exulted: "No te puedes imaginar la enorme ilusión que me hace este viaje y lo positivo que espero que sea para mí. I'm arriving! I'm happy! I'm free!" [You can't imagine how excited I am about this trip and how positive I hope it will be for me . . .] (Letter to Brown, Madrid, 23 August 1980). She again came to the United States in the fall of 1982 to be a visiting professor at the University of Virginia. Whenever Martín Gaite traveled to the United States she made it a point to spend time in New York. As she put it, in this country New York City "era y sigue siendo mi centro" [was and is my center] ("La libertad" 139). Her exuberant pose on the roof of a friend's apartment building captures the sense of freedom that she associated with the city (figure 2.2).

Figure 2.1. Carmen Martín Gaite in New York City, 1980

Figure 2.2. Carmen Martín Gaite in New York City, 1980

While living in the United States she kept close watch on what was going on back home. In 1982 the Socialists (PSOE, Partido Socialista Obrero Español, or Spanish Socialist Workers' Party) under the leadership of Felipe González won in national elections, effectively sealing Spain's transition to democracy. In a letter near the end of October 1982, Martín Gaite wrote: "Estoy muy contenta porque en España han ganado los socialistas y es un equipo de gente muy bien preparada. Esperemos que no les haga la vida imposible la ultraderecha. Ese es el único peligro." [I'm very happy because in Spain the Socialists have won and their team is well equipped to govern. Let's hope that the far right doesn't make life impossible for them. That's the only danger] (Letter to Brown, Charlottesville, 30 October 1982). The Socialists would successfully push back against conservatives for many years to come, eventually ceding power in 1996 (and periodically regaining it in the twenty-first century). Although the author had her issues with the Socialists, who demanded a fealty that she was reluctant to give to any political party, she was pleased that they had displaced the political heirs of dictator Francisco Franco, who had been in power from 1939 to 1975—most of her adult life.

Soon after returning to Spain, in early 1983, Martín Gaite published her landmark book of literary theory *El cuento de nunca acabar*, subtitled "Apuntes sobre la narración, el amor y la mentira" [Notes on narrative, love, and lies] and—to her surprise—it became a bestseller. The book's appearance coincided with the airing of a television miniseries based on her first novel, *Entre visillos*, as well as her starring role in a television special she wrote about Salamanca, part of the series *Esta es mi tierra* [This is my land] in which famous authors introduced viewers to their home towns. In a letter in May of that year she summarized her newfound celebrity in her home country:

El libro [*El cuento de nunca acabar*] es el primero de todos los míos que se ha situado por mérito propio en la lista de los best-sellers. En menos de un mes se ha agotado la primera edición y mañana sale la segunda. La gente lo compran como si fueran rosquillas. Y me he convertido de la noche a la mañana en una "autora de éxito", a la que todo el mundo quiere entrevistar, escuchar y llevar a la televisión y a la radio.

[The book is the first of all of mine to land on the bestseller list purely on its own merits. The first edition sold out in less than a month, and the second edition comes out tomorrow. It's selling like hotcakes. And overnight I have become "an important author" whom everyone wants to interview, listen to, and put on television and on the radio.] (Letter to Brown, Madrid, 2 May 1983)

She also wrote the screenplays for a television miniseries based on the life of Santa Teresa de Jesús [Saint Teresa of Ávila], in collaboration with director and friend José Luis Borau (in which she has a walk-on role as a nun, Sor [Sister] Gaitera).

Her travel schedule was packed. In the same letter, she listed all the places she had been. Along with her visit to Salamanca for filming, "he viajado también a Dublín, Barcelona, Amberes, Ginebra, Valladolid, Granada y Córdoba, he dado conferencias aquí en las Universidades Autónoma y Complutense . . . he ido a la recepción que dio el rey el 23 de abril . . . en fin, que no paro." [I've also traveled to Dublin, Barcelona, Antwerp, Geneva, Valladolid, Granada and Córdoba, I've given lectures here at the Autonomous and Complutense universities . . . I've gone to the reception that the king gave on 23 April . . . in short, I haven't stopped for a minute] (Letter to Brown, Madrid, 2 May 1983).

Perhaps owing to her hectic schedule, she did not manage to finish a novel between her third and fourth stays in the United States. The only works of fiction that she published were her two short (under 100-page) novels for children: *El castillo de las tres murallas* [The three-walled castle] (1981) and *El pastel del diablo* [The devil's pie] (1985); both feature independent young women who defy authority in order to find truth and happiness. In the fall of 1984 she returned to the United States for a semester as visiting professor at the University of Illinois, Chicago. There she worked furiously on a novel set in Spain in the 1970s. But it would not soon be published. When she returned home, she suffered the worst misfortune of her life: her twenty-eight-year-old daughter with Rafael Sánchez Ferlosio, Marta Sánchez Martín, died in April 1985. After her daughter's death Martín Gaite turned away from creative writing. Interviewer Juan Cantavella recalled her telling him that she could not write fiction while her wound remained open: "'Espero que esto pasará pronto y volveré a escribir novelas. Entonces podré hurgar dentro de mí misma, sin que me duelan tanto los recuerdos', nos decía hace años." ["I hope that this will end soon and I'll go back to writing novels. Then I can delve inside myself, without my memories causing so much pain," she would say years ago] ("Carmen Martín Gaite" 43).

Instead of fiction, Martín Gaite turned to research. In 1987 she published two important books. The first was *Usos amorosos de la postguerra española* [*Courtship Customs in Postwar Spain* 2004], an engagingly written piece of scholarship on the social and educational systems that shaped young people—especially young women—in the postwar era. It won that year's Premio Anagrama de Ensayo [Anagrama Prize for Nonfiction]. The other volume was *Desde la ventana: Enfoque femenino de la literatura española* [From the window: A female perspective on Spanish literature], a collection of long essays on literature by women. Her play *A palo seco* [On my own] was performed this same year and published in 1994. She received important honors in the years after Marta's death. In 1985 she was named an Honorary Fellow of the Modern Language Association (designating her as one of the world's greatest living authors) and in 1988 she was recognized with the Premio Príncipe de Asturias, awarded by the future king of Spain for cumulative literary achievement. Still, it was not clear that she would ever write another novel. *Caperucita en Manhattan* rehabilitated Martín

Gaite so that she could return to writing fiction—any kind of fiction—after her greatest tragedy. In order to do so, she needed to recover her innate optimism.

A Modern Red Riding Hood in New York

Caperucita en Manhattan is a complicated reimagining of the folk tale that was first brought into print by French author Charles Perrault in 1697. Differences between the original version or hypotext and Martín Gaite's novel involve new perspectives on characters and themes; in her study *Recycling Red Riding Hood*, Sandra L. Beckett classifies Martín Gaite's novel as an "expansion" text (299–331). The book's structure is like a play in two acts: the first part is "Sueños de libertad" [Dreams of freedom] and the second, "La aventura" [The adventure]. These parts comprise thirteen chapters (five in the first part, eight in the second part) spanning 200 pages. Each chapter features a descriptive title reminiscent of a nineteenth-century novel, drawing the reader into the tale, from the very first chapter entitled "Datos geográficos de algún interés y presentación de Sara Allen" [Geographical facts of some interest and introduction of Sara Allen]. Part one of the novel establishes the heroine's backstory. Ten-year-old Sara Allen lives in Brooklyn in the 1980s, long before this borough became fashionable. She longs for the excitement of Manhattan: "Los niños que viven en Brooklyn no todos se duermen por la noche. Piensan en Manhattan como en lo más cercano y al mismo tiempo lo más exótico del mundo, y su barrio les parece un pueblo perdido donde nunca pasa nada." [Not all children who live in Brooklyn go to sleep at night. Some of them stay awake thinking about Manhattan being the closest but at the same time the most exotic place on earth, and their own borough seems like a hick town where nothing ever happens] (15). Sara's parents have mundane occupations and outlooks. Her father is a plumber and her mother works in a geriatric center. But her mother's true passion is baking, and strawberry tarts are her specialty.

The young girl identifies with her maternal grandmother, a woman who is far from conventional. She is former chanteuse named Rebecca Little, whose stage name is Gloria Star. She lives in the Manhattan neighborhood of Morningside, across from Morningside Park. This grandmother is both beautiful and brave: she is unafraid to go into the park, despite the threat of the "Bronx vampire" (evocative of the "Son of Sam" killer in the 1970s) who has murdered five women and is still at large. From the young girl's perspective, "todo tenía que ver con la libertad" [everything had to do with freedom] (23). Sara reads, writes, draws, prays to the Statue of Liberty, and invents her own lexicon of words she calls "farfanías," the most notable being "miranfú," which means "'va a pasar algo diferente' o 'me voy a llevar una sorpresa'" [something new is going to happen or I'm going to be surprised] (35). Sara learns to keep her dreams to herself, waiting for something to happen while studying a map of Manhattan. Although Sara accompanies her mother on visits to her grandmother by subway each weekend, she longs to go to Manhattan by herself and to stay there.

Part two of the novel delivers the adventure that its title promises. It introduces its most stunning new character, Miss Lunatic. She is a luminous old woman who roams the streets of New York pushing an antique baby carriage. Miss Lunatic resembles a homeless woman—or the old crone Celestina, whose wisdom is cited in the section's opening epigraph.[3] In fact Miss Lunatic is the spirit of Liberty: Madame Bartholdi, the 185-year-old mother and muse of the sculptor who created the statue in New York Harbor. She lives to help others, always materializing wherever she is needed, such as the outbreak of a fire or a fight. And she has no interest whatsoever in material rewards. For her, freedom and wealth are opposing concepts, as are freedom and fear: "Para mí la única fortuna, ya le digo, es la de saber vivir, la de ser libre" [The only treasure I covet, I assure you, is that of knowing how to live, how to be free] (94). She enjoys listening more than speaking and interacts with people of all nationalities and walks of life, eager to learn their stories. Miss Lunatic meets Edgar Woolf, a lonely pastry magnate who lives in a luxurious building shaped like a gigantic tart, overlooking Central Park. Mr. Woolf is frantically seeking a new recipe for strawberry tarts, because the one he has is so bad that it is ruining his brand, "El Dulce Lobo," or *The Sweet Wolf*. Mr. Woolf—known as "el Rey de las Tartas" [the King of Tarts]—has built a multimillion-dollar business from the modest tea room that he inherited (a classic enactment of the American Dream), and he fears that his success is threatened.

The day after her encounter with Mr. Woolf, Miss Lunatic meets Sara Allen when she discovers her crying alone in the subway. Taking advantage of her parents' absence for a funeral, Sara has come to Manhattan by herself. She is wearing a hooded red raincoat and carrying a strawberry tart in a basket. Miss Lunatic is struck by how much the girl resembles an illustration of Little Red Riding Hood in a book of Perrault fairy tales from her son's childhood, and immediately approaches to ask if she is lost. Sara's plan had been to walk through Central Park on her way to her grandmother's house, but she is paralyzed by fear. The older woman befriends the young girl—more accurately, they befriend each other—and adventures ensue. Miss Lunatic imparts her secrets and enables Sara to overcome her fear of freedom. Sara meets Mr. Woolf in Central Park, shares some of the strawberry tart, and arranges for him to get the recipe from her grandmother—the same Gloria Star on whom he had a crush as a young man. The final chapter is entitled "*Happy end* pero sin cerrar" [*Happy end* but without ending]. Sara leaves Edgar Woolf dancing with her grandmother and drinking champagne; she herself embarks on a magical trip to the Statue of Liberty involving a coin, an incantation, and an underwater passageway.

A Young Adult (YA) Novel Ahead of Its Time

While this entrancing story has been embraced by readers, it has been sidelined by critics. The reception history of *Caperucita en Manhattan* has been one of popular triumph without the critical notice necessary for entry into a literary canon (Brown, "Constructing"). The *MLA Bibliography* reports fewer than two dozen scholarly essays on this novel to date, a small fraction of the number of studies of the author's most famous novel, *El cuarto de atrás*.[4] Not only has critical attention been scant, it has also been misdirected—"faked out" by an initial classification, "literatura infantil" [children's literature], that has no relevance for this novel. Spain, unlike the United States, had no recognizable "young adult" or YA category for fiction until the twenty-first century, when "literatura juvenil" [literature for young adult readers or young adult fiction] came into its own as a category separate from "literatura infantil." Prizes, booklists, and scholarship underscore this lack. The Premio Nacional de Literatura Infantil y Juvenil [National Prize for Children's and Young Adult Literature], established in 1978, has never distinguished between the two categories, awarding prizes indiscriminately to books for either audience. Publishers' prizes, like their booklists known by the acronym "LIJ," also maintained this forced pairing throughout the twentieth century, with very few exceptions.[5] Although one prize was inaugurated by the publisher Edelvives in 2001, the Premio Alandar de Narrativa Juvenil [Alendar Prize for Young Adult Literature], similar prizes did not proliferate until the past decade.[6] With regard to scholarship, the Ministry of Culture database of Spanish publications since 1972 does not contain a single study of literature for young people prior to 1991, and numbers do not begin to build until the years 1995–2000 (*Base de datos*). This database, which gets its information from publishers when they apply for an ISBN, also fails to distinguish studies of children's books from those of YA fiction.

According to the Young Adult Library Services Association (YALSA), the goal of all YA stakeholders is to "engage, serve, and empower teens." Separation of YA fiction from children's fiction in Spain was propelled by the market for English-language novels for teenage readers, inspiring Spanish publishers to promote this new category through prizes and booklists. The 1999 publication of the Spanish version of the first Harry Potter novel, *Harry Potter y la piedra filosofal*—originally published two years earlier by J. K. Rowling as *Harry Potter and the Philosopher's Stone* and published in the United States as *Harry Potter and the Sorcerer's Stone*—was a likely catalyst. Even today, listings of top-selling YA novels in Spain are dominated by translations of J. K. Rowling and other English-language writers, with Spanish authors gaining ground.[7] The clout of YA literature can be explained by its economic success. Although sales figures are not available for Spain, in the United States the number of YA books published annually hovers around 30,000 with revenue approaching three billion dollars, according to data compiled in 2015. Sales are high precisely because the category extends beyond the YA demographic. Fully 55 percent of these books are purchased by adults over the age of eighteen, notably by readers who are between thirty-three and forty years old (Brown, "Rescuing" 204).

The lack of YA fiction as a distinct category in the 1990s, which Ángel Esteban del Campo has identified as unique to the Hispanic world (859), allowed *Caperucita* to fall into the same grouping as picture books for preliterate children. *Caperucita* was relegated to the children's aisle. Critics have consistently associated it with *El castillo de las tres murallas* and *El pastel del diablo*. A typical characterization is that *Caperucita* is one of Martín Gaite's three "contributions to children's literature" (Rolón Collazo 139). This classification endures even though *El castillo* and *El pastel* are quite different from *Caperucita*. When the former two were published together as a single volume, they were labeled stories, not novels. The publisher Lumen combined the two works as *Dos relatos fantásticos* [Two fantastic tales], and the book club Círculo de Lectores [Readers' club] produced a collector's edition entitled *Dos cuentos maravillosos* [Two fantastic stories]. This is in contrast with the series that *Caperucita* inaugurated for its publisher Siruela, as defined on the back cover of the first edition. Called "Las tres edades" [The three ages], the series is intended for all readers.

Caperucita en Manhattan is much more complex than the author's books for children. It illustrates the ways in which, according to Mike Cadden, "young adult novels are closer to novels for adults than they are to novels by children," substantiating the truism that "the YA novel is a subset of the novel for adults while the novel for children is its own creature" (307). Though *El castillo* and *El pastel* share features with *Caperucita*, their similarities do not diminish this distinction. While the two earlier books also have girls as protagonists and fantastical elements, they are less than half the length of *Caperucita*. The characters and plots of the first two books are much simpler, as befits their intended audience. The earlier books' professional "picture-book" illustrations are large and elaborate when compared with the small pen-and-ink drawings by the author that grace the last page of each chapter in *Caperucita*. The first two novels take place in the worlds of castles and monsters that are the province of children's books. *Caperucita* contains specific information about a real place, New York City, and presents scholarly research about the Statue of Liberty—information that is likely to be new even to Americans. A linguistic analysis of a sample page (page 26) of all three texts indicates that *Caperucita* is more complex than either *El castillo* or *El pastel*. While the number of different words used is roughly identical among the three pages, the sample of *Caperucita* features more sophisticated vocabulary than the other two, with lexical items that would not be part of a young child's vocabulary, such as *fosforescentes* [phosphorescent], *minúsculos* [minuscule], and *segregaban* [secreted].[8] Unfortunately, we do not have a quantitative measure to assess the quality of prose. Nevertheless, most will agree that *Caperucita* is beautifully written, reflecting both the author's talent and her everlasting preoccupation with her craft.

Misclassification is the only plausible explanation for the book's absence from studies of Martín Gaite's later novels (Blanco *Life-Writing*; Cruz-Cámara *Laberinto*; O'Leary and Ribeiro de Menezes). A partial exception is the scheme devised by José Jurado Morales (*Trayectoria*), who groups *Caperucita* with the earlier children's books and adds a fourth novel, *La Reina de las Nieves* (1994) [*The Farewell Angel* 1999], based on the rationale that all of these can be considered rewritten fairy tales. The sole volume in which *Caperucita en Manhattan* now appears as the first of her novels of the 1990s is volume 2 of the *Obras completas*, although the fact that all of her novels are published in chronological order elides the issue of classification. Even the forward-looking anthology *Beyond the Back Room* virtually ignores *Caperucita en Manhattan*, with brief references to it embedded in essays about other works (Womack and Wood). Only when the novel is resituated in its proper context, as a YA novel for all ages, is it likely to be restored to its rightful place in the Martín Gaite canon. As Beckett has observed, this novel invokes the original audience for the Red Riding Hood story: "Carmen Martín Gaite's *Caperucita en Manhattan* is an excellent example of the many contemporary retellings that address a cross audience of children and adults, thus restoring the story to the general audience it had in the oral tradition" (329).

Modeling Freedom and Fearlessness

Spanish educators have confirmed the merits of *Caperucita* as a YA novel, which is after all a category defined by its intended audience. The book has long been required reading for Spanish secondary-school students throughout the country. It also is taught to their older brothers and sisters in courses such as "Imaginario femenino en la literatura española" [The female imaginary in Spanish literature] at the University of Granada. Young adult readers in Spain (and presumably elsewhere around the world) have responded enthusiastically to the novel. The Spanish student website *El rincón del vago* [The dunce's corner] is replete with enthusiastic commentary, including astute observations about the differences between *Caperucita Roja* [*Little Red Riding Hood*] and *Caperucita en Manhattan*, and awareness of the special significance of the character who is unique to the Martín Gaite version, Miss Lunatic. Young readers also note how they found themselves swept up by the novel, finding it a joy to read—just as the author found joy in writing it.[9]

Caperucita en Manhattan captivates young readers by modifying Perrault's hypotext to emphasize freedom and fearlessness. Instead of bowing to authority and convention, Martín Gaite's Miss Lunatic refuses to acquiesce to either social or natural laws. As she counsels Sara, "Nunca hay que hacer caso de las

prohibiciones. . . . No suelen tener fundamento." [Don't ever pay attention to pro-
hibitions. . . . They are usually baseless] (132). Miss Lunatic is a marvelous character according Tzvetan Todorov's taxonomy of the fantastic in literature. Unlike
the purely fantastic mode, characterized by unresolved doubt or hesitation, the
marvelous seems to be real—like magical realism in Hispanic America ("magical" being simply a modifier of "realism"), also known as "lo real maravilloso"
[marvelous reality]. Thinking about Miss Lunatic, Sara ponders the nature of
reality, recalling that Alice's adventures in Wonderland turned out to be fictional
and wondering "¿Dónde estaba la raya de separación entre la verdad y la mentira?" [Where was the dividing line between truth and fiction?] (162). In Todorov's classic formulation, when the reader "decides that new laws of nature must
be entertained to account for the phenomena, we enter the genre of the marvelous" (*Fantastic* 41). Miss Lunatic accepts the marvelous (this is the word she uses)
as she embodies it. She further believes that embracing the unknown is the path
to discovery, telling Edgar Woolf:

> Las gentes que tienen miedo a lo maravilloso deben verse continuamente en
> callejones sin salida. . . . Nada podrá descubrir quien pretenda negar lo inex-
> plicable. La realidad es un pozo de enigmas. Y si no, pregúntaselo a los sabios.

> [People who fear the marvelous must find themselves continually stuck in a
> dead end. . . . Whoever tries to deny the inexplicable will never discover any-
> thing. Reality is a crater full of enigmas. And if you don't believe it, ask any
> genius.] (169)

Mr. Woolf repeats these words of wisdom when he makes his own discovery, in
his case of Sara's still-enchanting grandmother, Gloria Star.

Martín Gaite enhances accessibility for all ages by muting the most distress-
ing feature of the fairy-tale genre: danger. In fairy tales "the dangers are real and
they are everywhere," as Kelly Barnhill has commented: "Tread carefully, these
stories remind us." While Sara braves the subways and streets of New York and
her grandmother ventures into Morningside Park, neither woman is assaulted,
much less devoured. As Marisol Morales Ladrón has noted, *Caperucita en Manhattan* "erradica la violencia y las connotaciones sexuales de la historia original" [removes the violence and sexual connotations of the original story] (169).
(The novel further eschews X-rated themes such as the bestiality of Angela
Carter's contemporary Red Riding Hood story "The Company of Wolves.")[10]
Mr. Woolf suffers from the classic fairy-tale flaw of greed (a weakness shared by
the monarch in *El castillo de las tres murallas*, who eventually turns into a mute
reptile). But this wolf does not prey on women. The most tension-filled scene
between Edgar Woolf and Sara Allen is their fateful initial encounter. Sara meets
Mr. Woolf in the woods of Central Park. He is described in lupine terms with a
narrow face, reddish hair (reminiscent of fur), flaring nostrils, and eyes filled

with desire. Sara finds his demeanor unsettling; remembering Miss Lunatic's advice, she makes a conscious decision not to be afraid. But her apprehension turns out to be unwarranted. What Mr. Woolf covets is the strawberry tart. After tasting it he falls to his knees, begging for the recipe and offering Sara anything she wants in return (she chooses a ride in one of his chauffeured limousines). So benign are his intentions that Mr. Woolf associates Sara with the grandchild he never had.[11]

Beyond its entertainment value, *Caperucita* is admired for its ability to move readers emotionally, inspiring them to relate its message to their own lives. This is a key characteristic of YA fiction, according to one pioneering theorist of the genre: "Young adult literature exerts a powerful influence over its readers at a particularly malleable time in their identity formation" (Coats 315). One reader— who grew up to become Martín Gaite's publisher at Siruela—has poignantly recalled the impact that the novel, and its *hada* or magical being Miss Lunatic, had on her when she read it at seventeen:

> Y yo, en el mismo centro de mi laberinto, encontré de su mano la fuerza para caminar hacia la salida, en sus palabras la energía para enfrentarme a los lobos que aparecen en el camino de cualquier caperucita y en su ejemplo la capacidad para crecer como mujer y no sentir miedo ante el túnel negro que, como Sara Allen, todos tenemos delante en algún momento. Fueron unas horas que todavía conservo en mi memoria como si hubieran sido ayer.

> [And I, in the middle of my own labyrinth, took her hand and found the strength to head toward the exit. In her words I found the energy to confront the wolves that appear in the path of any Red Riding Hood. In her example I found the ability to grow as a woman and to be unafraid of the dark tunnel that, like Sara Allen, we all face at one time or another. Those hours of reading are still fresh in my memory, as if they happened yesterday.] (Grande 265)

The novel fulfills the classic arc of the fairy tale, which Barnhill has identified as "a story of reversal" through which protagonists' initial circumstances are upended. Usually this reversal happens thanks to forces beyond the main character's control: rightful inheritances are restored, family bonds are revealed, evil rulers are stripped of their power. The reversal in *Caperucita* is inspiring because it is brought about by the agency of the young woman herself, aided by the magical Miss Lunatic.

MOUTH-TO-MOUTH RESUSCITATION IN NEW YORK CITY

This novel accomplished an equally important reversal for its author. As critics have unanimously acknowledged, writing was therapeutic for Martín Gaite, and nowhere is this more evident than in *Caperucita*. Martín Gaite's biography is thoroughly intertwined with this work. José Teruel has described this phenomenon ("Un contexto" [A context]) and so has Martín Gaite. The circumstances under which *Caperucita en Manhattan* was begun in New York City and New York state are detailed in her poignant, posthumously published essay "El otoño de Poughkeepsie" [Autumn in Poughkeepsie] (*Cuadernos* 611–630). To review the relevant facts: When her only child died at age twenty-eight, the author was left alone in the world except for her sister and her friends. Marta was the person who mattered most to her. Not only had the author cared for her daughter throughout her life, but her daughter also cared for her when she needed it (for example, when Martín Gaite was mugged on the street in Madrid and needed help as she recovered from a broken left arm). When Marta moved out of their shared apartment in the spring of 1983 she found herself unexpectedly devastated. She wrote at the time:

> . . . Marta se fue de casa. Ahora vive en un apartamento junto al de Rafael. Lo comparte con un amigo.
>
> Creía estar preparada para esto e incluso muchas veces pensaba que cuándo se iría, porque la convivencia en algunos aspectos interfería con mi quehacer o me parecía incómoda. Pero de repente es como si me hubieran quitado uno de los puntales más serios para que no me caiga la casa encima, la vida encima.
>
> [. . . Marta has left home. Now she lives in an apartment near Rafael's. She shares it with a male friend.
>
> I thought I was prepared for this and even wondered sometimes when she would go, because some aspects of living together interfered with my activities or seemed awkward. But suddenly it's as if they've pulled out one of the most crucial supports that kept the house from collapsing on me, kept my life from collapsing on me.] (Letter to Brown, Madrid, 30 June 1983)

She could not know that when Marta moved back, it would be because she was dying. On 8 April 1985, Marta passed away. The official cause of death was pneumonia, which was medically accurate, but this was not the full story. Like so many of her generation in Spain, Marta became addicted to heroin; she died of AIDS-related complications. Sadly, Spain's government had no policy to fight the AIDS epidemic at that time, as Teresa Vilarós has chronicled (251). The shame that surrounded the illness meant that there was no support system for either victims or their survivors. In the words of psychotherapist Esther Perel, "What makes the trauma worse is . . . the isolation, the secrecy, and the shame that you have to then live with afterward" (qtd. in Schwartz).

Martín Gaite had agreed to go to Vassar College long before the fall semester of 1985, for what would be her last visiting professorship in the United States. She kept this promise although she was at a very low emotional ebb. Once she landed in New York, she stayed for a few days with her friend Juan Carlos Eguillor, a well-known Spanish illustrator who had done the drawings for *El castillo de las tres murallas* and who had an apartment in midtown Manhattan that year. He showed her an art project that he had begun but with which he was now floundering, about a character in New York City who resembled Little Red Riding Hood. At first Martín Gaite helped him with it, and they both enjoyed an initial flush of enthusiasm. Then, gradually, she took over the project. As she recalled, "[Juan Carlos Eguillor] me ha dado los papeles para que yo siga escribiendo por donde quiero" [(Juan Carlos Eguillor) has given me the pages so that I can continue writing however I please] (*Cuadernos* 618). This development reveals her affinity for modern techniques of sampling and remix over sole proprietorship, as Alex Saum-Pascual has demonstrated, and reflects her long-standing fascination with fairy tales, detailed by María Elena Soliño. The resulting book is dedicated to her friend: "A Juan Carlos Eguillor, por la respiración boca a boca que nos insulfó a Caperucita y a mí, perdidas en Manhattan a finales de aquel verano horrible" [To Juan Carlos Eguillor, for the mouth-to-mouth resuscitation that he gave to Red Riding Hood and me, lost in Manhattan at the end of that awful summer].

Martín Gaite took the nascent project with her to Vassar. She was almost unimaginably lonely there, housed in a solitary apartment in what by day was a psychiatric health center—a situation whose comic potential she noted in "El otoño de Poughkeepsie," marking the return of her sense of humor. Though at times the campus could seem like a refuge in the woods, Vassar was mostly an isolated and isolating enclosure for her, literally and figuratively walled off from the world. She had visited Vassar once before, in November 1983 (noted in *Cuadernos* 572–573), but the person whom she knew best there—the department chairperson who had invited her to be a visiting professor—had just left for another institution. As she recorded soon after her arrival: "Estoy sola, más sola que lo que he estado nunca en mi vida" [I am alone, more alone than I've ever been in my life] (*Cuadernos* 611). Fiction was, she thought, beyond the realm of the possible when she felt as devastated as she did. Although *Caperucita* was conceived in a convivial collaboration with a friend—"se nos ocurrían muchas cosas nuevas entre los dos, nos reíamos mucho" [between the two of us we had a bunch of new ideas, we laughed a lot] (*Cuadernos* 618)—the book's gestation would be protracted and solitary. As recorded on the last page of the novel, it was begun on 28 August 1985, in New York City, and finished on 28 February 1990, in Madrid.

Alone and in a foreign country, Martín Gaite constantly had to combat sadness and depression. In an early letter from Vassar's Poughkeepsie campus, she confessed: "Hay algunos días, te digo la verdad, en que la vida me pesa como una losa de plomo. Otros se me hace más llevadera. ¡Necesito tanta valentía, Joan querida, para seguir viviendo sin ella!" [There are some days, I'll be honest, when life weighs on me like a ton of bricks. Other days it's easier to bear. I need so much courage, Joan dear, to keep on living without her!] (Letter to Brown, Poughkeepsie, 26 September 1985). She made new friends at Vassar and her classes went well, but she was filled with trepidation as the weeks went by. Nearing the end of the semester, she worried about her return to Spain:

> Va pasando el tiempo y acercándose poco a poco la fecha de mi reincorporación a la vida en Madrid. Tengo mucho miedo, cuando pienso en ello. Aquí estoy viviendo como en una nube. Y a pesar de todo, hay días en que no puedo con mi alma, te lo confieso. Vivir day to day es un arte difícil cuando está uno a punto de cumplir 60 años y acaba de salir de una catástrofe tan terrible. Pero no queda otro remedio.

> [Time is going by and little by little the date of my return to life in Madrid keeps approaching. When I think about it, I'm very afraid. Here I'm living in a bubble. And despite everything, I confess that some days it's too much for my soul to bear. Living day to day is a difficult feat when you are about to turn sixty and have gone through such a horrendous catastrophe. But there's no other choice.] (Letter to Brown, Poughkeepsie, 20 October 1985)

Gradually she began working on *Caperucita* as her salvation, taking back enough in her suitcase to complete the novel back home.

At first the novel's development stalled. Traces of floundering are embedded in the first part, with its nonrecurring characters and slow-building plot. As she admitted later, "la novela se me empantanó" [the novel became mired down] ("La libertad" 148). With the inspired addition of the fantastic character Miss Lunatic, the longer second part becomes a thrilling adventure. I do not view the author's resuscitation through *Caperucita* as primarily abstract and intellectual, rooted in her affinity for the genre of the fantastic (Teruel, "Un contexto"). Instead, I believe that she was saved partly by New York City, whose energy was contagious, and by her feisty protagonist, Sara Allen. By nurturing a young girl who would go on to a triumphant life—even though it was in a fictional world—the author was able to pick up the pieces of her own life and, most importantly for her own salvation, return to the pleasures that fiction writing held for her.

THERAPEUTIC WRITING (1): MANHATTAN'S MAGIC

In *Caperucita* Martín Gaite conjured up a city and a heroine to restore the emotional equilibrium that had been shattered by tragedy. Although it might seem odd for a writer from Spain to be an expert on New York, in fact she researched the city just as she researched other topics. Her fascination with New York City long preceded her arrival, dating back to childhood. As she explained: "Las películas en blanco y negro de los años cuarenta, así como todas las menciones a un país próspero, moderno e idealizado por su lejanía, alimentaban en la niña provinciana que yo fui un afán de escapatoria hacia la isla de Manhattan, que luego he proyectado en mi protagonista de ficción Sara Allen." [The black-and-white films of the forties, along with other references to a prosperous, modern country—idealized for being so far away—stimulated my young provincial self to dream of escaping to Manhattan. This dream was later projected onto my fictional protagonist, Sara Allen] ("La libertad" 138). The seed of Martín Gaite's knowledge of Manhattan was planted during her first visit in 1979 and bloomed while she was a visiting professor at Barnard College in the fall of 1980. The latter stay is documented in her posthumously published notebook of collages *Visión de Nueva York* [Vision of New York] (2005), which deploys images where words will not suffice. Several critics have addressed the author's depiction of New York City in *Caperucita*; Alison Ribeiro de Menezes is especially perceptive in her analysis of the symbolic importance of the city, deeming it a "portico" or future-facing gateway "offering entry into a symbolic realm of self-understanding" (48).

Caperucita offers a tour of Manhattan landmarks as Miss Lunatic traverses them—dispensing wisdom, potions, and even reading recommendations along the way.[12] This is the "geografía narrativa" [narrative geography] of the city that Martín Gaite had proudly mastered ("La libertad" 139). She takes the idea of social construction of urban space to its imaginative extreme, adding a magical subaquatic passageway between Battery Park and Liberty Island that might qualify as a mystical "Thirdspace" as theorized by Edward W. Soja: "an-Other way of understanding and acting to change the spatiality of human life" (10). Martín Gaite profiles the denizens of Manhattan with a sure eye. They include affluent businesspeople in a hurry, tourists seeking photographs rather than experiences, self-satisfied ladies who lunch, gang members who target one another, young mothers with their hands full, salaried employees who relinquish their dreams, and police officers who swallow their fear to do their job. The novel captures the essence of Manhattan neighborhoods from rich to ragged, often to comic effect. One hilarious scene involves Miss Lunatic crashing a midtown movie shoot with Sara at a restaurant where the servers wear roller skates. Although at first they are denied entry by a snooty production assistant, the director ends up enchanted by Miss Lunatic and begging her to be in his film, saying that she could have been dreamed up by cinematic master Federico Fellini. Practical information abounds. Martín Gaite dispels the misconception that Manhattan is all there is, acknowledging that some people think it comprises all of New York City's boroughs because "impone su ley a los demás y los empequeñece y los deslumbra" [it imposes its rules on the others and diminishes them, outshines them] (13). Helpful hints for travel within the city—including distances and public transportation routes—are part of the package.

Martín Gaite got a few things wrong, possibly on purpose.[13] There is no "Morningside" neighborhood in Manhattan, only the more prosaic Morningside Heights. (Morningside Park is in Morningside Heights.) In American

English, the character's name would be Mr. "Wolf" and not "Woolf," as with the British author whose novels Martín Gaite knew so well. And the trumpeted analogy used to explain the shape of Manhattan, devised by Sara and enthusiastically repeated by adults around her, is unlikely to be understood by Americans. The observation that Manhattan "se trata de una isla en forma de jamón" [is an island in the shape of a ham] (13) is meaningless even to a New Yorker, because most Americans have never seen a ham that was not in a can—or shrink-wrapped in plastic. Ultimately, the New York of this novel is her very own. As novelist Miguel Delibes sagely observed in the preface to his travel memoir *USA y yo* [USA and I]: "un país no es solo lo que ese país sea sino lo que le añade la perspectiva de cada observador y aun la disposición síquica y mental de éste" [a country is not only what it actually is, but also what each observer's perspective and state of mind brings to it] (311).

The New York City of *Caperucita* is mostly remembered from her earlier stay at Barnard. Even though some details seem unimaginable now, the setting of this novel is largely realistic because it is the New York of the late 1970s and early 1980s—bankrupt, filthy, and economically diverse. Martín Gaite was especially concerned with homeless people, whom she observed walking the streets and talking to themselves (in the days before cell phones), often pushing a shopping cart containing their worldly possessions; in a later novel, a character would refer sympathetically "los *homeless*" (*Irse de casa* 251), whose suffering persists today. Martín Gaite also had new experiences in the city while she was at Vassar, and these feature prominently in the novel. One memorable visit was on her sixtieth birthday, 8 December 1985. We had lunch at the restaurant Windows on the World on the 107th floor of the North Tower of the World Trade Center, which afforded a stunning view of the topography below. Later that afternoon the author discovered what would become the model for Mr. Woolf's "tart-shaped" apartment building: Hampshire House on Central Park South. My godfather, a movie producer, owned the penthouse in that building, which she loved. (Hampshire House also had been immortalized by Frida Kahlo, though neither of us knew this at the time.)[14] He welcomed us with champagne, which would be the preferred drink of the worldly Manhattanites in *Caperucita* (Mr. Woolf, Gloria Star, and Miss Lunatic). When Martín Gaite mentioned that she admired Woody Allen, whose 1979 film *Manhattan* was billed as "a love letter to New York," my godfather offered to introduce them. In her last Vassar letter, dated 14 December 1985, she described her birthday as "mágico" [magical].

THERAPEUTIC WRITING (2): SARA'S SALVATION

The best magic of all—the magic that resuscitated her—came from writing the story of a girl who triumphed with the help of a maternal figure. Martín Gaite herself has been identified by critics with Miss Lunatic and this is accurate ("¡Miss

Lunatic, soy yo!" [I am Miss Lunatic!], she used to exclaim).[15] The character's description of what makes life worth living is very close to the author's personal manifesto in her Autobiographical Sketch. Miss Lunatic explains that, for her, living involves taking her time, listening, telling the truth, having patience, and sharing a glass of wine or breaking bread over conversation. Living also means accepting solitude: "Vivir es saber estar solo para aprender a estar en compañía" [Living is knowing how to be alone in order to learn how to be with others] (92). Talking to herself just before she meets young Sara, Miss Lunatic could be speaking for her creator, warning her not to fall back into depression:

No quería darle coba a aquella desgana de vivir, se resistía a dejarse resbalar por la pendiente de las ideas negras. «Si caes al pozo, estás perdida—le dijo aquella voz interior—. Porque una vez allí, ya no ves nada,» era dejar de vivir.

[She didn't want to harbor that lack of interest in living. She fought against letting herself slip down the slope of dark ideas. "If you fall into the abyss, you're lost," said that inner voice. "Because once you're there you don't see anything anymore," you stop living.] (119)

Upon meeting Sara, this depression lifts—both for the character and for her author. Miss Lunatic "sintió como si su viejo corazón se calentara ante las llamas de una inesperada hoguera" [felt as though her old heart was warmed by the flames of an unexpected hearth] (121). In a felicitous twist, Little Red Riding Hood comes to lead her progenitor out of the woods.

As with New York City, Martín Gaite's fascination with young people had autobiographical roots. The author enjoyed spending time with children—delighting in what sociologists call "sanctioned regression"—and children adored her. My evidence of this joy comes from seeing her play with my two children, reading to them and playing games, sometimes getting down on the floor with them to be at their level (see figures 2.3 and 2.4). Ton Carandell has shared memories of these same activities with her children in the 1950s, specifically the summer of 1957, at the summer home she shared with her husband, José Agustín Goytisolo, in Reus, Catalonia:

Carmiña desayunaba con algún otro madrugador y siempre con mi hermana Tere, entonces de diecinueve años, y conmigo. Era muy alegre y cuando acababa el desayuno los niños la rodeaban para que jugara con ellos. Mi hermana Ita, de ocho años . . . ; Juan, de seis y Cristián, de cinco, la seguían para que les cantara alguna canción y les gastara bromas con algún juego de palabras. Las dos pequeñas, Marta y Julia, mi hija, también colaboraron en el jolgorio, riendo y llamándola para que les hiciera cosquillas.

[Carmiña ate breakfast with any other early risers and always with my sister Tere, then nineteen, and with me. She was very cheerful and when breakfast

Figure 2.3. Carmen Martín Gaite with Alexander Asher Brown at El Boalo, 1991

Figure 2.4. Carmen Martín Gaite with Sarah Elizabeth Brown at El Boalo, 1991

was done the children all gathered around wanting her to play with them. My sister Ita, who was eight . . . Juan, age six and Cristián, age five, followed her around so that she might sing them a song or make them laugh with some kind of riddle. The two little ones, Marta and my daughter Julia, also took part in the fun, laughing and calling her to come tickle them.] (Carandell and Riera 43)

By the time she wrote *Caperucita*, Martín Gaite had already created two intrepid young female protagonists: Altalé in *El castillo de las tres murallas* and Sorpresa in *El pastel del diablo*. Two other girls were intertexts for *Caperucita*: her daughter and mine. After Marta died, we talked a lot about what it meant to raise a young woman in the harsh modern world. There were wolves lurking everywhere, ready to pounce. When my daughter was born in 1987, she changed the name of the main character to hers, calling it a "godmother's gift."

The relationship of fairy godmother to protégé was a natural one for her, and it is immortalized in *Caperucita*, from the time that Miss Lunatic exclaims: "¡Cómo me gustaría descargar mis fardos más secretos en alguien más joven, digno de heredarlos!" [Oh, how I would like to unload my bundles of deep secrets on someone younger, someone worthy of inheriting them!] (110). More than just leaving a mark on another person, the author wanted to help young people grow, just as she had done with her daughter. This desire subtends all of the author's fiction for young readers and reaches its fullest expression in her novel for young adults. As Ribeiro de Menezes has observed, Martín Gaite respected childhood as much as adulthood, so that her literature for young people "sets out to convey in more direct form many of the preoccupations of her adult fiction, particularly as regards the possibilities for girls of self-realization and the acquisition of intellectual autonomy" (51). In her last reference to me about young people, written in the summer of 1997 following her final visit with my children, she wrote:

Les deseo a esos niños lo mejor en la vida, como un hada anacrónica. Porque en mis deseos va incluido el de que no renuncien a sus sueños, fantasías e idealismo. Ni al riesgo.

[I wish those children the best in life, like a timeless fairy godmother. Because among my wishes are that they never give up their dreams, fantasies and idealism. And that they never shy away from risk.] (Letter to Brown, Madrid, 14 July 1997; frontispiece)

These wishes were the same ones that she had for her own daughter, who had a life of freedom and adventures as she was growing up. And they are the wishes that Miss Lunatic confers on the little American girl who pulled her out of the abyss, Sara Allen, when she says goodbye. "¿Qué voy a hacer sin ti? Me quedo como metida en un laberinto" [What am I going to do without you? It's as though I'm left stuck in a labyrinth] (158), Sara says to Miss Lunatic. "Procura encontrar tu camino en el laberinto" [Manage to find your way in the labyrinth]

Figure 2.5. Collage-card for Sarah Brown by Carmen Martín Gaite, 1991

(158), Miss Lunatic replies. "Quien no ama la vida, no lo encuentra. Pero tú la amas mucho" [Those who don't love life won't find it. But you love life very much] (158), she affirms, adding that she will always be with Sara in spirit. Her card for my young daughter illustrates how the author empathized with children's sadness when they are forced to say goodbye (figure 2.5).

Caperucita en Manhattan became its author's path out of the labyrinth, her transition back to loving life, and writing, in her newly empty Madrid home. She had once again recovered the thread of a story, as she described in a 1978 letter about *El cuarto de atrás*: "Y sobre todo me anima y me divierte cuando, como ahora, consigo recoger el hilo que parecía haberse roto. Es como si reviviera." [And above all it encourages and delights me when, as is happening now, I manage to pick up the thread that seemed to have snapped. It's as though I were revived] ("Carta").

―――

Caperucita's fantasy-tinged adventure, delightful prose, wise cultural commentary, factual content, sense of humor, and message of triumph over fear are strong enough to engage readers of all ages. The novel's inimitable blend of the real and the imaginary illustrates the author's penchant for presenting the extraordinary from a realistic perspective and the realistic with an extraordinary twist. *Caperucita* has won devoted readers around the world. It also had a profound effect on its author. Having lost herself in the adventure of Red Riding Hood and having found within herself the courage she needed to resume life in Madrid, Martín Gaite would go on to her most fertile literary decade for the novel. Assessing her output, Jurado Morales observed that she published more novels in the 1990s (six) than in the entire period spanning the 1950s to the 1980s (five), a statistic that becomes more dramatic in his invaluable five-column chart, with blank columns for the years 1963–1974 as well as for 1978–1990 (*Trayectoria* 13). Without Sara Allen and Miss Lunatic's Manhattan, that chart would surely have been different, most likely with a final blank space for what instead were her most prolific years. Rather than the mouth-to-mouth resuscitation mentioned in the book's dedication, the resuscitation that Martín Gaite got from *Caperucita en Manhattan* was of another kind: a renewal that allowed her to continue her illustrious career.

CHAPTER 3

Nubosidad variable

CONTEMPORARY FEMINISM IN
POST-TRANSITION SPAIN

Martín Gaite's first novel of the decade written exclusively for adult readers became her most triumphant. *Nubosidad variable* (1992) [*Variable Cloud* 1995] holds a special place in the author's oeuvre, surpassed only by *El cuarto de atrás* in terms of scholarly attention (*MLA Bibliography*). It has captivated general readers as well as scholars. An immediate bestseller when it appeared, the novel has remained in print for over a quarter of a century and been translated into eight languages. Martín Gaite had a premonition that it would be a success. In a letter from Madrid composed while waiting for her copies of the book to arrive from the publisher, she wrote: "Estoy con muchas ganas de verlo, como comprenderás. Me ha quedado muy bien, creo. Y lleva en la portada un collage de mi invención." [I'm eager to see it, as you can imagine. I think it turned out well. And it has an original collage of mine on the cover] (Letter to Brown, Madrid, 28 March 1992).[1] The novel's appeal is readily apparent. It is a riveting, exquisitely crafted story of two fascinating Spanish women who reinvent themselves as they write to one another, set in the tumultuous years after Spain's transition to democracy. The novel's techniques and themes have been elucidated by critics, with special attention to those associated with writing (Nuria Cruz-Cámara, "*Nubosidad variable*"; María Luisa Guardiola, "*Nubosidad variable*"; Jesús Pérez-Magallón), female cultural symbols (Lee-Ann Laffey; Janet Pérez, "Structural"), and women's friendship (Lélia Almeida, Antonia Ferriol-Montano). *Nubosidad variable* also has broader cultural significance. The novel inserts women into post-Transition history using tenets of postmodern and twenty-first-century feminism. These precepts shed light on the intellectual biography of this iconoclastic author, as they point to cultural forces that shaped contemporary Spain.

Written in the late 1980s and early 1990s, *Nubosidad variable* is set in the same period. The last line on the last page specifies the novel's dates of composition:

"Madrid, abril de 1984–enero de 1992" (391) ["Madrid, April 1984–January 1992"
374].[2] For Martín Gaite, this was a period of change that laid the groundwork
for the rest of the decade. She was gratified by new levels of critical and popular
recognition in Spain, now approaching the veneration that she had already
achieved in the United States, and by honors that recognized her life's work. Two
bestsellers attracted new readers as they captivated those already familiar with
her work: *Usos amorosos de la postguerra española* (1987) [*Courtship Customs in
Postwar Spain* 2004], a volume of essays which won the Premio Anagrama de
Ensayo, and *Caperucita en Manhattan*. Martín Gaite had decided to change publishers, choosing two with which she felt the most rapport: the Anagrama publishing house in Barcelona and Siruela based in Madrid. All of her books in the
1990s would be published by one of these two firms, and new contracts for older
works were instituted when existing agreements expired. In 1988 she received
her most important honor since the Premio Nacional de Literatura: the Premio
Príncipe de Asturias from the future king of Spain, an award recognized around
the world. In 1992 she received the Premio Castilla y León de las Letras [Castilla
and León Prize for Literature], given by Spain's largest and most historic autonomous region—also the one that she came from (Salamanca being one of the
nine provinces of Castilla y León). The author invited her sister Anita to accompany her back to their native city for the ceremony; as Anita wrote shortly before
they left: "el día 23 vamos a recoger el premio Castilla y León que le han conce-
dido y se lo entregan en Salamanca. ¡Me hace ilusión!" [On the 23rd we're going
to get the Castilla and León Prize that they've given her and are presenting in
Salamanca. I'm excited!] (Letter to Brown from Anita Martín Gaite, El Boalo,
17 March 1992).

Even though the writing of *Nubosidad variable* began years earlier (as she typically developed a number of projects simultaneously), Martín Gaite did not
devote herself to it until two years before its completion. In 1990, soon before
the November publication of *Caperucita en Manhattan*, the author acquired
needed support for her writing when she hired a personal assistant, Angelines
Solsona. Although Angelines was untrained (when Martín Gaite met her she had
last been employed as an assistant in a hair salon), she was industrious. She
gamely did everything from typing and photocopying to running errands and
washing dishes, freeing the author to concentrate on her work. She was also a
young, cheerful presence in Martín Gaite's Madrid apartment. I became ac-
quainted with Angelines when she and I worked together to prepare final copies
of the "creative conversations" that Martín Gaite wrote for our textbook. The
author's letters to me as she was writing *Nubosidad variable* often included
regards from Angelines, typically "Muchos recuerdos de Angelines" [Angelines
sends her best] (Letter to Brown, Madrid, 18 April 1990). Sometimes she sent
regards from both her sister and her assistant, revealing that Angelines was a
valued presence in her life. Angelines also freed her employer to travel without

worry, since she handled her mail and other affairs when she was away. Among many other places, Martín Gaite traveled to Argentina in 1990 for a week-long conference devoted to her literature. After two weeks at a spa in Arnedillo, Spain, to recuperate from all of her activities—which she characterized as too numerous to list—she resumed work in earnest in the fall of 1990, reporting that "mi novela ha avanzado despacio pero con buena salud" [my novel has advanced slowly but soundly] (Letter to Brown, Madrid, 22 October 1990). Six months later, she shared that the novel was very far along but that "no sé cuándo la terminaré porque es una de las más ambiciosas que he emprendido nunca" [I'm not sure when I'll finish it because it's one of the most ambitious I have ever undertaken] (Letter to Brown, Madrid, 25 April 1991). She did manage to complete it in time for the Madrid Book Fair of 1992, where it was launched with a flourish.

Inscribing Two Women into Post-Transition Spanish History

Nubosidad variable captures a crucial time in Spanish history, now known as the post-Transition years. This was the era of Socialist (PSOE) leadership under Felipe González, whose election as prime minister in 1982 marked the end of the transition to democracy that began with dictator Francisco Franco's demise in 1975. When they came into power the Socialists had three goals. The first was to rebuff terrorism. The country's memory of the attempted military coup of 23 February 1981 was fresh, and the Basque terrorist group ETA was still active (the acronym stands for Euzkadi Ta Askatasuna or Basque Country and Freedom, known in English as the Basque National Liberation Movement). As Martín Gaite explained in 1981, following her return to Madrid after a semester in the United States:

> Estoy aquí desde primeros de febrero. Han pasado tantas cosas en España desde mi vuelta que todo el viaje a Norteamérica me parece un sueño distante y lejano. La situación política aquí es grave y nos tiene intranquilos a todos. Se me han quitado mucho los ánimos de trabajo que traía. Pero hay que procurar rehacerse y seguir adelante.

> [I've been back since the beginning of February. So many things have happened in Spain since my return that my entire North American trip seems like a distant and remote dream. The political situation here is serious and has us all worried. I've lost a lot of the enthusiasm for work that I brought back with me. But it's imperative to regroup and move forward.] (Letter to Brown, Madrid, 26 March 1981)

The second goal of the Socialist government was entry into the European Economic Community or Common Market, precursor of the European Union, which it achieved in 1986. The third objective was economic stimulus. The goal of staving off terrorism was not contentious, but the other two were fraught. A controversial vote to retain NATO membership along with mandated privatization or "reconversion" of state-owned entities (resulting in job losses) ushered in the go-go, reindustrialized Spain that forms the backdrop for *Nubosidad variable*.

The novel demonstrates how under the Socialists, political clout and entrepreneurial success went hand in hand. Politics are invoked indirectly; as the author explained in the year she began writing the novel: "Las referencias políticas en mis libros están puestos más para explicar un ambiente, para completar la descripción de un ambiente" [Political references in my books are put there mostly to shed light on a setting, to fill out the description of an environment] (Interview with Brown, 23–24 November 1984). The setting for *Nubosidad variable* encompasses the last years of La Movida (loosely translated as "The Movement"), the youth-oriented urban cultural phenomenon driven by "ganas de experimentar, de conocer, de romper los moldes y superar barreras" [the urge to experience, to explore, to shatter molds and break through barriers] in the words of José Manuel Lechado (15). Although La Movida is now remembered for its members' experimentation with sex, drugs, and rock music, *Nubosidad variable* captures a more refined aspect of this phenomenon. Museum openings, fashion shows, and concerts all attracted La Movida's celebrities and attendant media. Unlike most youth movements, this one was viewed favorably by political leaders. The prime minister's wife attended art openings in real life and was shown doing so on television, as is mordantly described in the first chapter of the novel.

Nubosidad variable is an expansive novel. Its nearly four hundred pages comprise seventeen chapters apparently written by two alternating narrators, followed by an omniscient epilogue. Along with a number, each chapter bears a pithy title (rendered in British "sentence" style—with only the first word capitalized—by Margaret Jull Costa, whose translation benefited from Martín Gaite's willingness to answer questions as she translated the novel into English). These chapter names range from the first one's practical "Problemas de fontanería" ["Plumbing problems"] to chapter five's more cryptic "Pulpos en un garaje" ["Octopuses in a garage"] to a reference to the surrealistic Dalí painting in the last numbered chapter, "Persistencia de la memoria" ["The persistence of memory"]. The narrators of these chapters were childhood friends but have lost contact for thirty years. Sofía Montalvo is a brilliant wife and mother whose imagination has been stifled in an unhappy marriage. Mariana León is a successful, emotionally repressed psychiatrist who never married; her long-term love interest is bisexual and bipolar. After Sofía and Mariana meet unexpectedly they begin their reacquaintance gingerly, through writing. The plot unfolds through first-person missives intended for the other woman. Sofía keeps a journal in which she transforms her experiences into narrative, while Mariana writes descriptive letters with multiple entries. Sofía begins and ends their correspondence, writing nine odd-numbered chapters that interdigitate with eight even-numbered chapters by Mariana.

In a twist on the dynamic exchange peculiar to the genre, only the first chapter by each woman is delivered or mailed, making this a static epistolary novel comprising interlocking monologues (reminiscent of the noninteractive dialogue of the author's 1974 novel *Retahílas*). The notion that writing is a solitary act, likened to a private striptease, is embraced by both protagonists. Writing is elevated to a therapeutic activity through which each correspondent gains transformative self-knowledge. As Catherine O'Leary and Alison Ribeiro de Menezes have noted, each narrator is primarily concerned with herself. Although Sofía and Mariana's writings are "presented as a form of mutual revelation and salvation," the focus of each correspondent is inward rather than outward: "Behind this concern for one another lies the contradiction that each woman is primarily focused on solving her own problems" (128). In the epilogue, Sofía and Mariana have a dramatic reunion after nearly a month of writing to one another. They read each other's chapters and, with a metaliterary wink from the author as the work's creation becomes its subject, fashion their writings into this novel. Sofía Montalvo is a veiled portrait of the author, down to the name Sofía. This was Martín Gaite's grandmother's name and an alias she had used before. She submitted the manuscript of her first novel *Entre visillos* to the jury for the Premio Nadal, then the most important literary prize in Spain (which her novel went on to win), using her maternal grandmother's full name: Sofía Veloso ("Bosquejo" 233; "Sketch" 243). Sofía's creativity bubbles beneath the surface of her consciousness, finding little outlet in her day-to-day life. Her eloquent writing style reveals her literary gifts. Her artistic impulse is expressed in the collage that she composes as she writes in a similar fashion, evoking the small, fanciful collage (featuring letters, clouds and clocks) that Martín Gaite devised for the original cover. The author's only other published collage, a self-portrait, was created around the same time (figure 3.1).

When the novel opens, Martín Gaite's alter ego Sofía is still vibrant and youthful-looking, but she feels adrift. Her marriage has become a shell, two of her three adult children have moved out, and her husband is having a serious affair. Sofía's closest emotional connection is with her now-absent oldest daughter. Their relationship mirrors the mutually protective one that Martín Gaite shared with her late daughter, Marta, to whom the novel is dedicated: "Para el alma que ella dejó de guardia permanente, como una lucecita encendida, en mi casa, en mi cuerpo y en el nombre por el que me llamaba" (9) ["For the soul that she left on constant guard, like a tiny light, in my house, in my body and in the name that she called me by" n.p.]. Mariana León is personally unlike the author, and compared with Sofía she is not as fully developed as a novelistic character. It is probable that she is a fictionalized version of one of Martín Gaite's close friends, a psychiatrist whose practice resembled Mariana's.[3] Stunningly

Figure 3.1. "Collage autorretrato" [Collage Self-Portrait] by Carmen Martín Gaite, 1992

beautiful, Mariana is also cool, rational, and controlled. She sees love as a game and sex as just a temporary palliative against loneliness. Mariana resists any kind of attachment, leaving her unmoored. "Nunca he tenido un novio estable" (214) ["I've never had a steady boyfriend" 201], she confesses. One of her patients accuses her of being incapable of love—something the patient finds ironic since everyone is in love with Mariana. Exhausted and drained by her suicidal boyfriend as well as her needy patients, Mariana decamps for Puerto Real, a seaside town in Andalucía near Cádiz. There she tries to finish an essay on eroticism. Tellingly, this project has stalled because she is too defended against passion: she overintellectualizes the subject, not realizing that "precisamente el erotismo es como una marea que rompe los diques de lo inteligible" (108) ["eroticism is like a rising tide that breaks all the bounds of intelligibility" 97].

Sofía and Mariana create a multivocal discourse that emphasizes the personal narrative of each. It is up to the reader to assemble their stories, as foreshadowed in the epigraph by Natalia Ginzburg (a favorite author of Martín Gaite's, whose novels she translated into Spanish). It begins: "Cuando he escrito novelas, siempre he tenido la sensación de encontrarme en las manos con añicos de espejo, y sin embargo conservaba la esperanza de acabar por recomponer el espejo entero. No lo logré nunca." (9) ["Whenever I write a novel, I always feel as if I were holding the shattered fragments of a mirror in my hands, and yet I'm always hopeful of being able to put the mirror together again. I never will manage it" n.p.]. The two protagonists fulfill the need for an interlocutor that was a recurring theme for the author, whose first collection of essays bore the title *La búsqueda de interlocutor y otras búsquedas* [The search for a conversational partner and other searches]. Martín Gaite called this search "la cuestión . . . que se plantea más tarde o más temprano simultáneamente con el deseo de romper la soledad" [the question that comes up sooner or later together with the wish to end one's isolation], namely "la búsqueda de un destinatario para nuestras narraciones" [the search for a recipient for the stories we tell] (*Búsqueda* 25). For Jacqueline Cruz, *Nubosidad variable* marks the culmination of this quest in the author's oeuvre (187). Having missed three decades of each other's existence, Sofía and Mariana come close to being the untarnished conversational partners that Martín Gaite wrote about in the essay "Los malos espejos" [Defective mirrors]—someone who knows so little about another person that he or she reflects back what is there without bias. In other ways they are memory keepers.[4]

Even though each writer is focused on her own situation, their correspondence results in mutual salvation. This happens through what Marcia Welles—implicitly invoking "the talking cure" of Freudian psychoanalysis—describes as "the writing cure" experienced by Sofía and Mariana (258). The one letter from Mariana that is actually physically sent helps fortify Sofía's resolve to extricate herself from her marriage. Sofía moves to her children's apartment, makes peace with the past, and decides that from now on she will not be forced to do anything that she does not want to do. With Sofía's assistance, Mariana also breaks free from the personal and professional responsibilities that are suffocating her, mirroring the story of her unfinished novel whose plot is "la escapatoria de una mujer madura" (227) ["mature woman escapes" 214]. By the time the women reunite on the beach in Cádiz, each is poised to triumph over her own challenges. They achieve a dramatic catharsis as they work to combine their manuscripts; their collaboration is intense and passionate without being sexual. The man who ostensibly caused their rift in the past is revealed to have been incidental, and men in the present are now also relegated to secondary status. Their trajectories fulfill the "coming out" arc that has been ascribed to third-wave feminism in literature. In this case the term does not refer to coming out of the closet to claim an intrinsic sexual identity. Rather, it refers to narrators' acceptance of their own essential feminism as innate and immutable: "what all these stories share, in addition to the confessional mode in which they are written, is a scenario in which the narrator . . . discovers that she is, and always has been, a feminist," as Justyna Wlodarczyk observed in *Ungrateful Daughters* (89).

WOMEN'S STORIES AND WOMEN'S WRITING

Nubosidad variable builds on its novelistic predecessors, illustrating Virginia Woolf's maxim from *A Room of One's Own* that "we think back through our mothers if we are women" (79). Martín Gaite's novel first evinces and then surpasses the "reclaiming of women's stories" that characterized Spanish feminism in the novel from the postwar era through the end of the twentieth century. This trajectory began with censored novels of the 1940s and 1950s that depicted female subjects in stifling traditional environments, with novels such as Carmen Laforet's *Nada* (1945) [translated using the same title, 2008] and Martín Gaite's *Entre visillos* (1958). It accelerated after censorship ended in the late 1970s, with novels that showed women participating in both public and private spheres: examples include *El cuarto de atrás*, Esther Tusquets's *El mismo mar de todos los veranos* (1978) [*The Same Sea as Every Summer* 1990] and Rosa Montero's *Crónica del desamor* (1979) [*Absent Love: A Chronicle* 1990]. By the end of the twentieth century, the focus on women's experiences became frank and intimate: Almudena Grandes's *Las edades de Lulú* (1989) [*The Ages of Lulu* 1994] and Lucía Extebarria's *Beatriz y los cuerpos celestes* [Beatrice and the heavenly bodies] (1998) typify these stories of female protagonists in pursuit of their own desires as well as their creators' market-oriented, apolitical stance.[5] In the twenty-first century a resurgence of historical engagement, mirroring this preoccupation in the surrounding culture, produced novels such as Dulce Chacón's *La voz dormida* (2002) [*The Sleeping Voice* 2006] and Carme Riera's *La mitad del alma* [Half of the soul] (2004).

While expanding the telling of women's stories, Martín Gaite renovated a genre that since the eighteenth century had been associated with women: the epistolary novel. (The fact that important epistolary novels ostensibly by women were in fact authored by men only confirms this association.) Commonly thought of as a dialogue involving an exchange of letters and/or diary entries between two correspondents, the genre also encompasses monologue and multiperspectival techniques, with the latter incorporating documents by others. In her essay "Buscando el modo" [Searching for the way], composed as she was writing *Nubosidad variable*, Martín Gaite analyzed women's use of the epistolary genre. She observed that letters and diaries have always been ideal conduits for women's literary expression, affording protection from scrutiny (since they are private) as well as a truly receptive audience. In the essay she explained her fundamental belief that if the ideal recipient (the "tú" or familiar "you") for a writer's message does not exist in real life, that person must be invented. For women writers, this is key: "Es la búsqueda apasionada de ese 'tu' el hilo conductor del discurso femenino, el móvil primordial para quebrar la sensación de arrinconamiento" [It is the passionate search for that "you" which is the common thread of female discourse, the primary motive for rebelling against a sense of being marginalized] (*Desde la ventana* 59). Martín Gaite viewed the diary form as an outgrowth of letter writing, reflecting the same progression—from concrete to abstract—as the search for the ideal recipient of a woman's writing (*Desde la ventana* 60).

Martín Gaite enjoyed playing with genre conventions, and she does so in *Nubosidad variable*. As Welles has pointed out, the protagonists move beyond the epistolary genre's convention of transmitting information as they become increasingly literary:

> *Nubosidad variable* purports to be an epistolary novel, a genre that, because of its pseudodocumentary form, is realist in convention and expectation. But the reader's expectations are manipulated ingeniously. The mimetic intent of the narrators to reproduce and communicate each other's reality becomes more self-consciously novelistic; their writerly concerns more obtrusive. (257)

Critics have associated the novel's genre innovation with female agency. Cruz has linked it to a "reivindicación de lo femenino" [reclaiming of the feminine] (137), as the two women dispense with men and create a work of literature that is worthy of publication with a premiere publishing house, Anagrama (as it would be, with support from the real-life publisher and friend who is mentioned in the text: Jorge Herralde).[6] María Luisa Guardiola has established a parallel between liberation from genre constraints and the protagonists' newfound freedom: "Al trascender la dinámica de la narrativa epistolar, se alcanza por ende la emancipación de las dos amigas interlocutoras, a la vez que libra el género de sus limitaciones convencionales" [As the conventional dynamic of the epistolary novel is transcended, so too are the female friends and interlocutors freed from conventional limitations] ("*Nubosidad variable*" 672).

Though Martín Gaite's execution of the epistolary form in *Nubosidad variable* is original, the function of letter writing remains immutable. As Thomas Mallon has noted, the intent of letters throughout history has been to overcome distance (13). For Martín Gaite, the exchange of letters brought her closer to family and friends; she also rewarded those whose interest in her work prompted them to write to her, replying to letters from scholars in Spain and around the world. She corresponded with everyone she cared about—a necessity not only before email, but before long-distance phone calls became affordable. In the 1970s and 1980s long-distance calls were prohibitive in Spain because the telecommunications monopoly Telefónica charged exorbitant fees for them. (I recall a week I spent at the Hotel Wellington in Madrid in 1978—now immortalized in *Cuadernos de todo* [443–444]—after which my phone bill exceeded the tab for lodging.) Overseas calls were so special that the author sometimes arranged them in advance, as with this telegram message dated Madrid, 25 March 1979:

TELEFONEAME MANANA A LAS DIEZ DE LA NOCHE HORA
ESPANOLA
BESOS
CALILA

[CALL ME TOMORROW NIGHT AT TEN O'CLOCK SPANISH TIME
KISSES
CALILA]

Her letters to me are full of another type of exhortation: to continue writing. These requests range from the friendly, "Aquí quedo recordándote y a la espera de tus noticias, cuando tengas ganas de escribirme" [I'm here remembering you and waiting for your news, when you feel like writing] (Letter to Brown, Madrid, 28 September 1978), to the affectionate, "No me olvides, pienso siempre en ti" [Don't forget me, I'm always thinking of you] (Letter to Brown, Madrid, 17 February 1980), to the more insistent, "Hoy solamente escribo para desearos toda clase de felicidades en estas fechas navideñas. Y para pedirte, por favor, que me escribes" [Today I'm just writing to send you all the best wishes of the Christmas season. And to ask you to please write to me] (Letter to Brown, Madrid, 18 December 1983), to the playful but specific "Escríbeme please. Una carta larguita, ¿sí? Un beso" [Write to me, please. A nice long letter, okay? Sending a kiss] (Letter to Brown, Charlottesville, 30 October 1982).

Martín Gaite's regard for the epistolary form was distilled in a 1964 letter she wrote to fellow novelist and friend Juan Benet—one of the first in the posthumously published volume of their correspondence:

No sé por qué usamos tan poco en nuestro tiempo la comunicación epistolar; yo mantengo que si se fomentara esta forma de trato tan desacreditada (no me refiero, claro, a las cartas para dar noticias o recados, ni a las cartas llamadas «sentimentales»)—uno de los pocos lujos que en era de tanta prisa nos podemos permitir todavía para tratar de llegar a los demás—, se aprendería también a hablar y a escuchar más sosegadamente en las otras ocasiones, cuando te echaras a la gente a la cara.

[I don't know why it is that today we so rarely engage in epistolary communication. I believe that if we encouraged this devalued form of interaction (and obviously I'm not referring to letters used to convey news or messages, nor love letters)—one of the few pleasurable ways of communicating that we still have in this harried era—that we would also learn to speak and listen more calmly in other contexts, when saying things to people's faces.] (Martín Gaite and Benet, *Correspondencia* 32)

The last line of this statement underscores the continuum Martín Gaite established between written and verbal communication, which she also prized. As she explained in 1980, the right circumstances for conversation do not always present themselves, and writing is a viable communicative substitute ("Bosquejo" 234; "Sketch" 244).

The author used letters not only to communicate, but to distill her thoughts. For her, writing was a way of seeing. She explained this function, which was independent of publication, in a letter to Benet: "Se escribe, y aunque se deje sin publicar todo lo escrito, como hizo Kafka, está vigente siempre la intención de decir cómo miramos, de fijar esa dirección nuestra a lo que está en torno mientras uno lo ve" [One writes and, even if you leave everything unpublished the way Kafka did, the goal is always to express how we look at things, focusing on what is around us as we are seeing at it] (*Correspondencia* 98). Martín Gaite practiced writing-as-seeing throughout her adult life, not only in her literature but in her more than one hundred notebooks (going back to 1961). Letter writing was for her a stimulus for further thinking and writing, beyond the epistolary exchange.[7] She did not conceive of letters as quests for replies, but rather as discrete exchanges of ideas. In the closing of one of her letters to Benet, she vividly expresses this concept, which would be reflected in the letters and journal entries of *Nubosidad variable*: "Un ruego: si me escribes—que ojalá lo hagas—o cuando te vuelva a ver, no contestes a esta carta. Pero háblame por tu cuenta de todo lo que quieras." [One request: If you write to me—which I hope you do—or when I see you again, don't reply to this letter. Instead talk to me of your own volition about whatever you like] (*Correspondencia* 39). More than any other novel by this author, *Nubosidad variable* celebrates the act of writing. Sofía asserts, "no hay mejor tabla de salvación que la pluma" (210) ["there's no better salvation than the pen" 198], words that reflect the deeply held conviction of her creator.

Martín Gaite's Third-Wave Feminism

Even as *Nubosidad variable* encompasses the stories and structures of its precursors and contemporaries, it offers a wider lens on society than other women's novels of the nineties—a perspective that would not become widespread for more than a decade. Written and set during the years immediately following Spain's Transition, the novel chronicles the zeitgeist from a female perspective, illuminating a period that is iconic and contested. *Nubosidad variable* actualizes Martín Gaite's humanistic view of gender, which advocated personal freedom. The novel reflects the same viewpoint as the two nonfiction books that interrupted its creation, a volume of feminist social criticism and a collection of feminist literary criticism.[8] A recently recovered interview from the 1970s clarifies Martín Gaite's conception of gender—including a passing reference to performativity long before Judith Butler had introduced the term—and demonstrates that in this area as in others, she was an independent thinker whose beliefs persisted over time. The novel's seemingly disparate structural and thematic elements can now be seen to belong under the rubric of contemporary, third-wave feminism. These include multivocality, an emphasis on personal narrative, rejection of doctrinaire theory, critiques of sociocultural and socioeconomic inequality, and an embrace of diverse modes of gender expression. Through its postmodern form and content, *Nubosidad variable* enacts present-day feminist tenets, presaging Chimamanda Ngozi Adichie's invitation (expressed through her celebrated title) to build a more inclusive world through gender equality: *We Should All Be Feminists*.

In Spain during the post-Transition years, feminism meant the international women's movement of the 1960s, 1970s, and 1980s. For Spanish feminists, sociopolitical concerns were paramount. Their rallying cry was for "reivindicación" (partially translatable as "vindication"), a term that includes both a defense of and a demand for women's rights. (*Reivindicación feminista* was also the title of the journal published by the newly inaugurated Ediciones del Feminismo [Feminist Editions].) This movement is now classified as second-wave feminism. The label reflects the fact that this was the successor to the first wave of feminism that began in the nineteenth century—arriving in Spain in the early twentieth century. In 1914 the Royal Spanish Academy added "feminismo" [feminism] to its dictionary (though it would be another sixty-four years before it admitted its first female member). The dictionary defined the concept as "una doctrina social favorable a la condición de la mujer a quien concede la capacidad y derechos reservados hasta ahora a los hombres" [a doctrine favorable to the female condition that recognizes in women the competence and rights hitherto reserved for men], as reported by María Antonia Fernández (829). The first feminist movement, spearheaded in English-speaking countries as well as in Spain by affluent political conservatives such as those belonging to the Asociación Nacional de Mujeres Españolas [National Association of Spanish Women], founded in 1915, addressed women's "shared exclusion from political, social and economic life" (documented by Gillis, Howie, and Munford 1). In Spain, first-wave feminism did not flourish until the establishment of the Second Republic in 1931. The Spanish Constitution of 1931 gave women the vote as well as other unprecedented rights, including the power to avail themselves of contraception, civil marriage, and divorce. During the Civil War of 1936–1939 female Republicans literally fought for egalitarianism. But when Franco came to power he set back the clock for Spanish women. His regime rescinded rights granted under the Second Republic and established mandatory social training for females that paralleled military service for males. The Sección Femenina [Women's Section] of the fascist Falange was formed to educate women into traditional marital and maternal roles through its Servicio Social [Social Service]. Martín Gaite was forced to fulfill five hundred hours of this indoctrination, which she would memorably describe in both fiction (*El cuarto de atrás*) and nonfiction (*Usos amorosos de la postguerra española*).

Feminism became linked with anti-Francoism during his dictatorship, and resistance continued to dominate the movement after his death. Second-wave feminism of the 1960s and 1970s, known as "women's liberation" on both sides of the Atlantic, was many times stronger than its first-wave predecessor. It was also much more fractured and fractious. In Spain, second-wave feminists included women of varied socioeconomic status, affiliations (with national and regional political parties as well as unions), and theoretical stances ("difference feminists," who rejected existing power structures, and "equality feminists," who lobbied for parity within them). Regardless of these distinctions, feminists were tarred with the same brush in both the media and academia. Writing soon after *Nubosidad variable* was published, Constance Sullivan observed that "feminists continue to be portrayed in both of these cultural institutions as aggressive man-haters, wild women on the margins of society" (53). A minor character in *Nubosidad variable* typifies the abrasive feminists of Sofía's and Mariana's university years in the 1960s: "una chica de gafas que hablaba de la emancipación femenina, se mordía las uñas y decía tacos, costumbre aún llamativa entre mujeres de la época" (231) ["she wore glasses, talked about female emancipation, chewed her nails and swore, a custom still unusual amongst women of the time" 218].

Martín Gaite echoed the era's widespread aversion to strident female protes-tors, but her objections went deeper. The author decried the movement's lack of intellectual rigor, epitomized by placard messages such as "No to Men!" in photo-graphs that originally illustrated her 1971 essay "Las mujeres liberadas" [Liber-ated women] (*Triunfo* 33). Martín Gaite criticized what she called "una rebelión indiscriminada" [an indiscriminate rebellion] based on rhetoric rather than a nuanced understanding of the institutions that were being challenged ("Las mujeres liberadas," *Búsqueda* 96). In a little-known, recently rediscovered interview with journalist Juby Bustamante—the friend to whom "Las mujeres liberadas" was dedicated—the author explained her theoretical stance in per-sonal terms:

> Bien, puedo decirte que yo me siento perfectamente en mi piel siendo mujer. Que desde niña me he sentido a gusto en tal condición. Que nunca he sufrido ese "complejo de castración" de que hablan los psicoanalistas. Y que me niego a cooperar en esa manía por marcar las diferencias, por dividir el mundo en dos bandos irreconciliables, en los que no creo. Puede que haya una razón para esa agresividad y ese rencor que utilizan las feministas . . . puede que la haya, pero no lo comparto. Creo que insistiendo en las diferencias, nada arreglaremos.

> [Well, I can you that I feel perfectly at ease being a woman. That I've always been comfortable in this state. That I've never felt that "castration complex"

to which psychoanalysts refer. And that I refuse to be part of the craze for mapping differences, for dividing the world into two oppositional camps, which I don't accept. There may be a reason for feminists' combativeness and resentment . . . if it exists, I don't share it. I think that we won't accomplish anything by insisting on our differences.] (Bustamante 8)[9]

In a more widely distributed and extensively cited interview following the 1974 publication of *Retahílas*, Martín Gaite endorsed an adjective used to describe the novelistic character who was most like herself: "antifeminista" [antifeminist]. She qualified her so-called antifeminism to interviewer Javier Villán by saying that what she truly believed in was freedom for women as well as men (Villán 22). This ideal of free choice presages Adichie's childrearing mandate: "Teach her that the idea of 'gender roles' is absolute nonsense" (*Dear Ijeawele* 14).

More than any of her fiction before or after, *Nubosidad variable* dramatizes the author's feminism. This is true even though Martín Gaite's feminism has been a delicate subject for many years. The controversy is not related to her literature: most of her novels have female protagonists[10] and many of her essays address women's concerns. Rather, the dispute stems from the author's rejection of the term. Martín Gaite consistently refused to be called a feminist. She was not alone among contemporary Spanish women writers in repudiating this label, but she did so long before others such as Soledad Puértolas or Cristina Fernández Cubas. This stance placed her in the company of a number of Spanish writers and intellectuals, from the nineteenth century forward, who advanced ideas that would be considered feminist while rejecting the term "feminism" in favor of "humanism."[11] Martín Gaite's earliest and best-known rejection of the label "feminist" was in the aforementioned essay "Las mujeres liberadas." Reissued versions neglect to mention its context: this short opinion piece was written for a special issue of the journal *Triunfo* devoted to the subject of marriage.[12] In the essay she declared that she had no use for the aggressive tactics—nor for the denigration of marriage—associated with the women's movement of the day.

Martín Gaite's "feminist purpose"—a term coined by Roberta Johnson to signify her enduring preoccupation with feminist concerns—is indisputable ("Teaching" 209). Scholars have recognized and explored feminist content in her literature since the 1970s, noting that she became increasingly engaged with feminist thought over time (Blanco "Feminism"; Brown *Secrets*; Gracia; Sullivan). The progressive feminism that characterizes her nonfiction essays from the 1960s through the 1990s, convincingly documented by Sullivan and elucidated by Johnson ("Teaching"), also subtends her fiction.[13] The author's evolution was heavily influenced by the intellectual currents that she encountered during her visiting professorships in the United States, as she chronicled in *Desde la ventana*.[14] Martín Gaite's most enduring feminist theme has been a critique of the passive, dependent female role imposed by the Franco regime and idealized in the *novela rosa* [romance novel], as Nuria Cruz-Cámara has shown (*Laberinto* 60). By the time she wrote *Nubosidad variable* Martín Gaite was also well aware of French feminisms (a theoretical world unto themselves), including the concept of *jouissance* or sensual pleasure through writing; Barthes's 1973 book of theory *Le plaisir du texte* [*The Pleasure of the Text* 1975] is cited in the novel. As Ofelia Ferrán has observed, "the connection between pleasure and writing is often evoked" by both Sofía and Mariana (160). Stylistic aspects of French feminism are also evident: the free associations and intense energy that Hélène Cixous associated with *écriture féminine* (a uniquely feminine style of writing) are evinced in the prose of both protagonists, and especially in Sofía's eloquent chapters.

While the rejection of traditional gender norms for women is a constant in her fiction, today it is apparent that Martín Gaite's inclusive and expansive definition of feminism fits perfectly with the "third wave" of feminism that began to emerge in both the United States and Spain the 1990s. This more sophisticated feminism, rooted in postmodernism, arose in part to address contentious aspects of the 1970s women's movement, as Gillian Howie has observed (2). Three key elements of third-wave feminist theory counteract problematic aspects of the second wave. As a result of the upsurge of postmodernism, with its acceptance of indeterminacy, doctrinaire grand narratives are no longer considered valuable for organizing beliefs: "third-wavers embrace multivocality over synthesis and action over theoretical justification." In response to increasingly fraught definitions of what it means to be a woman—and in recognition of the postmodern acceptance of difference without opposition—the definition of female identity now centers on diverse individual experiences: "the third wave foregrounds personal narratives that illustrate an intersectional and multiperspectival version of feminism." And in response to "the divisiveness of the sex wars" that accompanied the women's liberation movement, third-wave feminism "emphasizes an inclusive and nonjudgmental approach that refuses to police the boundaries of the feminist political . . . and replaces attempts at unity with a dynamic and welcoming politics of coalition" (all quotes from Claire Snyder's "What Is Third-Wave Feminism?" 175–176).

Antimaterialism, Environmentalism, and Social Justice

Alongside its formal qualities of multivocality and personal narration by Sofía and Mariana, both of which are defining characteristics of third-wave feminism in literature, *Nubosidad variable* explores sociocultural themes that are now recognized as feminist. The novel is consonant with Leslie Heywood and Jennifer Drake's theory of third-wave feminism as a movement that extends beyond gynocentric concerns. Third-wave feminism "is not focused on narrowly defined 'women's issues,' but rather on an interrelated set of topics including environmentalism, human rights, and anti-corporate activism" (13). These broader cultural and economic concerns are central to *Nubosidad variable*. They are especially important to Sofía, whose opinions and experiences are traceable to those of her creator.

Antimaterialism is the strongest sociocultural critique in *Nubosidad variable*. Its feminist element is explicit, with money linked to machismo. Sofía is disgusted by the rampant materialism of the post-Transition years, often called *el pelotazo* (literally "the hit," as in being hit by a ball, but with the connotation of having a massive amount of money thrown in one's direction). The most striking symbol of greedy excess is the bathroom renovation that is taking place in Sofía's own home: a ridiculously lavish endeavor that she wryly nicknames "El Escorial" after the imposing Renaissance monastery of San Lorenzo de El Escorial outside Madrid. On the national level, the economic expansion associated with Spain's acceptance into the Common Market in 1986 is also viewed with alarm. Recalling the art opening at which she and Mariana were reunited (featuring paintings by Sofía's grandiose bathroom architect), Sofía observes:

> En los tiempos que corren lo barato no gusta nada, está desprestigiado por principio, ya se sabe. Pero anoche me dio la impresión de que además resulta incluso un poco ofensivo en ciertos ambientes hablar de personas, de instituciones o de actividades que no mueven mucho dinero, pero no así como quiera, dinero a paletadas, manejan cifras que es que ya no le entran en la cabeza a un cristiano, qué exageración. (77)

> [These days nobody likes anything cheap, it automatically loses in prestige. Indeed, last night I got the impression that in some circles it's even considered slightly offensive to speak of people, institutions or activities that don't make a lot of money, and not just a lot, we're talking money by the shovelful; they deal in figures beyond the imagination of most ordinary people, it's ridiculous.] (67)

The movers and shakers who dealt in vast sums were all gender-conforming males. "Una de las características de esta sociedad de los ochenta ha sido la aparición de una clase empresarial y política que ha idolatrado el éxito" [One of the characteristics of society in the eighties was the appearance of an entrepreneurial and political class that idolized success], Salvador Oropesa has noted, adding that "en una sociedad esencialmente machista como la española . . . estos triunfadores de los ochenta han sido generalmente hombres" [in an essentially male-dominated society like Spain's . . . those who triumphed in the eighties were generally men] (60). In the novel, Sofía's husband Eduardo is emblematic of this class of men, typifying the arrogance that accompanied ambition. Sofía comments sardonically on "las aguas estancadas del alma de Eduardo" (198) ["the stagnant waters of Eduardo's soul" 186], whose burning desire to make money became apparent early in their marriage. For him, money is a "panacea" (14 [4]).

Eduardo is nominally liberal: as a student in the 1960s he had been a member of the progressive anti-Franco resistance (belonging to FUDE, the Federación Universitaria Democrática Española [Spanish Democratic University Federation]), and he now reaps benefits reserved for card-carrying Socialists. But his views on marriage and the family are regressive. He wants his wife to play a role as his accessory, demonstrating his status and success—a role that, much to his displeasure, she declines.

A telling description highlights the author's ability to judge character: the daughter of the family maid compares Eduardo to Mario Conde, the prosperous head of the Banco Español de Crédito or Banesto. Two years after *Nubosidad variable* was published, the "caso Banesto" or Banesto affair showed that he had misappropriated millions of pesetas, and he was sentenced to twenty years in prison.[15] Mario Conde epitomized the brash attitude of successful entrepreneurs of the day. Spain's Socialist government, along with its financial institutions, focused intently on the future, lending credence to Joan Ramon Resina's contention that the Transition's only goal was to situate the country "en un presente que quería ser absoluto: el presente del mercado" [a present that aimed to be all-encompassing: the present of the marketplace] (28). The old postwar mantra of "Prohibido mirar hacia atrás" (*Usos amorosos* 13) ["It was forbidden to look back" *Courtship Customs* 12] seemed to be in force again in the culture at large. The country was preparing for three star turns on the international stage in 1992: the Summer Olympics in Barcelona, Expo '92 in Seville, and Madrid as European Cultural Capital. Memory was set aside. As Jo Labanyi recorded near the end of that decade, "it has become common to criticize contemporary Spain for historical amnesia, particularly with the PSOE government's marketing of Spain as a youthful, modern nation, epitomized by the 1992 celebration" (159).

In this youth-obsessed environment, older women were devalued. After the Transition, the first thing that newly powerful men did was leave their wives. "Se trata de hombres viejos y jóvenes que efectivamente inician una nueva etapa en su vida y en la de España" [It has to do with old and young men who in effect are entering a new stage in their life and in the life of Spain], recalled Francisco Umbral in his chronicle of the era, *La década roja* [The red decade]: "Para ello, el primer estímulo es empezar con una compañera nueva" [To do so, the first impetus is to start with a new female partner] (207). The successful architect in *Nubosidad variable* has a young blond in the house where he lives (so young that Sofía at first mistakes her for his daughter), while his estranged wife—whose father helped him launch his business—suffers with their children in a lesser neighborhood. Sofía's husband is having an affair with a young redhead. And Mariana supposes that a recent, younger lover must now be dating someone closer to his own age: "una yuppie de treinta años" in New York (186) ["a thirty-year-old yuppie" 174]. Fiftysomething Sofía and Mariana each battle a midlife crisis, though this can be easily misdiagnosed because it does not conform to the male model of this predicament in life and literature (Oropesa 59). Sofía's deepest questions are existential: "¿Qué hago yo en este sitio? ¿Qué quiere decir 'yo'?" (113) ["What am I doing here? What does 'I' mean?" 102], while Mariana faces a Jekyll-and-Hyde "desdoblamiento" [splitting] of her personal and professional selves. Instead of motorcycles and mistresses, Sofía and Mariana propose a new, less stereotypically gendered model of crisis resolution—one involving friendship and writing.

Anticorporate sentiment goes hand in hand with antimaterialism, and it is something that Sofía feels with her entire being. In a speech that recalls the listing of negative words associated with the Civil War in *El cuarto de atrás* ("estaba harta de oír la palabra fusilado, la palabra víctima, la palabra tirano, la palabra militares" [55]; ["I was sick and tired of hearing the words *shot to death*, the word *victim*, the word *tyrant*, the word *soldiers*" 48]), Sofía angrily describes the business conversations that swirl around her at a party, deriding the popular term for one million pesetas ("un kilo"):

> Otros, los más, seguían hablando de dinero y de los negocios que tienen éxito. Se oían bastante las palabras tema, problemática, cotización, proyección de futuro, coyuntural y obsoleto. Pero sobre todo kilos. No kilos de filetes, ni kilos de oro, ni kilos de papel, kilos de nada, una masa informe, pastosa y marrón en la que se chapoteaba compulsivamente, que pringaba hasta los ojos, kilos de mierda. (85–86)

> [Others, the majority, were still talking about money and which businesses were booming. The words you heard most were "theme," "issues," "price," "future prospects," "collateral," and "obsolete." But most of all, you heard the word "million." Not millions of steaks, not millions of gold bars, not millions of sheets of paper, but millions of nothing, a formless, sticky, brown mass in which people splashed compulsively about, in which they were immersed up to their eyeballs, millions of kilos of shit.] (75)

These sentiments have longstanding connections to feminist theory: material feminism emphasizes capitalism and patriarchy as determinants of women's oppression. Throughout the novel, Sofía rejects the profits from her husband's business dealings. The wealth she gladly accepts is not from Eduardo, but from her mother, in the form of a large apartment that she left to her three grandchildren (Sofía's children) in her will. This inherited home nurtures the next generations: Sofía's two unemployed older children live there, her youngest often stays there, and Sofía herself moves in when she leaves her husband. Although Sofía's mother was a difficult and opinionated woman, she makes possible a matrilineal inheritance that protects her descendants from economic pressure. Sofía's antimaterialism also has autobiographical relevance. Throughout her life, Martín Gaite insisted that wealth was less important than freedom: "Siempre he evitado, aun a costa de vivir más modestamente, los empleos que pudieran esclavizarme" she declared ("Bosquejo" 234) ["Even at the cost of living more modestly, I have always avoided any employment that might enslave me"] ("Sketch" 244).

Erosion of the environment is another personally resonant theme in the novel, examined through the lament of a beekeeper who has lost his bees to a disease called *barroasis* (varroosis). In real life this ailment wiped out the bees at Martín Gaite's family's country home in El Boalo. Speaking with Sofía, the man compares the disease to AIDS, for which there was as yet no treatment (another personally resonant theme as this was her daughter Marta's cause of death). The beekeeper, now supporting his family as a truck driver, recites a long list of depredations:

Hablan de que están inventando una vacuna, ¿pero quién ha vacunado nunca a las abejas?, ¿de cuando acá?, si es que no puede ser, las dos vaquerías que hay en mi pueblo parecen farmacias de tanto potingue para que no se les pongan pachuchos los animales, y los peces de los ríos muriéndose y muchas especies del coto de Doñana, que ya las tienen como entre algodones, lo habrá usted oído decir. Y, claro, es que está todo envenenado, el aire, el agua, todo. (49)

[They say they're going to try and come up with a vaccine, but who ever heard of vaccinating bees, honestly, it's just not possible. The two dairies in my village look like pharmacies what with all the concoctions they use to keep the animals from falling sick and then there are the fish dying in the rivers and loads of animals in the nature reserve at Coto de Doñana, where, as it is, they keep the animals wrapped in cotton wool, you must have heard about it. And it's because everything is poisoned, the air, the water, everything.] (38)

Mariana is even more fatalistic. She takes the long view of human suffering, recalling that when she trained as a physician there was no cure for tuberculosis, and bemoans the fact that "siempre tiene que haber alguna plaga" (181) ["there will always be some kind of plague" 168].

Each narrator in *Nubosidad variable* also advocates human rights and social justice, most often through the elevation of workers from the lower classes to positions of equality with those who employ them. As with all of her social criticism, Martín Gaite shows rather than tells, rejecting theory by refusing to embed it in the characters' discourse. Social hierarchies of the past are symbolized by Sofía's brother-in-law, the son of a gardener whose "deseos de revancha social" (279) ["desires for social revenge" 266] fueled his ambition to become rich and buy the house where his father had worked. Sofía is not bothered by her brother-in-law's upward mobility, though she is saddened by the fact that he took advantage of a family that had fallen on hard times. Sofía's conservative mother (returning in a dream) mourns the disappearance of the old taboo against romances across social classes, noting that Sofía need look no farther than her own husband as an example of someone who came from nothing and married above his station (356; *Variable Cloud* 340).

Neither of the novel's protagonists makes sharp class distinctions. Sofía has coffee and conversation with the truck driver (and former beekeeper) after he makes a delivery to her home, breaching class barriers to have an authentic intellectual exchange. Both Sofía and Mariana have conversations with housekeepers in which the upper-class woman gratefully receives words of wisdom from the servant. Sofía listens to the salty observations of her housekeeper and accepts her insight based on experience; they both agree that a good man is hard to find. Mariana engages with a thoughtful housekeeper in Cádiz while staying briefly in her employer's mansion. When the housekeeper asks: "Tanto afanarse, tanto moverse de acá para allá, tanto querer abarcar. ¿Y para qué, si no hay amor?, ¿me lo puede explicar, usted que tiene tantos estudios?" (103) ["All this work, all this rushing around taking on so many responsibilities, and what for, if there's no love? Can you explain it to me, you with all your studies?" 93], Mariana bows her head, admitting that she has no answer. Later a server at a local bar gives Mariana advice about a romantic affair and she—a practicing psychiatrist— proceeds to weigh it carefully, valuing his insight. Mariana and her date share drinks with the waiter and when she leaves she gives him a kiss, disregarding class barriers.

Martín Gaite's acceptance of difference applies to gender as well as class. Her conception of gender aligns with Judith Butler's theory of gender performativity, which emphasizes the sociocultural construction of sex and gender through repetitive conduct or performance.[16] The author's position reflects Butler's avowed intent in *Gender Trouble*, which "was to open up the field of possibility for gender without dictating which possibilities should be realized" (3). For Martín Gaite, imposed conformity of any kind threatened individual freedom. From the beginning of her career, she exposed the tyranny of prescriptive gender roles. As Elizabeth Ordóñez posited for *Retahílas* and Nuria Cruz-Cámara has shown for her subsequent novel *La Reina de las Nieves* (1994) [*The Farewell Angel* 1999], gender mutability is embraced by the author and conveyed through her fictional characters (Cruz-Cámara *Laberinto* 37–44).

In *Nubosidad variable* neither of the two main characters is fulfilled by the domesticity traditionally associated with her gender. Sofía comes closer to the societal norm because she has complied with the conventional role of wife. But she reveals that this position was thrust upon her: she married because she was pregnant and saw no alternative. She also rebelled against her vows by having a brief affair during her marriage. (In an ironic plot twist, Sofía reveals having spent a disappointing week in London with the former flame who supposedly caused her rift with Mariana—joining him after delivering her daughter to an English school. This episode conjures up the author's own week in London after picking up her daughter from summer school in Brighton in 1971.) While Sofía loves her children and is especially attached to her oldest daughter, she chafes at the self-sacrificing maternal role for which her generation was socialized. As Mariana expresses for both of them: "¡Qué condena llevamos las mujeres con esta retórica de la abnegación, cómo se nos agarra a las tripas, por mucho que nos pasemos la vida tratando de reírnos de ella!" (61) ["What a burden all of that rhetoric about self-denial is to us women; it grips us in our vitals, however much we try to laugh it off" 51]. Sofía does not feel particularly successful in her domestic role, a sensation exacerbated by her husband's critical comments. Mariana's life choices enable her to avoid spousal criticism, but she is not immune from feelings of inadequacy. For her these feelings are associated with her professional self, whom she refers to in the third person as someone named "la Doctora León" who "devoró a" (26) ["devoured" 16] the Mariana León of her youth. In addition to being an unmarried physician (not a traditional female role), Mariana evinces personal characteristics that are popularly associated with masculinity. Foremost among these are a need to control, a tendency to intellectualize emotions, and a predilection for sex without emotional attachment. These qualities are not poses, but rather are innate to her performance of gender.

Diversity of gender expression is even more evident among secondary characters, whose nonconformity forces them to protect themselves from potential censure: "personas acostumbradas a fingir y a defenderse" (54) ["people accustomed to pretence and to defending themselves" 43]. Mariana's longtime love interest and intellectual soulmate identifies as bisexual but is almost certainly gay; reflecting the medical profession's stance at the time, Mariana tries to treat his "problemas homosexuales" (23) ["problems with his sexuality" 13] in both her office and her bed, partly to extricate him from the drug culture of his friends. Sofía's only son seems to be genuinely attracted to both men and women, with a woman in his bedroom and an androgynous gay man in his kitchen. Two secondary characters are gay, one of whom is Sofía's brother. A caring son and successful biologist in the United States, this brother stayed in close contact with their mother, who professed not to understand why he never married. Jesús Pérez-Magallón has gone so far as to compare the novel's secondary characters to the unconventional figures that populate Pedro Almodóvar's films ("fauna almodovariana," 187). They gather in the rambling, chaotic apartment inherited from Sofía's mother, aptly nicknamed "el refugio" or "the refuge." Although they shorten this to "refu" among themselves, the full name that the children gave the apartment is longer: "el refugio para tortugas" ["refuge for tortoises"]. This descriptor reveals how they see themselves and their friends as being out of sync with the world around them.

In the novel Martín Gaite makes use of "gender analysis before feminist theory had come to make distinctions between sex, sexuality, and gender and to prioritize the latter as a category of analysis," just as Sullivan observed in the author's essays (45). Martín Gaite's overarching goal was to deemphasize what she saw as arbitrary divisions in order let each person be him- or herself. As she asserted in the Bustamante interview:

> Que no estén los papeles tan divididos, porque esto es agobiante. Es el carácter de las personas, no el sexo, lo que define la cuestión. Conozco mujeres con enorme carácter y hombres muy dulces. ¿Por qué forzarse en "cumplir" con el personaje? Según cada uno sea así funcionarían las cosas mejor.

> [There shouldn't be a strict separation of roles, because that's oppressive. It's each person's nature, not their gender, that defines their existence. I know masculine women and feminine men. Why force oneself to "fulfill" the role of a character? Each person should be how he or she is, that way things would run more smoothly.] (9)

From the first chapter of *Nubosidad variable* to the epilogue, repercussions of repressive gender norms are explored through narratives of two women's lives, with an emphasis on false dichotomies. Through Sofía and Mariana, the novel problematizes the two paths available to middle- and upper-class females in a traditional society: matrimony or study. These options lead to different roles in life, corresponding to what sociologists term ascribed status (through association with a spouse) or achieved status (through personal attainment). The novel enacts its author's dissatisfaction with this oppositional formulation:

> A las mujeres se les suele enseñar, errónea y tradicionalmente, a no ver más que dos salidas: o casarse, o la de hacerse una bachillera (como las llamaba entonces . . .). Y estas dos eran soluciones contrapuestas. . . . Se veían como irreconciliables, y cada vez se tienden más a ver así.

> [Women were traditionally taught, mistakenly, that there were only two paths forward: marriage or becoming a learned woman (as they were then called . . .). And those were two opposing choices. . . . They were seen as irreconcilable, and this view kept being reinforced.] (Bustamante 9)

Martín Gaite went on to explain in the same interview that women, like men, needed preparation for self-fulfillment. "A la mujer le han hablado de 'papeles,'" she asserted, "pero no de intereses verdaderos" [Women have been spoken to about "roles" but never about their true interests] (9). As the protagonists of *Nubosidad variable* discover, self-realization can come only through expression of intrinsic desires and never through imposed roles, be they familial or professional.

———

Nubosidad variable illuminates issues that persist today. The novel's multivocal narratives, antimaterialism, environmentalism, concern for human rights, rejection of theory, and embrace of gender diversity have only recently been gathered under the rubric of third-wave feminism. Through its dual protagonists *Nubosidad variable* goes beyond individual "women's stories" to create a multifaceted critique of post-Transition Spain, inscribing women into the history of the period through the genre-bending epistolary interactions of two female friends. The era's *machista* materialism is the object of Martín Gaite's most vehement criticism, reflecting her own revulsion. Other social realities are also called into question. These include degradation of the environment, from animal extinction in a wildlife preserve to other plagues; entrenched class differences, with an embedded class of servants whose humanity goes unrecognized; and socially imposed gender binaries that strangle individual expression. Exploration of these issues illustrates postmodern definitions of feminism that had not yet been articulated by theorists when the novel was published. These characteristics make *Nubosidad variable* Martín Gaite's most prescient work of literature, as well as the one that fully expresses her inclusive view of gender. This remarkable novel reestablished her status as one of Spain's most important authors, reaping both critical and popular acclaim. Fortified by this success, Martín Gaite could go back to face the personal demons that resided in the novel she had put aside to write this one, *La Reina de las Nieves.*

CHAPTER 4

La Reina de las Nieves

REWRITING A TRAGEDY OF SPAIN'S TRANSITION

Martín Gaite's third novel of the nineties was supposed to have been the first of the decade. Despite its publication date, *La Reina de las Nieves* (1994) [*The Farewell Angel* 1999] belongs to the late 1970s and early 1980s. The author's novels for adults are all set close to the time they were written, as José Jurado Morales has noted (*Juego* 148). "La historia se desarrolla a finales de los setenta, que es cuando se me ocurrió" (12) ["The story is set firmly in the late 1970s, which is when I first started working on it" n.p.], Martín Gaite explained in a two-page "Nota Preliminar" ["Preliminary note"] that traces this novel's unusual development. She recalled that her note-taking for the novel began in 1975 and that she started writing in earnest in 1979. In the fall of 1984, while she was a visiting professor in Chicago, she made great strides with the manuscript. She was determined to finish the book upon her return to Madrid. But fate intervened: "A partir de enero de 1985," she recalled in language that evokes Andersen's tale, "y por razones que atañen a mi biografía personal, solamente pensar en la Reina de las Nieves me helaba el corazón" (11) ["However, for private and personal reasons, from January 1985 on, the very thought of the Snow Queen froze my heart" n.p.]. When she returned to her Madrid home in late December 1984, her twenty-eight-year-old daughter Marta Sánchez Martín, whose father was the novelist Rafael Sánchez Ferlosio, was seriously ill; she died on 8 April 1985.[1] Martín Gaite was devastated. Gradually she reconstructed her life, first immersing herself in nonfiction[2] and returning to the realm of fiction in 1990 with her young adult novel *Caperucita en Manhattan*. For years she avoided the project that took its title from Marta's favorite fairy tale.

After the enthusiastic reception of *Nubosidad variable* in 1992, she at last retrieved her notebooks for *La Reina de las Nieves*, prepared to face its contents. The reencounter with its protagonist was painful: "Y la pesquisa se inicia aun arrostrando las emociones imprevisibles que puede acarrear todo reencuentro, que viene a ser casi siempre como hurgar en una herida" (11–12) ["And so the search began, even though it meant facing the unpredictable emotions that are likely with any re-encounter, which is almost always akin to opening up old wounds" n.p.]. Martín Gaite drew strength from the stability of her life in Spain, where she would remain for the rest of her days; although she gave talks around the country and abroad, she would never again accept a visiting appointment that involved relocation. Nationally, the political situation was relatively calm. The Socialists under Felipe González remained in power (despite corruption scandals, they won national elections in 1993) and the economy was still strong (even though a decline was beginning to be felt). The country's sociocultural and political circumstances were a continuation of those described in *Nubosidad variable*, with added triumphalism following the successes of 1992. These included hosting the Olympics in Barcelona and Expo '92 in Seville, as well as Madrid's being honored as the year's European Cultural Capital, the national team rising to the first division in European soccer, and inaugurating the country's first high-speed train (the AVE, an acronym that also means "bird"). Although terrorism was still a threat, attacks by the Basque national liberation movement ETA were sporadic and on a smaller scale than in the past, with twenty-seven lives lost in 1992, fourteen killed 1993, and twelve deaths in 1994 (documented by Mónica Ceberio Belaza). Consequently, the generalized level of anxiety surrounding these attacks receded. (One visible manifestation of the reduced threat level was the reappearance of trash cans in public places—removed during the period when ETA bombs were a constant menace.) At home in Madrid, Martín Gaite's personal assistant Angelines Solsona—who would remain in her employ until the author's death—continued to make it easier for her to write by performing the chores of daily life. The author's sister, Ana María (Anita), also helped her preserve time for writing. Anita took charge of the sale of their parents' large Madrid apartment at Calle de Alcalá 35 (arranging a lucrative lease-purchase agreement with an American company) and oversaw the management of their country home in El Boalo outside Madrid (handling everything from renovations to taxes). Anita bought a Madrid apartment at Calle de Hermosilla 165, in the same Salamanca district as her sister's home, which was a mutual convenience.

At the same time, Martín Gaite's career trajectory was ascendant. In addition to her fiction, nonfiction, and conferences, she put out a book of previously published, sought-after but often difficult-to-obtain writings entitled *Agua pasada (Artículos, prólogos y discursos)* (1993) [Water under the bridge (Articles, prologues, and discourses)]. Her two volumes of short stories were consolidated and published together with her one-act monologue *A palo seco* [On my own] as *Cuentos completos y un monólogo* [The complete stories and a monologue] (1994). She also wrote the screenplays for a successful television miniseries, directed by her friend José Luis Borau. The series was based on a precocious seven-year-old girl named Celia who lived in Spain in the 1930s—the protagonist of a beloved collection of novels for young people by author Elena Fortún. The episodes aired in January and February of 1993 and enraptured viewers.[3] Together, these propitious circumstances helped Martín Gaite tackle the novel that she had started years before. In late 1993 she confided: "Yo ando dándole vueltas a una novela que dejé interrumpida hace ocho años y pico: 'La reina de las nieves.' Creo que resucita. Pero es top secret." [I'm playing around with a novel that I left off writing a little over eight years ago: The Snow Queen. I think that it's coming back to life. But it's top secret] (Letter to Brown, Madrid, 9 November 1993). Martín Gaite managed to finish the book in time for the Madrid Book Fair in the spring of 1994, after which it became a bestseller.

Readers were surprised to find that the author's latest novel was set in what seemed like the distant past. They discovered that Martín Gaite had begun two novels in the same fateful year: 1975. Her best-known work, *El cuarto de atrás*, took Franco's death in 1975 as the impetus for rebutting "the official story" of his dictatorship as a virtuous crusade against infidels, as David Herzberger has shown. Her dedication of my copy of *La Reina de las Nieves* refers to her previous novel, in which the symbol of a back room evokes both a childhood playroom and a mysterious region of the mind. The inscription begins: "Como ves, querida Joan, siguen saliendo historias del cuarto de atrás . . ." [As you see, Joan dear, stories keep emerging from the back room . . .] (Dedication to Brown, 16 September 1994). Fittingly for a cultural historian, this second novel, *La Reina de las Nieves*, would explore the next traumatic period in Spain's history: its transition to democracy (1975–1982). Political issues from the Transition continue to resonate in Spain, and a spate of recent studies examine the period in search of keys to current conflicts.[4]

La Reina de las Nieves is not a political novel. Rather, it uncovers the collateral damage of social upheaval in the wake of Spain's transition to democratic rule. While ostensibly mining clues to the development of its handsome and charismatic protagonist Leonardo Villalba, the novel tries to answer a broader— and darker—question. Why would a gifted, privileged young adult descend into heroin use? Although the novel is associated with a children's tale, the real "snow queen" of this novel is heroin, and Martín Gaite samples the conventions of detective fiction to investigate its evil power. Somehow heroin wiped out an entire generation of Spanish young people in the 1980s, who became known as the "generación perdida" or "lost generation." The novel's quest for answers had personal resonance. Martín Gaite's only child Marta became addicted to heroin and died from complications of AIDS. In *La Reina de las Nieves* the author achieved catharsis by rewriting the ending to the tragic story of her daughter's generation.

A Cultural History of Spain's Transition

In *Reina* as in previous novels, Martín Gaite hones in on the disparity between received wisdom and her own observations. For the Transition, the contemporaneous and best-known version of events was not only positive, it was ebullient. After Franco's death there was exuberance over new freedoms and possibilities. "Euphoria" and "celebration" (Spanish cognates *euforia* and *celebración*) were the two words that best described initial collective sentiment, and for obvious reasons: "Los primeros años del postfranquismo . . . marcan el fin de un régimen autoritario y represivo, el fin de la tiranía, de la censura social, ideológica y política y la llegada, tan esperada, de la democratización, que se aúna . . . con una voluntad de integración europea" [The first years of the post-Franco era . . . mark the end of an authoritarian and repressive regime, the end of tyranny, of social, ideological and political censorship. They mark the long hoped-for arrival of democratization, which was linked . . . with the desire for integration into Europe], in the words of Teresa Vilarós (5). The most prominent symbol of this celebration was La Movida (usually translated as "The Movement"), an umbrella term for a loose assemblage of cultural happenings, rock music, sexual and other experimentation—primarily in Madrid but also spreading to other urban areas.[5] "La Movida fue un reflejo en la juventud urbana del deseo generalizado de libertad. . . . Ya nadie soñaba con gestas patrias ni con trasnochados imperios, aunque tampoco con revoluciones ni utopías: lo que quería la gente era divertirse" [La Movida was a reflection of urban youth's general desire for freedom. . . . By now no one dreamed about heroic nations or empires of old, though neither did we dream about revolutions or utopias: what people were interested in was having fun], according to a historian who was in his twenties at the time, who admitted that this led to a culture of *pasotismo* [apathy] (José Manuel Lechado 15). The prevailing attitude among young people was one of "apolitical hedonism," with Almodóvar's first film *Pepi, Luci, Bom y otras chicas del montón* (1980) [*Pepi, Luci, Bom and Other Girls Like Mom*] a prime example of this generation's "excess of 'sex, drugs and rock 'n' roll'" as described by Mark Allinson (266). Within and beyond Spain, the media trumpeted a new dawn of an apolitical cultural revolution, a narrative that Alberto Medina has likened to a bildungsroman or "happy coming-of-age story" for the nation. Attention was focused on "youth having fun, uninterested in politics and creating spontaneous, exuberant culture linked to the avant-garde" (302).

While La Movida did supply pleasure, Spain's reality was much darker. The gap between the idealized narrative of Spain's peaceful transition to democracy and the often-bleak realities experienced by its citizens has been labelled *desencanto* [disenchantment]. While the Transition introduced cultural expansion through an explosion of new options, the country was also constrained by an economic crisis that had undercurrents of political anxiety. From 1973 to 1985 Spain suffered one of the most severe economic downturns in its modern history, characterized by high rates of inflation and unemployment (both exceeding 25 percent) accompanied by a lack of investment and growth. Massive unemployment among young people had severe repercussions for the generation that was coming of age; since they comprised nearly 25 percent of the population, their predicament was the most serious in the nation (Allinson 266). Political uncertainty was pervasive. In October 1977 the Ley de Amnistía [Amnesty Law] forgave all political crimes committed before that date, so as not to impede the changeover to democratic rule. But the first free elections in June 1977 were not widely seen as a step in that direction: the winner was former Franco associate Adolfo Suárez, one of the politicians who, to use the phrase of that era, had simply "changed his jacket."[6] The specter of a military coup, which was memorably attempted in a siege on the Corte de los Diputados [Parliament] on 23 February 1981, was a nagging fear. So was the threat of politically motivated terrorism, with strengthening of the Basque terrorist organization ETA (described by Santos Juliá, 442) and 124 deaths in the year 1980 alone (documented by Juan Francisco Fuentes, 1181). Many worried that Spain was too unaccustomed to democracy to be able to fully achieve it. The high hopes for political and social reform that accompanied the popping of cava corks when Franco died gave way to a sense of exasperation, especially among young people.

At the same time, illegal drugs flooded the country. Together with the new sociocultural freedoms and the severe economic problems (as well as the persistent political anxieties) of the day, this influx created the "perfect storm" that would drown the lost generation. A United Nations report from 1987 observed that illicit traffic and drug abuse in Spain skyrocketed from 1977 onward, "particularly cannabis and heroin" among the younger generation:

> Drug use predominantly affects young people. The use of two or more drugs simultaneously or successively, often involving alcohol, is reported as the most common pattern of drug use among youth. Drug use has become incorporated into the current youth culture. . . . Heroin abuse . . . has been increasing rapidly, achieving epidemic characteristics, particularly among youth. . . . The number of regular heroin users increased by 58.2 percent from 1980 to 1985. (Rodríguez and Anglin 1)

The drug crisis during these years reflected what Spanish researcher Juan F. Gamalla described as the biggest attitudinal and behavioral shift involving drugs in the country's history. While heroin was rare in Spain in 1976, it became increasingly widespread over the coming years, with "heroinomanía" [a heroin craze] beginning in 1977 and rising in successive waves until reaching its zenith between 1983 and 1986 (Gamalla).

For young people during the Transition and the decade after, "drugs were sense-numbing, a means of opting out of the established community for an alternative . . . marginal culture" associated with "nightlife, alcohol, music and fashion" (Allinson 269). The official report issued by the Spanish government in response to the crisis, the *Plan Nacional sobre Drogas, 1980–1985* [National drug plan, 1980–1985] documented nearly two million cannabis users and 80,000 users of heroin (qtd. by Joaquín Santodomingo Carrasco, 54), at a time when the country's population was around thirty-nine million and the number of Spaniards between the ages of fifteen and thirty was roughly ten million (PopulationPyramid.net). In Spain as elsewhere, drug use led to transmission of needle-borne viruses, the worst of which was AIDS. (Unlike in many other countries, pharmacies in Spain sold syringes without a prescription until well into the 1980s.) Pop icon Alaska recalled this devastation in personal terms: "Todas las generaciones tienen accidentes, enfermedades tempranas. La nuestra fue la generación del *caballo* [la heroína] y del sida. Siendo muy jóvenes perdimos a gran parte de la gente que teníamos alrededor por unos motivos u otros. He perdido antes a gente de mi edad que a mis mayores." [All generations have accidents and early illnesses. Ours was the generation of *horse* (heroin) and AIDS. We lost a great number of people around us when we were very young, for one reason or another. I've lost people my own age before my elders] (1). In Spain in the 1980s—unlike in the United States—AIDS remained invisible in the culture at large. As Vilarós has observed, "las representaciones culturales del sida, que surge coincidiendo con la llegada al poder del gobierno socialista . . . son en estos años prácticamente inexistentes" [cultural representations of AIDS, which surged at the same time that the Socialists came to power . . . were practically nonexistent in those years] (246).

Conventions of Detective Fiction

While *La Reina de las Nieves* features sociocultural analysis, it is by no means a treatise. The novel is an engaging work of fiction, the creation of a master prose stylist whose narrative gifts are continually on display. It dazzles the reader with its vivid descriptions, original metaphors, wise observations, and gripping dialogues. At times all of these elements are combined, as in Leonardo's recurring, jazz-like riffs on memories as prehistoric beasts. He compares distant memories to woolly mammoths; each person has his or her own, and they can barge into the present without warning. As in all the author's later fiction, there are references to international literature, music, film, architecture, and art.[7] The novel's complex story is organized like a collage, a favored art form of its creator.[8] The 330 pages of *La Reina de las Nieves* comprise three parts, each of which begins with a new chapter 1. The first and third sections of the book contain four chapters each, recounted by an omniscient narrator. These portions frame the longer middle section of the work, consisting of fifteen chapters that are ostensibly drawn from Leonardo's notebooks. All of the chapters have evocative titles that pique the reader's curiosity, including references to people (such as "La extraña inquilina" ["The strange tenant"]), places (from "La isla de las gaviotas" ["The island of seagulls"] to "La Puerta de Alcalá" [the Alcalá Gate, a neoclassical triumphal arch made of granite that is a landmark in Madrid]), and existential crises (including "Salto en el vacío" ["Leap into the void"] and "Averías del alma" ["Breakdowns of the soul"]). The four chapters of the first part present a series of cinematic scenes in two different locales: a picturesque, mysterious coastal village (evidently in Galicia) with a mansion called La Quinta Blanca and a drab, two-person cell in the old Carabanchel prison in Madrid. Characters are introduced obliquely, often without names, and the reader is left wondering which of them—and which events—will be important to the story.

Leonardo's notebooks constitute the central portion of the narrative. Including flashbacks and dialogues along with first-person narration and fragments of other texts, they situate the puzzle pieces of the first section and advance the melodramatic plot almost to its conclusion. Upon his release from prison, Leonardo learns that his parents died a week earlier in a car accident in Chicago. He returns to the stately family home in Madrid. There he begins searching for his identity, which has been shrouded in family secrets—secrets that contributed to such profound alienation that he left home and wandered for seven years, becoming a heroin user. Leonardo recalls how the woman he knew as his mother, a mentally unstable American heiress, was cold and controlling, unlike his warm paternal grandmother. When this grandmother had died five years earlier, Leonardo had inherited her home, La Quinta Blanca, and had immediately sold it. Now he tries to buy it back from its present owner, the beautiful and brilliant Casilda Iriarte. As the family solicitor sorts through the details of his inheritance, Leonardo passes the time smoking hashish, frequenting seedy clubs, and perusing family correspondence. Near the end of the novel, he discovers that Casilda Iriarte is his birth mother. She and Leonardo's father Enrique Villalba grew up in the same coastal village and fell in love as children. Casilda was the granddaughter of the lighthouse-keeper and Enrique was the scion of the family who lived in La Quinta Blanca. When their child Leonardo was born, they agreed that Enrique's wife, who did not want to bear children, would raise him as her own, and that neither his wife nor Leonardo would ever know the truth about his parentage. Casilda married a distinguished older man and became a renowned writer, returning to Spain as a widow. By the time that Leonardo's notebooks end, two months after his release from prison, he is preparing to go to La Quinta Blanca to spend Christmas with Casilda, at her invitation. The last four chapters chart the felicitous reunion of mother and son: each has been waiting for the other for a long time. Leonardo's identity crisis has been solved, and his heroin use is evidently behind him.

This story has little obvious connection with the 1844 Hans Christian Andersen tale of the same title. The characters and plot of Martín Gaite's novel diverge sharply from those of their namesake, to the point where the English translation uses a completely different title, *The Farewell Angel*—referring to the novel's protagonist.[9] Set in Denmark in the nineteenth century, Andersen's seven-part tale involves the rescue of a young boy named Kay by his innocent playmate Gerda after Kay is abducted from their village by the evil Snow Queen. While this fairy tale is (unusually for this genre) a feminist story—featuring a girl who saves a boy through her heroic actions—the plot bears almost no relation to the story of Leonardo Villalba. Nevertheless, Martín Gaite associates her novel with Andersen's. In the first of two dedications, she thanks her predecessor: "Para Hans Christian Andersen, sin cuya colaboración este libro nunca se habría escrito" (7) ["For Hans Christian Andersen without whose collaboration this book would never have been written" n.p.]. Two chapter titles and some of their contents also reference Andersen's hypotext: chapter 4 in the second part (taken from Leonardo's journals) is entitled "El rapto de Kay" ["The kidnapping of Kay"] and chapter 4 of the third part (the novel's last chapter) bears the title "El cristalito de hielo" ["The splinter of glass"]. Critics have followed the author's lead and categorized *La Reina de las Nieves* as a fairy tale. Jurado Morales has placed it in a separate category within Martín Gaite's novels written during the democratic era, which he calls "Los mundos de ficción" [Fictional worlds], alongside *Caperucita en Manhattan* and two children's stories (*Trayectoria* 291).[10]

Catherine O'Leary and Alison Ribeiro de Menezes have summarized the opaque but intentional connection between the two versions of *The Snow Queen*. Their analysis is based on the outcome of both plots as well as on the fact that the fairy tale is repeatedly referenced by Leonardo, who identifies with Kay. They observe that Andersen's tale can be viewed as a "motif" used to convey "that Leonardo's past contains a mystery which, when solved, will bring about his redemption and enable him to live a more fulfilling life in the present" (145). Textual references to Andersen's story in Martín Gaite's novel have been compiled by critics (notably by Rosa Penna and Enrique Turpín) and forces of good and evil, common to all fairy tales, have been elucidated by Nuria Cruz-Cámara ("Utopía"). Even when scholars have explored other aspects of *La Reina de las Nieves*—particularly its treatment of narration (Dorothy Odartey-Wellington "Triunfo"; Carlos Uxó González), its Romantic elements (Cruz-Cámara "Recreación"; Vilma Navarro-Daniels "Teaching") and its portrayals of women (María Elena Bravo; Dorothy Odartey-Wellington "Madres"), the fairy-tale lens for critical analysis has remained in place.

While this framing paradigm has yielded important insights, it is incomplete. Only a less obvious reading model for *La Reina de las Nieves*, associated with detective fiction, accounts for the powerful social criticism in this novel's pages—of harsh realities during the Transition. No fairy tale introduces its hero as he is vomiting into a prison toilet, as does *La Reina de las Nieves*. The revulsion and despair expressed in this scene correspond to emotions felt by survivors of that era. With its collage structure, goal of "hooking" the reader, idiosyncratic protagonist, and issues of memory and identity, *La Reina de las Nieves* actualizes many of the conventions of the detective novel as it sheds light on the Transition and the lost generation of young people left in its wake.[11] Martín Gaite herself recognized the insufficiency of fairy tales, as well as *las novelas rosa* [romance novels], as vehicles of social criticism. Both genres, she felt, "eran una especie de nada existencial almibarada y ñoña . . . [que] sobreexcita en vano el sabor de la aventura, pero no analiza nada ni da remedios al indefinible *malaise*" [were a kind of silly and sugar-coated nothingness . . . (that) vainly overpromise a sense of adventure, but never analyze anything or propose solutions to the indefinable malaise] (*Cuadernos de todo* 606). This interpretation also fits with literary currents in post-1975 Spain. As a mirror of society, the detective novel became an ideal conduit for examining the new realities of democratic Spain, as critics of the genre (José Colmeiro, Joan Ramon Resina, and many others) have demonstrated. In the words of prizewinning author Carme Riera, who knew and admired Martín Gaite, "lo que antes se llamaba novela social ahora se llama novela negra" [what used to be called the social novel is now called detective fiction] ("Cuando").

Detective fiction was a genre that the author knew well. It was the subject of her daughter's master's thesis in English philology, and Martín Gaite enjoyed reading the books that she helped acquire for Marta when she visited the United States. (The description of the Dashiell Hammett mystery *The Thin Man* on her daughter's nightstand in the last chapter of *El cuarto de atrás* was taken from real life.) Although *Reina* opens with a dead body (of a former nanny in the coastal town), it is by no means a murder-solving "whodunit." Nor is it obsessed with violence, as is the "thriller." Instead the novel evinces characteristics of the third type of detective fiction in Tzvetan Todorov's taxonomy, the "suspense novel":

> The suspense novel keeps the mystery of the whodunit and also the two stories, that of the past and that of the present; but it refuses to reduce the second to a simple detection of the truth. As in the thriller, it is this second story which here occupies the central place. The reader is interested not only by what has happened but also by what will happen next; he wonders as much about the future as about the past. The two types of interest are thus united here—there is the curiosity to learn how past events are to be explained, and there is also the suspense: what will happen to the main characters? ("Typology" 50–51)

Todorov observed that detective fiction always contains dual stories: "the story of the crime and the story of the investigation" ("Typology" 44), corresponding to those of "story" or *fabula* (the action itself) and "plot" or *syuzhet* (how the reader learns of the action) in Russian Formalist narratology, notably the writings of Viktor Shlovsky and Boris Tomashevsky (Lemon and Reis).

In *Reina*, the crime is one of stolen identity, and the plot involves solving the puzzle of Leonardo's past. Leonardo confides on more than one occasion that he sees himself as a detective. He describes his solitary efforts sorting through family papers, searching intently for answers to how and why he became the way he is. Throughout his quest the reader processes clues alongside him, as in a suspense novel. This "puzzle element" is characteristic of what Charles Rzepka defines as the "mystery story," which he distinguishes from "detective" and "investigation" stories. It is also consistent with the "clue-puzzle form" analyzed by Stephen Knight, which (fittingly for this novel) first came to prominence in novels by women in the nineteenth century. And the puzzle is solved within a highly specific environment: *Reina* is concerned with the milieu in which it is set, another distinguishing feature for Todorov ("Typology" 48). Curiosity and suspense combine to engage or "hook" the reader as new clues emerge about an unsolved mystery. The author's expert pacing technique heightens the reader's curiosity. As Leonardo uncovers information and approaches a breakthrough, the scene frequently shifts. A reminiscence or an interaction in the present interrupts his search, increasing tension. Nevertheless, the pace of this quest is sometimes slow. Leonardo is an "isolated amateur," a convention of "analytic detective fiction" according to the classification system of Marty Roth (11).[12] Under the guise of talking to himself, Leonardo encourages the reader to be patient with the process: "Tarda uno mucho en descifrar las cosas," he acknowledges, crediting his grandmother with this piece of advice. "La solución al misterio puede venir engastada dentro del mismo texto misterioso que la camufla" (160) ["You're right, grandma, it does take a long time to decipher things, it is all a question of patience. The solution to the mystery can be set within the same mysterious text that camouflages it" 142].

Leonardo's method of detection involves textual analysis. His spadework involves piecing together "las pistas contradictorias" (129) ["contradictory clues" 111] in letters from family members. Instead of a smoking gun, the circumstantial evidence that helps him crack the case of his own identity consists of textual and philosophical similarities between a book by Casilda Iriarte and letters from his father's love, Sila, revealing that they are one and the same person. "Efectivamente," he explains, "en el libro y en las cartas a mi padre aparecen metáforas casi idénticas, quiebros de ritmo semejantes, estallidos de rebeldía y de sensualidad tan sólo comparables al afán a contrapelo—que también comparten ambas—por reconstruir sobre bases inéditas la percepción del mundo" (235-236) ["In fact, almost identical metaphors appear in the book and in her letters to my father, similar rhythms, outbursts of rebelliousness or sensuality that share the same perverse eagerness to rebuild their perception of the world on new foundations" 214]. His insights about Casilda through her writings resonate deeply. Close to discovering who she really is, Leonardo reads letters to his father from Casilda and marvels, "Dan pistas que le ponen a uno la carne de gallina" (229) ["They contain clues that would make your hair stand on end" 207]. When Leonardo succeeds in breaking the code to his father's office safe (using an anagram of "Sila") his climactic discovery is compared to that of a crime sleuth:

El primer resultado de mi frenética pesquisa, comparable a la del detective ante
una pista que sospecha que le puede implicar, fue el barrunto de que Sila pudiera funcionar como diminutivo de Casilda. Hipótesis pronto confirmada
por el acoplamiento progresivo de una mujer con otra, a través de las coinci-
dencias textuales que delatan sin sombra de duda un estilo único. Me invadía
una excitación rara, a medida que iban apareciendo nuevas pruebas. (235)

[The first result of my frenetic researches, comparable to those of a detective
confronted by a clue which he suspects might implicate him, was the hunch
that Sila might well be a diminutive form of Casilda. This hypothesis was soon
confirmed by the progressive linking of one woman with the other, through
textual coincidences that betray, without a shadow of a doubt, a single style.
As new evidence appeared, I felt a strange excitement.] (213)

As Leonardo searches, he involves the reader in his mission, making his discoveries especially satisfying.

In addition to including the reader in his quest, Leonardo adheres to another
strategy of detective fiction, eschewing romance (Todorov "Typology" 49). Two
potential female love interests appear in the novel and one from the past (an
archivist who helped him get organized) is also described. The redhead who picks
him up when he is released from jail tells Leonardo that he is the father of her
unborn baby, eager for his response. She reminds him that he once said that what
he most wanted was a child of his own. Leonardo's philosophy of childrearing
is identical to the credo of his creator: "Yo le enseñaría a mi hijo a ser libre" (61)
["I'd teach my child to be free" 48], she recalls him saying. But the redhead is
involved with someone else and Leonardo does not pursue a relationship with
her. (Although the woman says that she plans to go to London for an abortion,
the baby is written off as a premature stillbirth late in the novel.) Casual hook-
ups are insinuated, fueled by hashish. When Leonardo goes home with a vacu-
ous woman he meets at a club, he finds himself drawn to her roommate, an
attractive and bookish young woman named Mónica. (In *Reina* the "good
guys"—most of whom are women—are storytellers who love to read, just like
the protagonist.) Leonardo and Mónica form a bond and seem as though they
could be soulmates. In a fateful twist, Mónica gives Leonardo a book by Casilda
Iriarte (entitled *Ensayos sobre el vértigo* or *Essays on Vertigo*, an existential malaise from which he suffers). But she is unobtainable from the start. When Leonardo meets Mónica she is packing to leave for Australia where the man she loves
is waiting, and he does nothing to make her change her plans.

A Different Snow Queen

Leonardo's indifference to romantic love also points to an aversion to commitment. This reluctance to commit characterized his generation, which came of

age in a time of instability. Martín Gaite once observed that the political is personal: "Todo el mundo comenta los acontecimientos políticos viviéndolos, y desde su punto de vista" [Everyone comments on political events according to how they experience them, and from their own perspective] (Interview with Brown, 23–24 November 1984). In *Reina*, Leonardo's milieu and his experiences actualize statistics about the Transition and its lost generation, confirming Helen Graham's conviction that the most powerful way of writing history is "telling big stories through individual human lives" (qtd. by Sebastiaan Faber, 92). Specific references to social and economic problems are concentrated in the first half of the novel, perhaps because these pages were written contemporaneously. Leonardo's cellmate in the Carabanchel prison thinks about being released but immediately has misgivings: "Se acordó de que tenía cuarenta años, del incremento del paro, de las dificultades de un preso para reinsertarse en la sociedad" (30) ["He remembered suddenly that he was forty years old; he thought about the rise in unemployment, how hard it was for an ex-con to find a place in society" 17]. The use of drugs to block out the surrounding world is introduced in the novel's early pages, when Leonardo and his cellmate retrieve their stash of marijuana concealed in a wall and smoke a joint together.

Recreational drugs are omnipresent in *Reina*, beginning with cannabis. Leonardo smokes hashish (cannabis resin) throughout the novel, sometimes mentioning that he is high as he writes in his journal. In Madrid nightclubs such as the one with the suggestive name "Ponte a cien" (a loose translation is "Get turned on"; the British translation renders it as "Go like the clappers" 190) and at parties in cramped apartments, Leonardo smokes as he has a drink. He takes pleasure in "el bienestar de los primeros efectos del hash" (80) ["the sense of wellbeing brought on by the first effects of the hash" 65] despite his sleazy surroundings. There is even a scene that involves making contact with a dealer and scoring "chocolate" (slang for hashish) in a club (196); in the English version "chocolate" is translated as "hash" (176). At times Leonardo smokes too much, experiencing uncomfortable symptoms: tachycardia, dizziness, and possible hallucinations. The mood-altering substances he ingests intensify his feelings of displacement. This is especially true in the basement clubs he frequents at night, which he describes as "locales ruidosos donde corren la droga y el dinero" (74) ["noisy clubs rife with drugs and money" 60], to the extent that at times he seems to disassociate from his surroundings. These stifling environments function as escape valves for young people who find the pressures of life to be overwhelming, offering what Leonardo calls "un remedo de refugio" (74) ["poor imitations of refuges" 60].

The ultimate escape for young people during the Transition was a more brutal drug: heroin. Although she usually wrote from experience, this was not a drug that Martín Gaite ever tried, and she felt powerless to understand it (Personal communication, July 1985). Like other Spaniards her age, Martín Gaite watched

in horror as the twin plagues of heroin and AIDS decimated the younger generation. Her laissez-faire acceptance of recreational drugs was quite different
from her view of heroin, as can be discerned in her novels. Characters smoke
marijuana in *Fragmentos de interior* (1976), Martín Gaite's first novel to be
immune from censorship, with a lyrical scene in which they experience synes-
thesia. Drugs play a key role in *El cuarto de atrás*. The mysterious man in black
offers the narrator psychotropic substances (colored pills and Portuguese ciga-
rettes) that loosen her memory and evoke the long-suppressed recollections at
the heart of the novel. On the second page of *Cuarto* the narrator compares jum-
bled images experienced in a trance-like state of insomnia with an intravenous
drug (page 20 of the Siruela edition that begins with an introduction), an association reminiscent of preoperative anesthesia. In her novels set after Spain legalized cannabis for personal use in 1982, characters smoke a joint as readily as
they sip a glass of wine. (One such episode in *Nubosidad variable* involves a vivid
dream in which Sofía converses with her dead mother after smoking hashish.)
But *Reina* is the first work by Martín Gaite to specifically reference a hard drug,
and it is part of a cautionary tale. The prison sentence that Leonardo serves is
related to a botched heroin shipment. His explanation is that he was set up by
his accomplices; regardless, his drug use nearly derailed his life, as it did for so
many others.

The evil Snow Queen of this novel—unanimously identified by readers as
Leonardo's adoptive mother—is actually a drug, heroin. Leonardo's description
of the effect of the Snow Queen's kisses resembles heroin entering a user's blood-
stream: "y entonces Kay ya se sintió completamente bien, porque no sentía
nada. Todo era igual, todo era eternamente blanco" (109–110) ["and then Kay felt
completely well again, because he did not feel anything. Everything was the same,
everything was eternally white" 93]. The Snow Queen stops kissing Kay after he
forgets everything, saying that if she continued he would die—as with a drug
overdose. (This scene also harks back to Andersen's tale, in which the Snow
Queen's third kiss would be fatal to Kay.) There is no scene of intravenous drug
use in the novel, perhaps because the author could not bring herself to imagine
the sordid act. But it is implied. Leonardo refers obliquely to his time in Tangiers with friends "cuando estaba empezando a meterme en el lío de las drogas"
(197) ["when I was just beginning to get into drugs" 177]. He also describes his
long convalescence from hepatitis, a disease that in developed countries is associated with drug users sharing contaminated needles (an analog for needle-borne
HIV transmission).

Leonardo acknowledges his drug use, as do those around him. Returning
home after a long absence, he recalls places associated with drugs, including
squalid apartments belonging to friends of friends. The odious majordomo of
his parents' home, noticing what he thinks is unusual behavior, asks Leonardo
what is wrong with him: "¿No habrás bebido . . . *o algo*?" (118, italics added) ["You

haven't been drinking *or anything*, have you?" 100; italics added]. Leonardo describes the drug culture that was his world: grungy Madrid clubs where he used to hang out with people who were evidently high: "hombres y mujeres oje-rosos, inquietos, excitados, pertenecientes a una grey condenada al extravío" (91) ["restless, hyped-up men and women with dark shadows under their eyes, all members of a fraternity of people doomed to drift" 76]. His drug use shapes the way he perceives experiences, as he observes: "resbalar de una percepción a otra no es algo inhabitual para quien ha tenido contacto con la droga" (315) ["slip-ping from one perception to another is not that unusual for someone used to taking drugs" 294]. When he returns from prison Leonardo comments on the advent of new, more lenient drug policies which avoid jailing offenders. He does not add that under the Socialists, drug law enforcement was neglected to the point that groups of neighbors banded together in vigilante squads to try to erad-icate nearby users and dealers on their own, in the absence of police interven-tion. At the time, some wondered whether the government's indifference to drug use was a conscious strategy to neutralize the younger generation (recounted by Esteban Ordóñez).

Writing and Recovery

Leonardo's generation was also Martín Gaite's daughter Marta's. While virtu-ally all critics have recognized Casilda Iriarte as Martín Gaite's alter ego, there is a second real-life correspondence between characters in *La Reina de las Nieves* that remains unexplored: between Leonardo Villalba and Marta Sánchez Mar-tín. Leonardo is the same age as the author's daughter: "más cerca de los treinta que de los veinte" (23) ["nearly thirty" 10]. They belong to the generation that came of age during La Movida. In *Reina* the daughter of the solicitor abandons both medical school and her family to run off with the drummer in a rock band—a choice that reveals the hedonism of the times, as well as the divide between parents and their grown children. This chasm has been lamented by a real-life parent, the father of Marta's boyfriend, Carlos, who like her "entró de lleno en esa generación de muchachos dispuestos a quemar su existencia. Había que apurarla hasta el límite (lo que para ellos era el límite), sin precaución ni cautela" [was fully immersed in the generation of young people who were pre-pared to burn up their lives. They had to push everything to the limit—what was for them the limit—without regard for safety or good judgment] (Castilla del Pino 449). Even if they had been inclined to exercise restraint and focus on a career, members of Leonardo's and Marta's generation entered adulthood dur-ing an era of youth unemployment that denied them what Spanish researchers called "a project or a place in the world" (Manuel Martín Serrano and Olivia Velarde Hermida, qtd. in Allinson 266). Employment opportunities in Spain were few and, when they existed, tenuous. In the novel Leonardo dabbles with various occupations. He notes that his "tentativas de trabajo" (144) ["attempts to get work" 127] have included periods as a photographer, painter, journalist, tourist guide, waiter, and part-time actor; he also worked abroad as a Spanish teacher in Italy (144 [127]). Marta similarly experimented with jobs as an editorial assistant, English teacher, and translator.

In addition to being a member of her generational cohort, Leonardo exhibits many of Marta's personal characteristics as I observed them over the nearly ten years that I knew her.[13] Like Marta, the protagonist of *La Reina de las Nieves* is talented, adventurous, generous, intellectually curious, and spontaneous. Also like her, Leonardo is somewhat adrift and reluctant to ask for parental help. As cultural critic Juan Cruz reported, quoting mutual friend Ignacio Álvarez Vara, Marta "era como una Peter Pan juvenil, siempre nos parecía que tenía veinte o veintidós años" [was like a young Peter Pan, she always seemed to us to be twenty or twenty-two years old] (qtd. in Cruz, "Volver a Carmiña" [Return to Carmiña]). Because of social privilege, Marta was sheltered from the responsibilities of adulthood, just like Leonardo. In the first chapter of the novel a wise old crone remarks "No hay cosa peor para la juventud que verse con dinero y tanto mimo, y más hoy en día" (18) ["being rich and spoiled is about the worst thing that can happen to a young person, especially nowadays" 6]. As Nuria Cruz-Cámara has described, "el panorama generacional que ofrece Martín Gaite en *La Reina*... pinta un cuadro de tintes oscuros" [the generational panorama offered by Martín Gaite in *Reina* paints a dark portrait] characterized by "desarraigo y la falta de dirección vital" [rootlessness and a lack of direction in life] and "un fracaso colectivo" [collective failure] ("Utopía" 125). Leonardo refers to his own situation as "catastrófica" (179) ["catastrophic" 159], and this descriptor also applies to "la juventud a la que pertenezco" (183) ["my generation" 163]. He adeptly captures the paralysis that accompanies too many choices: "Te parece que has ido donde has querido y que has hecho lo que te ha dado la gana, pero no, todo se reduce a andar zarandeado de tumbo en tumbo, a evitar esquinas y leyes y llamadas, a elegir entre las mil alternativas con que te tienta el mundo movedizo" (39) ["And you think you've gone where you wanted to go and that you've done what you felt like doing, but you haven't; you just lurch from one place to the next, avoiding corners and laws and phone calls, trying to choose between the thousand tempting alternatives offered you by this shifting world" 26].

This generation was rudderless, adrift in a sea that became increasingly rough. As they drive away from prison, Leonardo's redheaded friend accuses him of throwing away all the advantages he has been given: "Te has pasado la vida haciendo cosas que no te reportaban ningún beneficio... regalando tu dinero, tu talento, tu salud, todo, tirándolo por la borda..." (64) [You've spent your whole life doing things that never benefited you in any way... throwing away your money, your talent, your health, everything, just tossing it overboard..." 51].

Leonardo was never happy in the home where his unloving mother set the rules. But his sense of alienation grew during his years away from home—a period of increasing drug use. He became estranged not only from his sympathetic father, but from himself. Leonardo laments that his father "últimamente perdió mi rastro porque yo mismo lo perdí también, igual que la memoria, la paz y el equilibrio" (143) ["finally lost track of me because I lost track of myself, along with my memory, my peace of mind, my equilibrium" 126]. The inability to assume life's challenges as a functioning adult is a motif in the novel, symbolized by Eric Fromm's *Fear of Freedom* (*El miedo a la libertad*). Leonardo finds this book in Mónica's library while she is packing to leave; when she offers it to him, he declines, explaining that he has read it many times. He evidently identifies with this book, just as he does with Camus's existential classic *L'étranger* (so much so that "el extranjero" [the stranger] became his father's nickname for Leonardo when he wrote to him, though the novel's title remains in the original French). Martín Gaite may also have associated this generational fear of freedom with her daughter. In *Visión de Nueva York* there is a photograph of her with Marta (who came to visit in December 1980) on a boat in New York Harbor in front of the Statue of Liberty. Next to the photo is a Post-it Note in the author's handwriting: "La libertad siempre da algo de miedo cuando se ve de cerca, ¿no lo sabías?" [Freedom is always a bit frightening when you see it up close, didn't you know that?] (n.p.; transcription 181).

The detective-fiction model enables healing revisionism. "Most analysts of detective fiction see the genre as a form of wish-fulfillment," according to one historian of the genre (Rzepka 21). Martín Gaite firmly believed that the reader deserved gratification when deciphering a story. "A veces las historias se presentan desordenadas" [sometimes stories are presented in a chaotic fashion], she explained to Juan Cantavella soon after the publication of *Reina*, noting that even when events might seem indecipherable, the reader was entitled to a unifying thread: "No puedes desorientarle sin ofrecerle una solución" [You can't confuse the reader without offering a satisfactory solution] ("Carmen Martín Gaite" 30–31). While satisfaction is usually associated with vicarious pleasure for the reader, in this novel it is also palpably strong for the author. As O'Leary and Ribeiro de Menezes have pointed out, "the novel has a rosy tone of wish fulfillment at times" (143). In *Reina* Martín Gaite rewrites the ending to her daughter's story. Here the successful mother is able to save her gifted, risk-taking child even though she has been away for nearly all of his life. Such absence may possibly be an exaggeration of Martín Gaite's time away as a visiting professor in the United States between 1979 and 1985, totaling a year and a half (Brown "Los años americanos" 83).

The way that Casilda rescues Leonardo is through writing. Casilda's writing becomes a lifeline to her son, just as writing has been her personal salvation (her closest resemblance to her creator). Casilda's longtime butler observes that writing is a joy for her, even more so than conversation, comparing it to a long-lasting state of inebriation. Writing is also Casilda's means of communication when conversation is not possible, a theme that has persisted in Martín Gaite's literature over time. In addition to her essay "La búsqueda de interlocutor," Carlos Uxó González has observed the relevance of her essay "El interlocutor soñado" [The imaginary conversational partner], which describes a solitary precursor phase in which narratives are told to the self. As he observes, the most common way in which a "doubling" or the creation of a dual persona is actualized is through diaries ("La forma más habitual en que se concreta este desdoblarse es la de los diarios" [62]). Martín Gaite defined her search for an interlocutor in her only published autobiography: "Creo que si siempre pudiera uno comunicarse con sus semejantes de forma adecuada y en el momento adecuado, no necesitaría escribir, la escritura es como un sucedáneo para paliar esta incomunicación que hoy padecemos" ("Bosquejo" 234). ["I think that if one could always communicate with one's peers in the right way and at the right time, there would be no need to write. Writing is like a substitute used to alleviate the lack of communication that we suffer today"] ("Sketch" 244). By serving as each other's interlocutors, Casilda and Leonardo personify what literary historians Jordi Gracia and Domingo Ródenas have identified as the fundamental theme of the novel: "la misteriosa fuerza redentora de la escritura" [the mysterious redemptive power of writing] (733).

Casilda felt that her son was her conversational partner. Martín Gaite expressed the same sentiment about Marta: "Mi hija es muy amiga mía . . . y nos lo contamos todo" she wrote in 1980 ("Bosquejo" 234) ["My daughter and I are good friends . . . and tell each other everything"] ("Sketch" 244). Casilda wanted to connect with Leonardo and be there for him—to supply the kind of nurturing that he did not get from the woman who adopted him. As Casilda explains near the end of the novel, she has gladly assumed the *atadura* or binding tie of motherhood, another enduring theme for the author:[14]

Total, que no soy libre. Me he pasado treinta años llamándolo a través del mar, igual que llamaba a mi madre, y a veces venía y otras se volvía a ir, escribiendo para él, soñando con él. Sabía que algún día lo llegaría a ver, porque no se había muerto como mi madre, pero esperaba sin prisas. Estaba segura de que él recogía desde cualquier playa del mundo mis mensajes cifrados dentro de una botella. (307)

[In short, I'm not free. I've spent thirty years calling to him across the sea, just as I used to call to my mother, and sometimes he would come and at others he would go again, thirty years of writing to him, dreaming of him. I knew that one day I would see him, because he hadn't died as my mother had, but I wasn't in a hurry. I was sure that on some beach in the world he would pick up my coded messages inside a bottle.] (286)

Even though the messages were undated and out of order, Leonardo found them as she intended. As María Elena Bravo has observed, in *Reina* "the link[s] between narration and the writer/mother are obvious" (224). Through her writings, Leonardo recognized himself in his mother: "Añoro lo mismo que añora ella, escribo, sueño, muero y resucito como ella y con ella, a su compás" (236) ["I long for what she longs for, I write, dream, die and come to life again like her and with her, keeping time" 214]. Casilda also sees herself in her son. Beyond the fact that they look alike, they both turn to the written word to cope with the world around them. When Leonardo imagines reuniting with Casilda, he likens their reunion to "una cita de amor" or assignation (243) [translated as "going out on a date" 223] and plans to conquer her with words. Leonardo is of course successful: Casilda welcomes him with open arms, making him whole. Casilda has also fulfilled her quest. Before Leonardo's serendipitous arrival, Casilda had fallen into listlessness, as if she had suddenly become old. After their reunion, she has a son to rely on. He offers to be his mother's helpmate and companion until she sends him away, which he hopes she never does. As Jurado Morales has summarized "[La novela] toma como eje narrativo las carencias de . . . dos seres descolocados en el mundo que luchan por fortalecer su identidad" [The narrative of the novel revolves around the needs of . . . two people who feel out of place in the world, fighting to shore up their identity] (*Trayectoria* 320).

Closure brings recovery from loss. In *Reina* the successful resolution of the plot promotes equanimity, despite the fact that there is no way to undo past suffering. Resignation is a recurring motif. Even as a child Leonardo had acknowledged the power of fate. In the chapter whose title references the fateful kidnapping by a rapacious Snow Queen in Andersen's text, Leonardo recognizes that "no ha nacido nadie que nos pueda avisar de esas amenazas que cierne sobre nosotros el destino y que deja caer cuando nos ve más descuidados" (100) ["the person has not yet been born who can warn us of the dangers that Fate brandishes aloft and then drops on us when she sees we are distracted" 84]. This acceptance also applies to coming to terms with the heroin epidemic: "jóvenes que, en los años ochenta, cayeron en el abismo de las drogas ante la impotencia de las generaciones que los precedieron" [young people who, in the eighties, fell into the abyss of drug use as the preceding generations stood by helplessly], in the words of creators of the long-running fictionalized historical television series *Cuéntame cómo pasó* [Tell me how it happened]. One director of this series—recalling that in the 1980s he lost half his friends to the epidemic—explained how he and his colleagues used their own experiences to pull back the curtain on this era in 2015 (RTVE).

Leonardo evidently makes peace with the deception that damaged his psyche and left him vulnerable to drug use. When the family solicitor asks Leonardo if he has children, the answer is no, but the older man nevertheless explains the challenges of parent-child relationships: "Pues cuando los tengas, te darás cuenta de que nunca se sabe cómo acertar, lo disculpa uno todo, pero sin entenderlo. Los hijos, en cambio, puede que nos entiendan mejor, pero no nos pasan ni una" (162) ["Well, when you do, you'll come to realize that you just can't get it right; you can forgive your children anything, but you never understand them. Maybe our children understand us better, but they don't let us get away with a thing" 144]. The solicitor recalls that Leonardo's father did not want to pressure or over-whelm him; the implication is that he respected Leonardo's free will, even when he wished he would accept more guidance. But with the help of his mother, Leo-nardo manages to pull through. Thanks to her, he recovers his identity and his past (Casilda even maintained his old room with his belongings at La Quinta Blanca). Ruminating about his view of relationships, he could just as well be describing his own evolution during the Transition: "Sin duda existiría un pro-ceso de desencanto, pero también de madurez" (197) ["There doubtless exists some process of disenchantment, of maturity too" 177].

Not all members of Leonardo's generation were so fortunate as to be able to look back on their youthful mistakes; many found themselves trapped in a dead-end or, in a phrase with special resonance for the author, a "callejón sin salida" (47) ["cul-de-sac" 34]. Along with disillusionment, loss is another theme that permeates *Reina*. When Leonardo describes his grandmother's death, which he characterizes as a strange type of scar, his eloquence is poignant. As he realizes that he can no longer call to share things with her, the thought strikes him as if he were once again being hit with the news of her passing: "Y supe que la noción de la muerte es lateral y oblicua, que se nos cuela de través por ahí, desde la inmo-vilidad de las cosas huérfanas de su dueño, persistentes, parásitas, sin uso" (150) ["I knew that the notion of death is both lateral and oblique, it slips inside us from out there, from the stillness of all those orphaned objects which endure, parasitical, useless" 133]. The most awful specter is that of forgetting the loved one. Casilda laments how difficult it is to recall a dead person's voice, and Leon-ardo is terrified of forgetting the voice of his grandmother: "la posibilidad de que algún día llegara a olvidarla, a no poderme arropar con ella ... me pareció lo más horrible del mundo" (152) ["It occurred to me ... that the day would come when I would forget it ... and that seemed to me the most terrible thing in the world" 135]. Stories are always incomplete, Casilda observes in the penultimate chapter of the novel, and death does not end them: "Es una equivocación que se paga cara no contar con el rastro de los muertos" (305) ["That's a mistake we pay for dearly, not taking into account the traces left by the dead" 283]. Casilda and Leonardo demonstrate that keeping alive the memory of a loved one is at once a comfort and a mission for those they leave behind.

———

La Reina de las Nieves chronicles the years of Spain's Transition with a histo-rian's eye. The novel uses tropes associated with fairy tales and detective fiction to investigate the power of heroin—the villainous Snow Queen—over gifted and privileged young adults. Protagonist Leonardo Villalba stands in for the author's daughter Marta Sánchez Martín, both personally and generationally. His experiences illustrate the Transition's toxic combination of hedonistic freedom and economic crisis—conditions that foreclosed opportunities for an entire cohort of young people. Both Leonardo and Marta fell victim to the circumstances detailed in the novel, as did many other members of Spain's "generación perdida" [lost generation]. But the fictional hero, helped by his mother, manages to escape with his life. The happy ending of the novel's eponymous fairy tale is achieved. Critics have recognized that "Martín Gaite conceived of literature as catharsis" (O'Leary and Ribeiro de Menezes 271), and she herself acknowledged as much for this novel. Her somewhat cryptic description of *La Reina de las Nieves* in a 1995 interview becomes clearer when its biographical underpinnings are known. She called it "un canto al deseo de esclarecimiento, de salir de un pozo, de salir de una situación que parecía cerrada, mediante la inteligencia y mediante la memoria" [a hymn to the desire for clarity, for getting out from under, for leaving what seemed to be a closed room—and doing so through mindfulness and memory] (qtd. in Cantavella "Carmen Martín Gaite" 81). The novel's second dedication confirms that she was referring to her bereavement, as it invokes her daughter without naming her.[15] Reading between the lines, it is clear that Marta was the "farewell angel" of *La Reina de las Nieves*, and that the author did not want Spain's lost generation to be forgotten.

CHAPTER 5

Lo raro es vivir

EXISTENTIAL QUESTIONS IN UNCERTAIN TIMES

Martín Gaite's next-to-last finished novel was begun in 1994, the year that she was awarded Spain's Premio Nacional de las Letras Españolas by the Spanish Ministry of Culture in recognition of lifetime achievement. That year she also published an affecting generational memoir entitled *Esperando el porvenir*, in which she recounted experiences shared by the writers and friends who would become known as Spain's "midcentury generation." Between 1994 and 1996, at the height of her literary powers, Martín Gaite produced a beautifully written novel with a compelling story in an innovative narrative frame. *Lo raro es vivir* (1996) [*Living's the Strange Thing* 2004] is the fictional memoir of a week in the life of a fascinating thirty-five-year-old woman in Madrid in the mid-1990s. The novel documents a time of relentless social change and unrest in Spain: "nuestro caótico fin de milenio" (179) ["our chaotic *fin de millennium*" 150], as the narrator puts it. In the late 1990s Spain's fledgling democracy was on the brink of dramatic political change. The Socialist Party's historic rise to power in 1982, which came to symbolize the endpoint of the Spanish transition to democracy, would end in March of 1996, just weeks before Martín Gaite's book was published. After more than a dozen years of liberalizing legislation and nearly as many years of fiscal corruption and other alleged criminal activities, the reign of PSOE under Felipe González was nearly over. A very close vote would send the pendulum of power swinging back toward conservatives of the Partido Popular (PP) or People's Party, a refuge for former Franco supporters headed by José María Aznar.

The dreaded shadow of fascism hovers in this novel's opening and closing scenes. They feature the Valle de los Caídos [Valley of the Fallen], the huge Catholic basilica and monument outside Madrid, built by Republican prisoners after the Civil War to honor mostly Nationalist Civil War victims. There are 33,847 Spaniards buried there. Of this number 12,000 have never been identified; it is assumed that the majority of the unidentified are Republicans who were victims of the Franco dictatorship (reported by Elena Genillo). As historian Paul Preston observed in his classic study of the Spanish Civil War, "from 1939 until Franco's death Spain was governed as if it were a country occupied by a victorious foreign army," an army that was trained and deployed "for action against the native population rather than an external enemy" (*Civil War* 319–320). The Valle de los Caídos was—and still is—a repository of anguish for non-Franco supporters: a symbol of defeat and humiliation. Franco was buried there in 1975. Efforts to exhume and resituate his remains, supported by Socialists and stymied by the Partido Popular, finally came to fruition in October 2019, though the monument remains. Such a shrine is an anomaly in Europe. There are no monuments to Hitler in Germany or Austria, nor to Mussolini in Italy; meanwhile Spain has continued to maintain this pilgrimage site for fascists, with an estimated 250,000 annual visitors in 2018, according to Andrés Gil. Even though Martín Gaite previously refrained from explicit political allusions in her fiction, the gravity of the country's situation led her to do otherwise in this novel. Her "blatant reference to a highly politicized location" in *Lo raro es vivir* anticipates current disputes over the recovery of historical memory, as Catherine O'Leary and Alison Ribeiro de Menezes have noted (160).

Spain's debates about historical memory are rooted in the country's deferred reckoning with its past. Because the Transition had depended on a tacit *pacto del olvido* [pact of forgetting] in order to achieve reconciliation, instigated by the 1977 Ley de Amnistía that forbade prosecution for political crimes before that date, there was no truth telling. As political scientist Omar G. Encarnación has explained:

> Instead of justice and truth, forgetting and moving on prevailed in Spain. . . . Furthermore, the pact to forget effectively precluded an official condemnation of Franco's military coup in 1936. . . . Adding insult to injury, the pact facilitated the survival of numerous monuments across the Spanish territory honoring Franco, including the infamous El Valle de los Caídos, Franco's megalomaniacal monument on the outskirts of Madrid to his Nationalist crusade. (2)

In 2000, after the discovery of a mass grave of Republicans murdered by Franco-supporting Falangists in 1936, an organization was established to examine the country's history: the Asociación para la Recuperación de la Memoria Histórica [Association for the Recovery of Historical Memory]. Seven years later the Socialists attempted to legislate the recuperation of historical memory. They had unexpectedly been reelected in March 2004 after the ruling Partido Popular falsely accused Basque nationalists of carrying out the brutal bombings of Madrid commuter trains three days earlier (bombings which were in fact carried out by Islamic terrorists). The 2007 law passed by the Socialist majority became known as the Ley de Memoria Histórica [Law of Historical Memory]. It did not undo the 1977 amnesty law but did introduce measures that acknowledged the rights of those who suffered persecution or violence during the Civil War and dicta-torship, including the exhumation of mass graves. The law was opposed by mem-bers of the Partido Popular, who said it reopened old wounds; they defunded it once they returned to power in 2011.

Martín Gaite's invocation of the Francoist monument in *Lo raro es vivir* sit-uates the novel in circumstances that resonate in the twenty-first century. Many contemporary novelists have chosen to explore the Civil War and its repercus-sions (Javier Cercas, Javier Marías, Carme Riera, Isaac Rosa, Dulce Chacón, Alberto Méndez, Ángeles Caso, Jordi Soler, José María Marino, and Manuel Rivas, among others). For these writers, born after the war, knowledge derives from received wisdom (what Holocaust scholar Marianne Hirsch termed "post-memory") rather than first-hand experience, as Isabel Cuñado has elucidated in her essay "Despertar tras la amnesia" [Awakening from amnesia]. *Lo raro es vivir* presages the centrality of enduring sociopolitical divisions in twenty-first-century Spain, including the uneasy alliances among a number of political par-ties, beyond the duo of PP and PSOE—one of which is a new ultra-right party, Vox. Founded in 2014, by 2019 Vox had won enough seats in Spain's Congreso de los Diputados [Parliament] to become a major player in the national govern-ment. "The far right has made huge gains in the country's general election," reported Guy Hedgecoe for BBC News in November 2019, "becoming the third force in parliament."

Against the backdrop of a dynamic city in precarious times, *Lo raro es vivir* tells a story that is riveting, moving, thoughtful, and humorous. This is the only one of Martín Gaite's later novels to have a young adult female protagonist—someone who would have been the same age as her daughter, Marta Sánchez Martín, had she lived. It contains the author's last and most hopeful novelistic engagement with the issue that had haunted her since Marta died. Nearly a decade later, with a string of successful books and burgeoning acclaim in her own country (where recognition trailed her international status), she initiated this novel with newfound optimism. The passage of time had dulled some of the sharpest pain from her grief. Her assistant continued to carry out mundane tasks, enabling Martín Gaite to finish the novel in time for the annual Madrid Book Fair in late May. In a letter to publisher Jorge Herralde in April 1996—as she was finishing the novel and sending him the chapters in batches—she described her process: "Trabajo día y noche con mucha ilusión, en total encierro. Y voy que-dando muy satisfecha con lo que sale. Las musas me están portando." [I'm hap-pily working day and night, completely sequestered. And I'm pleased with what is emerging. The muses are carrying me along] (reprinted by Iker Seisdedos). The following month she would once again be the de facto Reina de la Feria del Libro [Queen of the Book Fair]. Ensconced in one of the hundreds of "casetas" or book booths in Retiro Park, she was a celebrity, signing books for fans of all ages who waited in long lines to meet her.

A Story of Reconciliation from Beyond the Grave

Lo raro es vivir traces the reconciliation of a mother and daughter in ways that are unexpected and poignant. This overarching theme subsumes existential questions about the meaning of life and death, since a crucial impediment to mutual understanding between parent and child in the novel is the fact that the mother is no longer alive. *Lo raro es vivir* is narrated by a protagonist who goes unnamed for two-thirds of the book. This omission, coupled with the narrator's sometimes cryptic free associations, foster the reader's sense that he or she is assembling the pieces of a puzzle. The narrator, Águeda Soler Luengo, is bright, beautiful, energetic, and disorganized. Her charismatic mother—also named Águeda Luengo—died eight weeks earlier, leaving her daughter with unresolved maternal issues. Águeda had always put her mother on a pedestal, admiring her above all others for her creativity and grace. At the same time, she felt that she was not as central to her mother's life as she wanted to be. Her mother did not try to mold her, nor did she attempt to intervene when she made poor decisions, despite the fact that the daughter secretly longed for her to do so.

The younger Águeda works as an archivist while attempting to write a doctoral dissertation that involves the recovery of historical truth. Her subject is a real historical figure: a fascinating but little-known eighteenth-century diplomat named don Luis Vidal y Villalba, whom Martín Gaite discovered when she was conducting archival research in the late 1960s and early 1970s.[1] Vidal y Villalba's exciting adventures in South America, where he encountered the indigenous leader Tupac Amaro and conspired with expelled Jesuits to help Chile and Paraguay gain independence, had a tragic ending. These exploits led to imprisonment in London, where both Vidal y Villalba and his faithful manservant were charged with conspiracy. Eventually Vidal y Villalba died in Gibraltar, having gone insane. In *Lo raro es vivir* the protagonist's scholarly career is relatively recent: when Águeda was in her twenties she had a more edgy lifestyle and occupation. She was a hard-drinking rock musician, composing a type of music she called "entrerock" [inter-rock] whose songs had titles such as "Lo raro es vivir" [Living's the strange thing]. Águeda's parents have been divorced for years (her father left them and started a new family) and during this time her mother has achieved international renown as a painter. Águeda left her mother's new home some time ago, moving to her own apartment. Now Águeda seems to be in the process of settling down. She has traded her bad-boy boyfriend Roque for a calm and thoughtful architect named Tomás, whose apartment she now shares.

Despite her newfound stability Águeda is capable of wild, almost hallucinogenic flights of the imagination, something that she attributes to the power that language and metaphors exert over her. During a visit to her grandfather's geriatric home she has a vision of her mother crying glass tears on a crystal planet, and she can vividly picture the afterlife as "una especie enorme de almacén" (59) ["a kind of huge warehouse" 45] in which the dead person's belongings are offered for sale, as at the venerable Madrid flea market El Rastro. Since she was a child Águeda has used her imagination to escape reality. She used to imagine that she was going into the forest when she descended into the subway with her mother, eager to "romper los lazos con lo previsible" (34) ["to sever ties with the unpredictable" 22]. As a grown woman, Águeda can use her intellect to humorous effect, as when she asks two suburban matrons whether they know of a certain Vidal y Villalba (to which one replies yes, she is sure that is the name of the town's new orthodontist). But Águeda can also be calculating, as when she pretends to be her mother—whom she resembles in both physique and voice—to delay her grandfather's realization that his daughter has died. The fact that her role as an imposter is (improbably) suggested by the doctor in charge of her grandfather's old-age home makes this a kindness rather than a cruelty, but it is nonetheless a deception that a conventional person would not undertake.

Águeda's narrative recreates a crucial sequence of days from two-and-a-half years earlier—a retrospective distance that does not become fully clear until the novel's Epilogue, written in the present tense. Two visits to her dying maternal grandfather serve as bookends for a week that begins on 30 June. With Tomás away in southern Spain working on a project, Águeda has the solitude necessary for deep reflection. She has a series of encounters with people who have had an impact on her life: friends and family. Among the latter are her former art history teacher Rosario Tena, who inspired her to become a scholar; her passionate but narcissistic and abusive ex-boyfriend Roque (whom she spots working as a street mime, aptly dressed in a devil's costume); her sympathetic boss Magda, who acts like a big sister; and her supremely supportive partner, Tomás (in nightly phone calls). She also interacts with her father (a cipher in the novel) and, through a series of recollections, her mother. Águeda searches for her own identity, using others to gain self-knowledge. As José Jurado Morales has observed, "los recuerdos de la familia, los amores y los amigos son el mejor trampolín para alcanzar una realización emocional y afectiva" [memories of family, lovers, and friends are the best springboard for reaching emotional fulfillment] (Trayectoria 397).

By the last chapter of the novel Águeda has resolved her ambivalent relationship with her mother and has overcome her negative view of motherhood generally. She stops blaming her mother for perceived deficiencies, realizing that "culpas, además, no hay, sólo causas" (149) ["there are no faults, only causes" 124]. Although her grandfather dies soon after their last visit (in which he sees through her disguise and recognizes his granddaughter), he leaves her a parting gift: the knowledge that her mother valued her more than anything in the world. Hours after she learns that, Tomás returns home; she becomes pregnant that night. In the present-day Epilogue the reader is introduced to Cecilia, the infant daughter of Águeda and Tomás, who lives with her parents in the home that Águeda inherited from her mother. The novel concludes with Águeda picking up her young daughter to look out the window, as if offering her the world. The baby girl responds with delight. The last lines of the novel contain one of the most beautiful endings in Martín Gaite's oeuvre. They describe how baby Cecilia looks out the window and embraces everything she sees: "Hace un gesto circular y parsimonioso con la mano como si quisiera investigarlo todo, abarcarlo todo" (223) ["She makes a careful, circular gesture with her hand as if she wants to investigate all of it, take it all in" 194].

A PROUSTIAN NARRATIVE

Despite its modest length (229 pages in Spanish, 194 pages in the English translation by Anne McLean), *Lo raro es vivir* is an intricate novel filled with surprises. Its eighteen chapters are short, ranging from five to twenty pages and averaging less than twelve pages in length. They have wryly evocative names such as "Primeras mentiras" ["First Lies"], "Bajada al bosque" ["Down to the Woods"], "Un gato que escucha" ["A Cat Who Listens"], and "Cuatro gotas del existencialismo" ["Four Drops of Existentialism"]. The reader's curiosity is piqued by each chapter title, which can only be deciphered by reading the relevant segment of text. Although Águeda can be indecisive ("Indecisiones" or "Indecisions" is the main heading in the notebook she uses to record her ideas), she is an engaging narrator. As with all the author's protagonists, Águeda is a person of good character who does not inflict harm intentionally, and she respects people of diverse ages and social classes. Even when she is highly critical, as when she describes her father's controlling new wife, her observations are more analytical than hostile. She scrutinizes herself with the same degree of frankness as she does others, acknowledging, for example, her own propensity for telling lies.

Águeda's verbal dexterity is striking. Her way of expressing herself reflects the author's gift for capturing the colloquialisms of a generation, a talent on display since the seemingly tape-recorded dialogue of her first novel, *Entre visillos*, analyzed by linguist Manuel Seco. Some expressions have a rough literal meaning; for instance, a friend of Águeda's exclaims "No jodas" (37) [literally "don't screw with me," though the English translation renders the expression more generally as "How weird!" 25]. Águeda has a gift for inventing (or preserving) original words for use by herself and her inner circle, recalling Natalia Ginzburg's concept of a family lexicon.[2] Águeda's expressive neologisms include "ponerse dostoievski," which involves becoming philosophical in the manner of Dostoevsky, and "ninfrar," which her mother invented to describe the plaintive vocalization that precedes crying. Águeda cites an expression used at work to foster closeness with her supervisor Magda. Interestingly, this expression was truly a Martín Gaite family saying—"r.p.f.," for "rabiando por fumar" (147) ["d.f.a.s.," for "dying for a smoke" 122–123] was coined by ex-husband Rafael

Sánchez Ferlosio (*Cuadernos* 443); Martín Gaite added a footnote explaining the abbreviation when she photocopied this notebook excerpt and mailed it to me in 1978. While her expressive language invites reflection, Águeda's narrative also has a sense of immediacy, with passages that seem to be addressed directly to the reader. Águeda is also the most amusing protagonist in Martín Gaite's repertoire, closely followed by the delightful Miss Lunatic of *Caperucita en Manhattan*. Águeda's sense of humor is wry, featuring the type of mordant quip at which the author excelled in conversation. For instance, she wonders why rented rooms don't include poison among the little bottles in the minifridge, since that is what anyone who found themselves there would surely want: "Veneno no tienen, nunca piensan en serio de las necesidades de la gente" (71) ["They don't provide poison, they never take the client's needs seriously" 55].

The novel's balance between meditation and action is Proustian.[3] Águeda's first-person commentary is interspersed with reported scenes with other characters, varying the pace of the narrative. The novel's tempo fluctuates between events and description, reflecting the author's own characterization of the book as having been written "en plan jazz" [like a jazz piece], as she told interviewer Xavier Moret ("Presenta"). Following Gérard Genette's analysis of what Émile Benveniste termed narrative or story and discourse (*récit* and *discours* respectively) in Proust's *À la recherche du temps perdu* [*Remembrance of Things Past*] and other works, it is possible to discern Martín Gaite's method for calculating the proportion of these elements, which are never wholly separate (Genette 137–143). She balances narrative discourse with enough plot to hold the reader's interest. As Martín Gaite related in *El cuarto de atrás*, when she was a girl it took her a long time to learn to enjoy any parts of a novel unrelated to the action. She dismissed these sections as useless "paja" [straw]—pages to be skipped over, as she used to do with the initial scene-setting pages of *Robinson Crusoe*: "tarda uno bastantes años en saborear la paja," she observed (160) ["It takes one quite a few years to learn to relish the chaff as well" 195]. For the memoir genre in Spanish (as in French and all other Romance languages), verb tenses distinguish discourse from story. Discourse in narrative uses the imperfect or iterative tense of verbs ("I always used to do it . . .") whereas actions take the preterite or singulative tense ("I did it"). In Martín Gaite's text as in Proust's, textual passages containing iterative recollections in the imperfect tense are suspended between unique, singulative preterite-tense events that advance the plot.

Also like Proust, Martín Gaite has a sharp sense of how much discourse the reader will tolerate, as he or she reads to find out what happens next. In *Lo raro es vivir* Martín Gaite inserts the most abstract consideration of philosophy into a dialogue between Águeda and a restaurant owner who is writing a book on existentialism, injecting immediacy into what could have been a treatise. Águeda's own musings on philosophical topics are pithy and often moving. Coming to terms with human mortality in a cemetery, for example, Águeda thinks about the universality of mourning, observing that regardless of what caused their death, "al fin y al cabo todos los ausentes . . . tienen en común que brillan por su ausencia," adding: "dejan una orfandad parecida, el mismo rastro de perpleji-dad" (94) ["After all, what those absent . . . all have in common is that they're conspicuous by their absence and leave a similar orphanhood, the same trace of bewilderment" 77]. These observations give rise to consideration of funerals in general, parents and children, identity and communication—all inserted into a suspenseful, singular adventure: a car trip during which Águeda becomes lost.

SETTING AS CHARACTER: MADRID COMES TO LIFE

Águeda does not get lost in Madrid. On the contrary, she has a superb grasp of the city and makes it part of her story, recalling Madrid's role as a supporting character in Martín Gaite's 1976 novel *Fragmentos de interior* (detailed in Brown, *Secrets* 123–126). The novel "exhibits an immense preoccupation with geographic spaces, demonstrating a keen perception about the links between spatial repre-sentation and identity," as Amy L. Tibbitts has described (77). Like the city itself, *Lo raro es vivir* is a novel of neighborhoods. Águeda traverses them alone as she thinks about her present and past. From the historic Barrio de las Letras [Liter-ary Quarter] to the newly chic Bernabeu Stadium neighborhood and in between, Madrid is elevated to the status of a secondary character, a sort of "Thirdspace" (Edward W. Soja's term for socially mediated spatial constructs) that incorpo-rates Águeda's imagined and lived conceptions of the city. The locale where Águeda becomes disoriented is the anodyne, half-built suburb of Las Rozas (which happens to also be the site of a prison where the subject of her disserta-tion, Vidal y Villalba, was held for a time). Las Rozas is located approximately fifteen miles outside the city. Águeda's father—at the insistence of his new wife—has recently moved to a new house on one of its many indistinguishable streets. Even the gardens in this half-finished *urbanización* [housing development] are lifeless, decorated "en plan 'mírame y no me toque'" (101) ["in the look-but-don't-touch manner" 83]. Águeda imagines that this sterile look is the result of the landscape designer being entranced by the magazine *House and Garden*, a sym-bol of the encroachment of synthetic North American tastes.

Las Rozas, which Águeda likens to the barbaric Wild West, contrasts with Madrid's distinctive and cultured neighborhoods. As the protagonist leaves Las Rozas and approaches Madrid, "the image of the city is directly linked to the image of awakening" (Tibbitts 81). In the city Águeda visits recognizable land-marks such as the Gran Vía, the Círculo de Bellas Artes and its open-air café, the Plaza de España with its statues of Don Quijote and Sancho Panza, and the Reina Sofía Museum. She also names some of the subway stations she traverses, such as Antón Martín and Santo Domingo, as she goes from one part of the city to another. Madrid is so alive as to have volition, as Águeda observes just before she encounters her former boyfriend Roque: "La ciudad a veces se convierte en una víscera que empieza a funcionar mal, y al llegar a una esquina determinada te asalta de improviso el dolor desconocido, como una punzada en el páncreas" (127) ["Sometimes the city seems to turn physically upsetting, and arriving at a certain street corner you're assaulted by a mysterious pain, like a punch in the stomach" 106]. Despite or perhaps because of its uncertainties, going outside is therapeutic for Águeda; as she explains, "la calle abre otra perspectiva" (66) ["the street will provide a fresh perspective" 53]. In this regard she resembles her creator. As Martín Gaite revealed to an interviewer about her protagonist: "Se parece a mí en que yo también me largo a la calle cuando tengo un día negro" [She resembles me in that I also go out to the street when I have a dark day] (Moret "Presenta").

Madrid is a repository of memory, folding Águeda's personal history into its own. Águeda appreciates history in general: not only is it her life's work, but she places great value on relics from the past (such as inherited belongings, without which she feels a house is not a home).[4] This appreciation extends to the history of her city. Águeda admires the Gran Vía, for example, and notes how fine and modern it was when it was inaugurated at the beginning of the twentieth century by King Alfonso XIII, in contrast with its present decadent and abandoned state in which it has been invaded by beggars and automated cash machines (125 [104]). Change is a constant in the city, with new businesses replacing the haunts of her past. Coming out of a café and noticing a Burger King with its yellow signage (another symbol of invasive North American tastes),[5] Águeda realizes that the locale is familiar. The Burger King now occupies the site of a former hangout of hers, a club called Fuego Fatuo [Fatuous Flame]. An acquaintance confirms that "en Madrid cambian mucho locales" ["the bars change so much in Madrid"], going on to cite their mutual friend: "Roque dice que se les caen las letras como si fueran dientes, y que es el primer síntoma de que empieza la piorrea" (41) ["Roque says the letters fall off the signs as if they were teeth, and it's the first symptom of encroaching gum disease" 28].

The narrator's physical associations between present and past illustrate Henri Lefebvre's contention that in the urban environment "nothing disappears completely" because "what came earlier continues to underpin what follows," leading to the field of "architectonics" which aims to "describe, analyse and explain this persistence" (229). Lefebvre defines the influence of preexisting space in cultural as well as physical terms: "pre-existing space underpins not only durable spatial arrangements, but also *representational spaces* and their attendant imagery and mythic narratives" (230). This concept was anticipated by Martín Gaite, who observed in 1975 that "cuando un lugar ha sido otro, esas escenas superpuestas te van tejiendo el tiempo de la narración actual" [when one place used to be another place, these superimposed scenes shape your sense of the time when the current narrative takes place] (*Cuadernos* 355). Tellingly, the exhibition of paintings that Águeda's mother was preparing when she died was entitled "Geografía urbana" (201) ["Urban Geography" 169], a favorite term of the author's, developed when she was living in New York City. (Águeda teases her mother when she hears this title, telling her that she's becoming something of a New Yorker.) In Martín Gaite's usage, urban geography included places, their histories (real and imagined), and their interrelationships.

AUTOBIOGRAPHICAL CONNECTIONS: MATERNAL-FILIAL BONDS

There are two autobiographical mother-daughter referents in *Lo raro es vivir*, one implicit and the other explicitly developed in the text. The implied association is with Martín Gaite's own mother, María Gaite Veloso, known as Marieta. Martín Gaite's mother approximated the maternal ideal. Kind, supportive, and generous, she was content to put others' needs ahead of her own. She was also highly intelligent and curious: an avid lifelong reader. As recollected in *El cuarto de atrás*, Marieta Gaite would have liked to have had a university career just as her brothers did, but back then—in the first decades of the twentieth century—it never occurred to her to ask. She died unexpectedly in December of 1978, two months after the passing of her husband (the author's father), José Martín. A week after losing her mother, Martín Gaite wrote:

> Querida Joan, te escribo con el corazón desgarrado para darte la triste noticia de la muerte de mi madre, ocurrida el día 9, un día después de mi cumpleaños. No tengo palabras para explicarte mi dolor: no puedo aceptar su ausencia y cada día que pasa me parece más intolerable la vida sin mirar su rostro sereno y luminoso de donde yo recogía toda mi fuerza para seguir adelante.

> [Dear Joan, I write with my heart torn apart to give you the sad news of my mother's death, which happened on the 9th, one day after my birthday. I don't have words to convey my pain; I can't accept her absence and every passing day seems less tolerable without seeing her luminous and serene countenance, from which I gathered all my strength to carry on.] (Letter to Brown, Madrid, 16 December 1978)

A brief postscript elaborated on her despair, ending "Esperemos que el tiempo—tan clemente y tan cruel—me ayude a serenarme. A olvidarla, nunca" [Let's hope that time—so merciful and so cruel—will help me recover my equanimity. As for making me forget her, never] (Letter to Brown, Madrid, 16 December 1978). Martín Gaite dedicated her only autobiography to her parents, noting that she would miss them always: "Nunca dejaron de alentarme en el trabajo ni de compartir todas mis alegrías ni de esperar mis cartas, cuando estaba ausente. Desde el hueco que me dejaron y dedicado a su memoria—que nunca me abandonará mientras tenga vida—escribo este esbozo autobiográfico . . ." ("Bosquejo"

Figure 5.1. Carmen Martín Gaite with her mother María Gaite Veloso, El Boalo, 1978

235) ["They never stopped encouraging me in my work, or sharing all my joys, or waiting for my letters when I was away. I write this autobiographical sketch from the empty space that they left in me and dedicate it to their memory, which will be with me for as long as I live"] ("Sketch" 245).

Accepted wisdom in the Martín Gaite family held that each sister resembled a parent: Carmen was like their Galician mother, and Anita was like their Castilian father, as she observed in a 2007 interview with Juan Carlos Soriano (267). Anyone who saw them together can attest that the author looked like her mother, especially as she got older (figure 5.1), though the resemblance was not as eerily similar as that of the two Águedas in *Lo raro es vivir*. As her sister explained, the author and her mother "tenían un hilo que, aún sin hablar, sabían de qué iban una y otra. . . . Por eso, Carmen en todos sus relatos habla como si fuera mi madre. Es que es ella." [They had a connection such that, even without speaking, they knew what the other was up to. . . . Because of that, in all her stories Carmen speaks as though she were my mother. She is her] (Soriano 278). In her 1980 essay "Retahíla con nieve en Nueva York" [A tale with snow in New York], dedicated to the memory of her mother, the author described her mother's intuitive understanding: "Mi madre, una de las personas más sabias que he conocido y desde luego la que más me quiso en este mundo y adivinó lo que me estaba pasando, aunque yo no se lo contara, sólo con oírme la voz o verme la cara cuando la iba a visitar . . ." [My mother, one of the wisest people I have ever known and also the person in the world who loved me the most, could guess what was happening to me, even though I didn't tell her, just by hearing my voice or seeing my face when I visited her . . .] (23). The essay goes on to recount her mother's constant encouragement, as she reminded her daughter that no matter how she might despair (always thinking that her most recent novel would be her last), she never ran out of ideas.

The conflicted mother-daughter relationship depicted in *Lo raro es vivir* is different from the close bond between Martín Gaite and her own mother. Rather, it mirrors the relationship of the author and her daughter, Marta Sánchez Martín. Águeda displays many of Marta's qualities—qualities that I witnessed during the last decade of her life. Like her surrogate Leonardo Villalba in the author's previous novel, *La Reina de las Nieves*, Marta was bright and inventive. She enjoyed making the kind of associations that are credited to Águeda in the novel, such as imagining she was going into the forest when she went on the subway; her father, Rafael Sánchez Ferlosio, revealed that Marta actually wrote a poem entitled "Un bosque singular" [A special forest], which he treasured (interview with Ignacio Echevarría). Like Águeda, Marta had the tenacity to stick with a subject until she mastered it, learning a second language to a level of proficiency that enabled her to earn money from teaching and translations. In Marta's case the second language was English rather than Águeda's Russian, but for both of them parental support—in the form of private lessons— was key to achieving this expertise. Both young women had highly educated parents. The family dynamic was also the same: after seventeen years of marriage, Sánchez Ferlosio began a new life with another woman (remaining with her until his death in 2019). Marta moved to her own apartment for a time when she was in her late twenties, reflecting the fact that, like her fictional counterpart, she had begun to consolidate her independence from her parents. In the novel Áugeda explains: "se fue consumando la ruptura con mi adolescencia de hija única, decidida a escapar, aunque fuese de mala manera, de la tiranía de unos padres separados y cultos, que dicen haberla educado para que vuele con alas propias y no caiga en sensibilerías" (187) ["I gradually erased the rupture with my adolescence, when, as an only child, I'd been determined to escape, even without grace, from the tyranny of my cultured and separated parents, parents who believed they'd raised me to fly with my own wings and not fall into self-pity" 157].

Marta was also a risk-taker who dissipated her talent, much like Águeda when she was in her twenties. As the author wrote in her posthumously published essay "El otoño de Poughkeepsie" [Autumn in Poughkeepsie], composed months after her daughter's death, Marta "nunca ordenaba nada, nunca tiraba nada, nunca acababa nada" [never organized anything, never threw away anything, never finished anything] (*Cuadernos* 613). When she was Marta's age, Águeda wrote popular songs that she never bothered to record. She joined her generational cohort in embracing the hedonistic ethos of the La Movida and what Nuria

Cruz-Cámara has identified as its liberating sense of euphoria ("Se movió" 269). Águeda also drank to excess. The difference between the novelistic protagonist and her real alter ego is that Águeda's addiction was not a "callejón sin salida" [dead end]. This phrase recurs in *Lo raro es vivir* as a euphemism for tragedy. The restaurant owner who is writing a book on contemporary existentialism reveals that his motivation is to depict why people like his brother, a drug addict, end up in a hopeless situation: "precisamente lo que quería retratar era esa confusión y desesperanza que lleva a callejones sin salida" (77) ["precisely because it was that kind of confusion and desperation, leading down dead end streets, that he wanted to address" 61–62].

The symbol of a dead end was part of Martín Gaite's lexicon in fiction and in life. The epigraph of her 1963 novel *Ritmo lento*, taken from the prose volume *Juan de Mairena* by twentieth-century poet Antonio Machado, compares the process of thinking to going from street to street, from narrow street to alley, until coming up against a dead end ("Pensar es deambular de calle en calle, de calleja en callejón, hasta dar con un callejón sin salida" [qtd. in *Ritmo lento* 17]). In *Ritmo lento*, "roads, streets, and alleys represent life; 'closed' alleys portray frustration," as Michael D. Thomas showed in his study of confinement and freedom in the text (63). The phrase contains an indirect reference to the childhood mantra that Marta, or "La Torci" [The Twister] as they called her, received from both parents. They recited the incantation to her in a sing-song melody like a lullaby: "No te preocupes / Que hay un pasadizo" [Don't you worry / There's a way out].[6] While in real life Marta's boyfriend Carlos Castilla del Pino led her to become involved with heroin and contract a then-fatal disease (as detailed in the senior del Pino's autobiography), in the novel Águeda escapes permanent damage.

Mother-Daughter Reversal and Redemption

The saving force in this novel is not maternal love, as in *La Reina de las Nieves*. Rather, Águeda is rescued by the love of a man who is so special that she dreamed of him when she was an adolescent, not yet knowing his identity. Tomás represents the opposite of men whom Águeda labels "enloquecedores" (153) ["the furthest thing in the world from the men I think of as the kind who drive you crazy" 128]. When she meets him, Águeda immediately senses that they are as different as night and day (which is also the chapter's title). This difference affects her positively because she is in the chaos of darkness, with her life in disarray: drinking heavily, in debt, and alone after her boyfriend Roque has left her. Recounting their meeting to her colleague Magda, Águeda confesses that she was in a state of ruin when she met him, like a rag waiting to be collected by the garbage truck (150 [125]). It is Tomás who brings her back to life, and he does so without *machista* [virulently "male-chauvinist"] paternalism. Tomás is almost too good to be true. In addition to his rationality he is perceptive, faithful, patient, generous, and attentive. Since he is known only obliquely, through Águeda, he is never fully developed as a character. His profession as an architect is emblematic of his personality: creative enough to be interesting (he can design new spaces) yet firmly tethered to facts and figures. In the novel he functions as a deus ex machina or unexpected power saving an apparently hopeless situation, rescuing Águeda from her own destructive impulses. "Desde que vivía con Tomás, no había necesitado volver a beber" (161) ["Since I'd moved in with Tomás, I hadn't needed to go back to drinking" 134], Águeda states, closing the door on the incipient alcoholism that could have threatened her life.

After surviving the reckless period she shared with much of her generation, Águeda proceeds to become "hooked" on something positive: historical research. While at first this seems far-fetched, in fact Martín Gaite herself became obsessed with archival research as she investigated her magisterial book on don Melchor de Macanaz, another misunderstood eighteenth-century figure.[7] Writing about her own experience, she warned: "los archivos son algo muy absorbente y, como te metas en ellos sin condiciones, no te libras ya en vida del insensible veneno que segregan" ("Bosquejo" 233) ["Archives are very absorbing, and . . . once you get involved in them unconditionally, you will be trapped for life by the imperceptible poison they secrete"] ("Sketch" 244). In the novel Águeda feels liberated rather than trapped by research. She enjoys archival sleuthing because it frees her from her own problems: through investigation she can forget the chaos in her own life. "Hurgar en el pasado remoto puede ser un lenitivo" ["Rummaging around in the distant past can be soothing"], a wise French mentor counsels, whereas, "el cercano hace más daño" (50) ["the recent past hurts more" 38]. This conversation takes place in a chapter entitled "Caldo del archivo" ["Archival Breeding Ground"], indicating the fertile nature of Águeda's search into the twists and turns of her riveting subject Vidal y Villalba's life—a search complicated by the fact that he was an imposter. Most importantly, Águeda's current vocation offers her a lifeline, enabling her to join the more fortunate members of her generation as a fully functioning adult.

The novel's connection to Marta's generational cohort is reinforced by its dedication to a good friend of Marta's: Lucila Valente (b. 1955), a daughter of the poet José Ángel Valente, with whom Martín Gaite shared the 1988 Premio Príncipe de Asturias for literary achievement. This prize was hugely important to Martín Gaite. She had a spectacular mauve silk dress made for the award ceremony by designer Jesús del Pozo.[8] Her acceptance speech also was stunning: she began by saying that for a woman of her generation, when a man and a woman were being honored together, the expected thing would be to have the man do the talking, but she was going to speak for herself. Anita Martín Gaite saw this prize as symbolizing her sister's return to the living after Marta's death: "Para mí fue un momento muy importante" [For me it was a very important moment],

she told an interviewer: "No por el premio en sí, sino porque la vi salir del infier-
no y dirigirse otra vez a la vida" [Not on account of the prize itself, but because
I saw her escape from hell and once again embrace life] (interview with Soriano
279). As Lucila Valente explained, there was an almost eerie association between
her father and Calila, as she naturally called her friend: "Siempre hubo esa trama
extraña: murieron sus dos hijos en parecidas circunstancias por problemas con
las drogas, les dieron el premio juntos y murieron casi el mismo día" [There was
always that strange plot: their two children died in similar circumstances due
to problems with drugs, they were given the same prize together, and they died
on almost the same day] (qtd. by Braulio García Jaén). After Marta's death, the
author and Lucila Valente became close, with Lucila visiting often. The novel's
dedication reveals the comfort that those visits brought. Written in verse form,
it reads "Para Lucila Valente / siempre sacando la cabeza / entre ruinas y equivo-
caciones / con su sonrisa de luz" (7) ["For Lucila Valente / always turning up /
amid ruins and blunders / smiling light itself" n.p.].

Instead of the daughter dying and leaving her mother to cope with loss, as
happened in real life, in *Lo raro es vivir* the roles are reversed. It is the daughter
who is left to grapple with the issues that alienated her from her mother, now
unreachable behind "la sólida muralla alzada . . . para siempre entre su viaje y
el mío" (55) ["the solid wall erected . . . forever, between her voyage and my own"
41]. Águeda does so by thinking back on her life. As Cruz-Cámara has shown,
this narrative tactic is a constant in Martín Gaite's fiction. In this novel as in
others characters not only remember the past, but impose order and meaning
on their memories as they access them, using the past to discover how they
became who they are in the present.[9] This process actualizes Martín Gaite's belief
in childhood as crucial to identity: "Creo que cualquier novela que podamos con-
siderar lleva referencias implícitas o explícitas a la infancia," she once explained,
"porque en ella reside la raíz de la memoria" [I think that any worthwhile novel
contains implicit or explicit references to childhood, because that is where the
root of memory is buried] (interview with Marie-Lise Gautier, 26). Águeda's
search into her own life parallels her historical quest, using some of the same
skills and also invoking the transformation of facts into narrative.

In *Lo raro es vivir* the protagonist's identity is inextricably bound up with that
of her mother, whom she both idolized and resented. Águeda likes to pretend
that she does not care about her mother, but Tomás calls her bluff, observing:
"No haces más que declarar que no la quieres, que pasáis una de otra, pero la
pasión te sale a flote" (163) ["You're always saying you don't love her, that the two
of you can do without each other, but you can't hide your passion" 136]. Águeda
esteems her mother for the same things that other people admire: her artistic
success, her beauty, and her charisma. The art history teacher (and aspiring artist) Rosario Tena develops a mild obsession with Águeda's mother's work, leading to a comparison of this character with the usurping actress in the classic film

All About Eve, while the doctor in charge of her grandfather's nursing home praises Águeda's mother's care for her father. What Águeda longed for from her mother was also care, because she felt that her mother did not love her enough. Águeda's grandfather counters this feeling with evidence, supplying a key story that she did not know. When Águeda's mother was seven months pregnant, she and her father were in a severe train wreck. All that Águeda's mother cared about was her unborn daughter, worrying that she would perish because of the accident. This story is almost identical to one that happened to the author's own mother when she was pregnant and a heavy armoire fell on her. Martín Gaite's mother explained that she was able to summon extraordinary strength to keep it from crushing her, only because she was terrified that the accident would hurt her unborn child ("Bosquejo" 226; "Sketch" 236). In both the novel and in the author's life, an averted tragedy reveals the strength of a mother's love. Speaking as her mother when she is with her grandfather for the last time, Águeda exclaims through tears: "¡Para mí es lo primero! Entre ella y yo no se cruza nada, ¡nada ni nadie, para que te enteres!, mi hija es lo que más quiero en este mundo . . ." (222) ["She is the first thing to me! Nothing comes between me and my daughter, nothing and no-one, for your information! My daughter is what I love most in this world . . ." 188].

As she reassesses her memories Águeda comes to terms with her mother's parenting style, which respected both her own and her daughter's independence. This parental approach—permissive rather than authoritarian—is identical to that of Leonardo's father in *La Reina de las Nieves*. It also was Martín Gaite's method of parenting her daughter, whom she described as her good friend ("Bosquejo" 234; "Sketch" 244). This style could be a by-product of being a single parent after Sánchez Ferlosio left; in a survey of North American mothers of this generation, 74 percent reported that becoming a single-parent household improved their relationship with their children, citing the mutual interdependency that developed between parent and child (reported by Genevie and Margolies, 375–376). Though their lives were intertwined, Águeda's mother was never controlling. Águeda explains to Rosario Tena that her mother had no desire to be her Pygmalion:

> Me ha pedido desde pequeña que no le permita angustiarse por mi vida ni intentar influir en ella, le dan miedo esas madres que de tanto echarles en cara a sus hijos lo que han hecho por ellos acaban creyéndose con derecho incluso a que les devuelvan lo que nunca les perteneció. (194–195)

> [She's asked me since I was little to prevent her from worrying about my life or trying to influence it, she's scared at the thought of mothers who throw all they've done for their children back in their faces, having convinced themselves that they're owed something that never belonged to them in the first place.] (163)

This parenting stance had the unintended consequence of making Águeda feel vulnerable: "A mi no me protege, desde luego" she adds (195) ["She doesn't protect me, naturally" 163].

In the novel as in life, the daughter's rebelliousness complicates the maternal-filial relationship. Recalling that when she was younger she bragged to friends about her trusting mother who did not barrage her with questions, Águeda reveals that she intentionally refused to answer when her mother did ask her things. In an unsent letter to her mother, Águeda lamented that what she had most wanted from her mother was that she ask for explanations (185 [155]). Consciously or not, the daughter had wanted to provoke her mother into castigating her: "Necesitaba que me hubiera echado una bronca. Lo necesitaba muchísimo" (167) ["I'd needed her to tell me off. I needed it so badly" 140], she once realized after telling her mother a particularly hurtful lie. Yet the daughter cherishes a memory of protecting her mother, possibly saving her life, when they were in Tangiers and her mother was pregnant, subsequently suffering a miscarriage. (In real life, Martín Gaite traveled with Marta to Tangiers when she was a teenager [*Cuadernos* 167–168].) Águeda also has a dream in which her mother is destitute and abused, evidently in need of protection that the daughter is unable to provide. Ultimately, Águeda recalls a happy reunion with her mother in the recent past, when they drank French champagne and ate luxurious canapés, laughing and enjoying one another's company.

Águeda's mother's physical presence in the novel is displaced onto a beautiful self-portrait in blue that she painted in Tangiers when she was around thirty—given as treasured gift to her daughter when she was a girl. In one of their conversations in the year she died, Águeda's mother asked her daughter if she could borrow the portrait for an exhibition. Disappointed that her mother had seemingly called just to ask for something and jealous of her commitment to her art, Águeda lied and said that she had sold it when she needed cash. In truth she had hidden the painting. When she comes to accept her mother's love, she retrieves the painting and displays it prominently. In addition to being a representation of her mother at around her age, the portrait is a near representation of Águeda herself, since they look so much alike. This ekphrastic device (featuring a vivid description of a work of art) symbolizes the rapprochement between mother and daughter. Near the end of the novel, Águeda comes to appreciate both her mother and her unique upbringing. She understands that:

> . . . en mi madre no había una persona sino varias, lo sabía hacía mucho, y aunque no las conociera a todas, intuía que ninguna de ellas estaba dispuesta a dejarse vampirizar por amores exclusivos, éramos de la misma raza. Pero había algo además que nunca me podía robar nadie: mi infancia privilegiada. (209–210)

[. . . I'd known for a long time that my mother was not one person but several, and although I didn't know them all, I guessed that none would be willing to allow herself to be bled dry by exclusive love; we were cut from the same cloth. But there was also something that no-one could ever take away from me: my privileged childhood.] (176)

Instead of viewing her mother's art negatively, as a competitor for attention, Águeda ultimately celebrates her mother's creativity by enshrining her portrait in a place of honor in her home.

THE REPRODUCTION OF MOTHERING

Águeda eventually enacts maternal acceptance in the most sincere way, by becoming a mother herself. In doing so she demonstrates the cyclical nature of the mother-daughter relationship that Nancy Chodorow famously characterized as the "reproduction of mothering," by which "women create and recreate this relationship" (vii), demonstrating that "the mother is very important in the daughter's psyche and sense of self, such that core psychological and interpersonal experiences for women can be understood in terms of this internal mother-daughter lineage" (ix). At the beginning of the novel Águeda vehemently disavows motherhood. She even responds negatively to a tile image of the Virgin Mary with baby Jesus (tellingly, it is the Virgen del Perpetuo Socorro [Our Lady of Perpetual Help]) outside her grandfather's geriatric home, caustically wondering what lies in store for her and worrying that "tendré que aguantar al mismo tiempo la maternidad y la leyenda" (12) ["I'll have maternity and mythology to put up with" 2]. When the director of the home wonders if she could be pregnant (after she faints for no apparent reason), she replies "—¿Embarazada yo?—protesté—. De ninguna manera, ¡Dios me libre! No quiero tener hijos nunca, nunca. ¡Jamás en mi vida!" (19-20) ["'Me, pregnant?' I objected. 'God forbid. I never, ever want to have children. Not in a million years'" 8].

By the end of what Tibbitts has called a "late-onset Bildungsroman" (67) or novel of personal growth, Águeda embraces the maternal role. *Lo raro es vivir* represents the zenith of the author's depiction of motherhood. In this novel— her ninth, counting *Caperucita en Manhattan*—Martín Gaite presents her "first fictional embodiment of fulfilling maternity," in the words of Kimberly Chisholm (111). As Andrew Bush has observed, the truest love in *Lo raro es vivir* is between mother and daughter, something that "stands at odds with the Freudian mythology of the Oedipus complex and constitutes an important contribution on the part of Martín Gaite to psychoanalytic theory" (186). The formulations of international feminist theorists also have been used to elucidate the mother-daughter relationship in *Lo raro es vivir*. These theoreticians moved beyond the developmental paradigms of Sigmund Freud and Jacques Lacan, both of whom situated the mother's importance in a nonspeaking, pre-Oedipal phase of development. North American Kaja Silverman's concept of the mother as a voiced, Oedipal figure who serves as an acoustic mirror for her child has been singled out as particularly relevant to the highly verbal mother and daughter in the novel (Chisholm 111). The central mother-daughter relationship can also be aligned with the writings of French feminist Luce Irigaray and Italian feminist Luisa Muraro, both of whom emphasized the circular nature of the mother-daughter relationship. This circularity has been likened to "genealogy," since Águeda must accept her maternal origins in order to situate herself in the world, as Caroline Wilson has posited (719). The symbolism of a home becomes a concrete expression of this circular pattern. While nurturing her own daughter, Águeda accepts protection from her mother, having moved into the duplex home that had belonged to her—now remodeled by her architect husband to suit their needs.

There is another significant way in which Águeda pays homage to her late mother: through her doctoral dissertation. Critics have explored the parallels between Águeda's historical quest and her search for her own identity (notably Cruz-Cámara in "Un aspecto"; Guardiola in "Novelización" and "Propuesta"; Navarro-Daniels in "La invención"; and Blanco in *Life-Writing* 165–172). Symbolic importance also resides in the broader area of goal fulfillment, through projected completion of the dissertation. The doctoral thesis, a perennial symbol of self-actualization, becomes a feminist symbol when the PhD candidate is a woman. On the penultimate page of the novel, Águeda reports that a week and a half earlier she resumed the story of Vidal y Villalba, and that she likes to work on it undisturbed in the mornings (much as her creator wrote during the quiet time after her daughter went to bed, described in her "Autobiographical Sketch"). Unlike Martín Gaite's daughter, Marta, who abandoned projects without finishing them, Águeda resists the temptation to succumb to "la enfermedad de las tesis doctorales" (202) ["doctoral thesisitis" 169], marshaling the discipline to continue, just as Martín Gaite did with her own thesis. As the author explained, she finished her dissertation after a lapse of more than two decades even though she had no plans to enter academia, affirming that "siempre me ha gustado terminar las cosas que empiezo" ("Bosquejo" 233) ["I have always liked to finish what I start"] ("Sketch" 243).[10]

The doctoral dissertation in *Lo raro es vivir* represents the passionate pursuit of a vocation. It enacts Águeda's mother's dictum that "la vida sólo es de quien la agarra y la conquista por su cuenta" (195) ["a life belongs to the person who grabs it and conquers it for themselves" 163]. The reader shares Águeda's journey of discovery as she follows her research subject from Spain to South America and uncovers his truths and lies. When she gets bogged down in presenting his story, Tomás advises her to proceed if she were writing a novel—a fitting suggestion since Martín Gaite herself was known for blurring the boundaries between genres. As the author described her historical book on Melchor de Macanaz to interviewer Carlos Pérez Cavero, "para mí era igual que una novela pero manejando materiales reales" [for me it was the same as a novel only I was working with real materials] (iv). Although at first Águeda responds negatively to Tomás's suggestion, saying that a novelistic narrative would not be a "real" dissertation, the possibility of a nonconforming thesis written by a woman suggests female empowerment. By the end of Lo raro es vivir, the daughter is recapitulating her mother's investment in a personally meaningful career. This choice, demonstrating that individual achievement and motherhood are by no means antithetical, much less mutually exclusive, validates her mother's life by imitating it. Tellingly, Águeda has appropriated part of the kitchen for her home office. While she had arranged this makeshift modification in Tomás's apartment years earlier, removing her papers apologetically when the space was requisitioned by the housekeeper, her husband has now formalized a permanent kitchen niche where she can do her work—a physical representation of the combination of domestic and career roles.

EXISTENTIAL QUESTIONS: LIFE AFTER LOSS

Lo raro es vivir is a novel with a quintessentially existential focus, concerned with the meaning of individual existence. Jurado Morales has demonstrated that, although this is not an existential novel in the literary-historical sense of the label (referring to a specific context after the Second World War), existentialism permeates every aspect of the work: its treatment of time and space, the themes of its dialogues, the development of the protagonist, the titles of some of its chapters, and of course its title (Juego 189–209). Águeda's mother's death triggers an existential crisis, as the protagonist looks for her place in the world in the absence of religious or other explanatory schemes. She comes to terms with her alienation and begins to define herself through actions. In Jurado Morales's formulation, Águeda's anguish enables her to actualize her freedom, searching for inner knowledge based on individual experience (Juego 207). The sense of being a solitary unit is also associated with the realities of the postmodern era, with increased fragmentation and decreased cohesion in nearly every sphere (from familial to local to global). María Luisa Guardiola has characterized the novel in universal terms as the author's response to the existential dilemma that existed at the end of the twentieth century, a time of especially great uncertainty in Spain ("Propuesta" 134).

While Lo raro es vivir tackles generalized problems of existence, it also encodes specific issues related to the author's life. Its underlying question is: Why am I still alive, while she—whom I loved so dearly—is not? In the novel it is the daughter who wonders and who is tasked with resolving issues between herself and her mother. In real life this question was even more disturbing because it was the daughter who predeceased the mother, an unnatural order. Death in a younger person (up to and including middle age) is what sociologists term an "off-time event." When this happens to a child, the surviving parent has fewer support systems than he or she would have had earlier in life. This is especially true if the child died from what others perceive as a "censurable" cause (for example, substance abuse). Martín Gaite's circumstances left her especially bereft. When my own father died, she wrote: "Espero que vayas consolándote de tu pena poquito a poco con la dulce compañía de tu maravillosa familia" [I hope that you find consolation for your grief little by little with the sweet company of your wonderful family] (Letter to Brown, Madrid, 28 March 1992). Yet she had had no such comfort: no other child, no spouse, no surviving parent. Besides her friends, the only person she had in the world was her sister.

The novel represents an inquiry into death and a journey through the stages of loss. Asked about the title, Martín Gaite offered a key to its subject matter: "Es que vivir es muy raro. Pienso que sobre todo los jóvenes tienen la percepción de que vivimos de milagro, la sensación de que la vida es un regalo continuo." [The fact is that living is strange. I think that young people, especially, have the feeling that we're just miraculously alive, the sense that life is an endless gift] (Moret "Presenta"). The tacit conundrum is why this gift can be snatched away in an untimely fashion, and how a survivor can cope in the absence of a cosmic explanation. In the novel the relevance of faith in God seems to coincide with C. S. Lewis's formulation in *A Grief Observed*, a book that Martín Gaite knew well: "The conclusion I dread is not 'So there is no God after all,' but 'So this is what God's really like'" (6–7). Like the loss of a child, Águeda's mother's death from an aneurysm in middle age represents an off-time event, though as her colleague Magda observes, this experience is devastating no matter when it happens: "que se te muera la madre es siempre algo tremendo. . . . Se van y te dejan mutilada, a partir de ahí es cuando empiezas a envejecer" (148) ["Losing your mother is always a terrible blow. . . . They've gone and they leave you maimed, that's the moment you start to age" 124]. After her mother's death, daughter Águeda traverses the five stages posited by psychiatrist Elisabeth Kübler-Ross in her classic study *On Death and Dying*, a project that is relevant to the formulations of contemporary philosophers "from Hegel to Heidegger": (1) denial and isolation; (2) anger; (3) bargaining; (4) depression; and (5) acceptance (observed by Sean Ireton 284–285). Originally used to describe the passages of the dying, these steps have become synonymous with stages of grief—with the final stage, acceptance, associated with hope.

Águeda's speculations about death have to do with wondering where her mother is now. This is a natural question for someone who is grieving; as C. S. Lewis wrote with emphasis about his late wife, he struggled to understand "*in what place* is she *at the present time?*" (23). In addition to the image of a giant warehouse, Águeda imagines an environment where people are confined—some in concentration camps that have existed for centuries—and where visiting investigators are handed a ticket that says: "'Abandona toda esperanza. A los muertos hay que dejarlos irse'" (60) ["'Abandon all hope. The dead must be left to make their own way'" 47]. Águeda recognizes that the most meaningful thing would be to hear from the dead, to know what they have to say, but that such events happen only in dreams. She concludes that only the dead understand the strangeness of life, but unfortunately, they can no longer write a book about it to help the living. The notion that the strangeness of life is tied to mortality becomes a motif. As Águeda observes in one of the many iterations of this sentiment, "Me rondaba a menudo la idea de la muerte y la consideración de lo raro que es vivir" (165) ["The idea of death often haunted me, as did the contemplation of how strange it was to live" 138].

———

In *Lo raro es vivir* the protagonist surmounts loss by achieving a mother-daughter reconciliation from beyond the grave. Águeda finds purpose in life, which builds resilience and helps her cope with grief. By the last chapter she is a changed woman. The doctor who runs her grandfather's nursing home observes that Águeda does not seem like the same person he saw one week earlier. He tells her that "de pronto me encuentro ante alguien que no se esconde, que va al bulto de las cosas, ante una persona de verdad. Y sé que ella se alegraría de estarla viendo así, como yo la veo" (216). ["I find myself with someone who doesn't hide, who goes to the heart of the matter, a real person. And I know your mother would be pleased to see you like this, the way I'm seeing you" 182–183]. In the Epilogue the full extent of Águeda's transformation is revealed, and it is clear that her mother would indeed have been proud. The daughter is poised to find fulfillment as a mother and as a woman who is passionately engaged with her profession, just like her own mother—and exactly like Martín Gaite herself. If writing represented wish fulfillment for the author, as critics have long suggested, then *Lo raro es vivir* marks the apogee of this endeavor. With this novel she reimagined the story of her daughter Marta and their relationship, culminating in a joy that she would never experience in life: a grandchild.

CHAPTER 6

Irse de casa

BACK TO THE FUTURE IN DEMOCRATIC SPAIN

When she began writing the last novel she would complete, *Irse de casa* [Leaving home] (1998), Martín Gaite was flush with success. Her previous novel, *Lo raro es vivir*, had been received enthusiastically by critics and readers across generations. She was riding the crest of a wave of acclaim that had been building since the publication of *Caperucita en Manhattan* in 1990. Her international stature as one of the world's eminent authors was now in sync with her status in Spain, a parity that was a long time coming in the still male-dominated culture of her homeland. She was "discovered" by so many Spaniards that she almost felt like a new writer who had made her debut in the nineties (as she explained to interviewer Rosa Mora).[1] And she was in great demand as a distinguished speaker. Martín Gaite had over two dozen national and international speaking engagements in 1996 and another two dozen in 1997, according to Emma Martinell ("Ampliación"). She delivered talks in England, France, and Italy, as well as in cities throughout Spain, on topics that ranged from her translations of Natalia Ginzburg novels to her conceptions of narrative time, space, and voice. During these years Martín Gaite delivered what would be her final talks in the United States; they would form part of the posthumously published anthology *Pido la palabra* [May I have the floor?] (2001).

A note on the last page of *Irse de casa* documents Martín Gaite's whirlwind schedule while she was composing the novel. Though she began taking notes for one of the characters in 1994, the actual writing took place from September 1994 to March 1998 and was spread across four locales on two continents (349). The first place she wrote was in El Boalo, the site of her country home outside Madrid. The second was Bayona la Real, a seaside town in Galicia (today known by its Galician name Baiona) where she spent the latter part of the summer of 1997. Before going to Galicia she was exhausted and anxious for some time alone: "A veces me gustaría retirarme a una isla desierta o volver a tener mi antiguo poder para soñar con ella," she wrote [Sometimes I'd like to retreat to a desert island or go back to having my old power to conjure one up] (Letter to Brown, Madrid, 14 July 1997; excerpted in Frontispiece). A few weeks later, on a beautiful card displaying the Galician shoreline, she wrote in a completely different tone: "Estoy aquí muy aislada y feliz, este año necesitaba el descanso como ninguno, ha sido tal la cantidad de actividades que no podía más. Disfruto del mar, del silencio y de la libertad. Además me están ocurriendo ideas muy bonitas." [I'm very secluded and happy here. I needed a rest this year more than ever, there were so many things on my schedule that I reached my limit. I'm enjoying the sea, the silence and the freedom. And I'm getting some very lovely ideas] (Letter to Brown, Bayona/Baiona, 9 August 1997). The third place named on the last page of *Irse de casa*, Washington, documented a stay on the other side of the Atlantic. This trip included time in our home in Swarthmore where she spent hours writing in a notebook, ensconced in a large chair next to a sunny window (figure 6.1). Finally, she completed the novel at home in Madrid, as was her custom,

Figure 6.1. Carmen Martín Gaite in Swarthmore, Pennsylvania, 1996

delivering the last chapters of the manuscript in time for the book to be presented at the Madrid Book Fair.

Martín Gaite's travels were a distraction from the political situation in Spain. In 1996 the Partido Popular—home of former Franco supporters and other conservatives—was entering the first of its two terms under Prime Minister José María Aznar. "Franco's Dark Legacy Hovers over Madrid's New Regime" was the postelection headline in one North American newspaper (over an article by Stanley Meisler). This party would be in power for the rest of Martín Gaite's life.[2] Aznar quickly introduced stringent economic reforms, with the rationale that they were necessary to enable Spain's adoption of the euro in 1999. Privatization of state monopolies (notably the phone company Telefónica and several energy companies) led to an influx of funds accompanied by a sense of dread about the future, expressed in the popular lament "pan para hoy y hambre mañana" [bread for today and hunger tomorrow]. Education, pensions, and public health were subject to budget cuts; wage freezes were introduced and unemployment remained high at close to 20 percent. In addition to his economic policies, which were seen as disproportionately beneficial to the rich, Aznar's social views were regressive. At one time or another during his career he espoused climate-change denial, driving after drinking, and the idea that Muslims should apologize for invading Spain in the eighth century. Martín Gaite's position of privilege gave her immunity from Aznar's budget cuts; if anything, she and her sister benefited from rising real estate values for their apartments in the upscale Salamanca neighborhood of Madrid. She was held in high esteem—considered a national treasure—by conservatives, just as she was by Socialists. Despite their efforts to ingratiate themselves (and she confided that the conservatives had much better manners than the Socialists), Martín Gaite was deeply mistrustful of this government, preferring to have nothing to do with its members. If ever there was a time for her to travel, this was it.

In her Madrid apartment, Martín Gaite continued to depend on her personal assistant, Angelines, to open her mail while she was away and tidy the apartment when she was home. *Irse de casa* is dedicated to Angelines in a charming manner, tacitly comparing Martín Gaite to Don Quijote and Angelines to Sancho Panza and using her assistant's given name: "Para Ángeles Solsona, mi fiel escudero en la lucha contra los fantasmas" [for Ángeles Solsona, my faithful squire in the battle against ghosts]. Angelines was very proud of this book dedication and not the least bit self-conscious about physical similarities between herself and Don Quijote's portly sidekick. By this time, Martín Gaite had emerged mostly victorious from her combat with phantoms. Her grief over her daughter's death would always be with her, but she had recovered her equanimity and optimism. She even told me once that she saw Marta as "una pionera" [a pioneer], since she was one of the first to confront the twin plagues of heroin and AIDS that would claim the lives of so many young Spaniards. Through whatever means, including rationalization and literary wish fulfillment, she had made peace with Marta's passing. She lived in the present, relishing her popularity across the generational divide. As she shared with interviewer Xavier Moret in the year the novel was published, Martín Gaite had an enduring concern for young people (who had always filled her home while Marta was alive): "Me interesa cómo son y lo que dicen, y por eso escribo sobre ellos" [I'm interested in what they're like and what they say, and that's why I write about them] (Moret "Novela"). She continued to mentor the next generations of Spanish writers, among them Soledad Puértolas, Belén Gopegui, Juan José Millás, and Marcos Giralt Torrente.[3]

A Tapestry of Stories

Irse de casa is masterly in both content and form. Two decades before the bestselling romance novel *El tiempo de costuras* (2009) [*A Time In Between* 2011] by María Dueñas, Martín Gaite originated the story of a Spanish seamstress who came from nothing—her only legacy the skills of her seamstress mother—to become a fashion designer on the world stage. The novel's structure is full of unexpected inventions and its themes of self-discovery, female empowerment, and patriotism are accompanied by wise social analysis. The framing device of "bookends" to bracket the central narrative, a technique favored by Martín Gaite throughout her career, appears for the last time in *Irse de casa*.[4] The first and last chapters have parallel titles, each invoking the word "pórtico" [portico] or sheltered place, usually at the entrance to a building. The initial chapter of *Irse de casa* is entitled "Pórtico de rascacielos" [Skyscraper portal] and the final one is called "Apertura a otros porticos" [Opening into other portals]. These framing chapters are both set in New York City, marking a novelistic return to what the author considered the most fascinating city on earth ("Bosquejo" 235; "Sketch" 245), eight years after *Caperucita en Manhattan*. The opening and closing chapters have been identified with a journey. Specifically, they have been interpreted by Nuria Cruz-Cámara (*Laberinto* 175) and Janet Pérez ("Presencia" 109) as symbols of a transformative "quest-romance" that begins and ends in the same place. Between these bookends are twenty-eight numbered chapters for a total of 340 pages, making this the second-longest of her novels of the nineties, exceeded only by *Nubosidad variable*.

The novel's two titled chapters bracket a riveting narrative. Protagonist Amparo Miranda is a successful, stylish New York fashion designer and wealthy widow who is about to turn sixty-four. She and her mother arrived in the United States from Spain when Amparo was a young woman. In New York Amparo first worked as a translator at the United Nations and later, with her husband's support, she founded a successful fashion company. She is known to most by her American name, Miranda Drake—also the name of her eponymous fashion line. Her patrician, older American husband Gregory Drake passed away some time ago, but she is recovering from another loss: her consort Ralph (a man much like her husband whom she refused to marry despite his entreaties) has recently died. To the surprise of her two grown children, Amparo suddenly decides to return to the provincial Spanish city where she grew up. She brings with her the somewhat anemic script for a film about her life written by her son, Jeremy—a metafictional device (referencing the story's own creation) that will also serve as an impetus for the plot as Amparo tries to flesh it out. Vilma Navarro-Daniels has called the script an "interlocutor" for the lead character, based on the "counterpoint between Amparo's memories and the script" ("*Irse de casa*" 9), while Joyce Tolliver has noted "a shifting of the boundary" between Amparo and the main character in the script (261). Conflation of the protagonist of the novel with the leading lady in the script is facilitated by the fact that at times the novelistic heroine sees herself as a character in a film.

After checking into a suite in the best hotel, Amparo spends a week exploring and observing the town on her own, never announcing her presence to those whom she knew forty years ago. The stories of people around her develop independently, even when Amparo's path intersects with theirs (something so infrequent that by the sixth day of her stay, she has met only three people who are not employees). Amparo uses her solitary journey to reflect on her origins and her life. Despite her efforts to remain anonymous, she is discovered by the person from her past who matters most: Abel Bores. He is the handsome and brilliant widower whom she had loved desperately when she was young, but whose upper-class standing left her—the daughter of an unmarried seamstress—feeling inadequate. In a denouement that would not be out of place in a romantic film, Abel glimpses Amparo in the town's cathedral and pursues her in the rain. They reunite and he takes her to a special birthday dinner, where he soon learns that this is the last day of her visit. They rekindle their romance, tenderly but chastely, and it is apparent that he is still her soul mate. The possibility of future encounters is clearly implied. Amparo intends to return to the town to produce her son's film, which bears the title of the street where she grew up: *La calle del Olvido* ["Oblivion Street" or "The Street of Forgetting" are the most faithful English translations, though Margaret Parker (116) as well as Catherine O'Leary and Alison Ribeiro de Menezes (174) render the name as "Forgetfulness Street"].

While the structure of *Irse de casa* can be viewed as a mosaic, as José Jurado Morales (*Trayectoria* 399) and Ester Bautista Botello (67) have noted, it is best understood as a tapestry: an intricately designed fabric of interwoven stories, with Amparo Miranda as the predominant motif. This is a postmodern tapestry whose fragmented pattern continually shifts the observer's focus from the center to the periphery and back again. The conceptual key to the novel's structure is supplied in its second epigraph, a quote from Brazilian author Clarice Lispector: "Un tapiz consta de tantos hilos que no puedo resignarme a seguir uno solo; mi enredo proviene de que una historia está hecha de muchas historias. Y no todas puedo contarlas." [A tapestry is made up of so many threads that I can't resign myself to following just one; I become entangled because one story is made up of many stories. And I can't tell them all] (*Felicidad clandestina*) [Clandestine happiness]. The author was fond of the metaphor of sewing for writing, declaring that "ponerse a contar es como ponerse a coser" [telling a story is like sewing] (*El cuento de nunca acabar* [The never-ending story] 23). Late in the novel, Amparo elaborates: "toda creación consiste en lo mismo, en saber coser los elementos dispersos, y entender cómo se relacionan entre sí, da igual que sean historias o pedazos de tela" [All creation involves the same thing—knowing how to stitch together the various elements and understanding how they relate to one another, regardless of whether they are stories of pieces of fabric] (320).

In *Irse de casa*, stories are necessary to breathe life into the film about Amparo. She tells her son as much in the closing chapter: "hay que meterle más cosas. Muchas más cosas" [you have to put in more things, many more things] (349), all based on truths. This reconfirms what a young actress had observed after reading Jeremy's screenplay in the opening chapter. The story of Amparo's life, she told him, requires other people: "Gente . . . lo que hay que añadir a ese argumento es gente. . . . La vida no es así, chico, somos muchos. Gente que vaya contando también sus historias . . . un choque de historias." [People . . . what that plot needs is people. . . . Life isn't like that, man, there are a lot of us. People who go along telling their stories, too . . . a clash of stories] (34). Instead of clashing, the stories of *Irse de casa* are intertwined. They are transmitted in cinematic fashion with a multiperspectival objective approach, as if the scenes were simultaneously recorded by several camera operators.[5] Ten of the numbered chapters are primarily devoted to third-person narration of Amparo's stay in Spain, featuring her internal musings about her experiences and encounters with a host of characters. The remaining eighteen numbered chapters offer a collection of interrelated stories and voices, including interior monologues as well as interactive dialogues, with Amparo surfacing now and again. Letters from one character to another are interspersed throughout, adding depth to their stories. There is no pattern to the distribution of chapter perspectives. Amparo's point of view sometimes alternates with others' voices and at other times there is more than one intervening chapter featuring other characters. Amparo also has a series of back-to-back chapters in the middle of the novel. This unpredictable sequencing increases the suspense associated with Amparo's journey, as its narration is repeatedly interrupted.

Amparo functions as a visiting outsider, through a voyage that Nuria Cruz-Cámara has compared to the one in the 1985 Robert Zemeckis film *Back to the Future*—a film that is mentioned by Amparo's son in the novel (*Laberinto* 176–178). Like Michael J. Fox's character Marty McFly in *Back to the Future*, who returns to a time before he was born and meets his future parents, Amparo makes a trip back to her distant place of origin. While the time-traveling Marty McFly succeeds in changing the course of his family's future, Amparo Miranda instead makes an internal adjustment that allows her to come to terms with her past. With the distance of time, she can assess her surrounding dispassionately. Some of the author's notes while she was writing *Irse de casa* show that she considered having Amparo become a more intrusive presence, interviewing local residents about unemployment and other issues to the point where they would think she was a sociologist (*Cuadernos* 668). But as Martín Gaite told an interviewer, "Los libros cambian a medida que los haces. Amparo se me fue convirtiendo en un ojo, se fue desleyendo en las vidas de los demás personajes" [Books change as you are writing them. Amparo changed on me and turned into a means of see-ing; she went along insinuating herself into the lives of the other characters] (Moret "Novela"). In Martín Gaite's first novel, *Entre visillos*, the same role of outside observer was played by the young German instructor Pablo Klein. He returns to teach in the provincial capital where he spent time as a child, seeing it with fresh eyes (Brown, *Secrets* 71–72). Martín Gaite used to say that Pablo Klein was her alter ego in *Entre visillos*, being the same age as she was when she wrote the novel; according to John Kronik, this character was the "implied author's mask-presumptive" who would be more recognizable if we did not know the author's gender (53).

Although—like Pablo Klein—Amparo Miranda differs from her creator, in *Irse de casa* she is easier to identify as the author's counterpart, being a Spanish woman of the same generation. (In sociological terms a generation spans thir-teen years, and the author was eight years older than her protagonist when she began the novel.) Carmen Martín Gaite and Amparo Miranda have a number of similar character traits: intelligence, curiosity, creativity, integrity, charisma, generosity, drive, patriotism, and openness to change. Amparo also shares Mar-tín Gaite's astute powers of observation. The observer's stance is embedded in her last name, Miranda—which invokes the Spanish verb "mirar" [to look], as Cruz-Cámara has observed ("Salamanca posmoderna" 33). Amparo was raised to watch others while revealing little about herself, always conscious of her infe-rior social status as the illegitimate child of a working-class mother. Growing up, when she heard stories about those around her, Amparo collected them for future use, again invoking the metaphor of a woven textile: "Recogía . . . esos informes . . . los archivaba entusiasmada en su memoria, una reserva de hilos de colores para bordar algún día un tapiz" [She collected . . . those accounts . . . avidly archiving them in her memory, a trove of colored threads with which to someday embroider a tapestry] (189).

Most of the threads that add color to this tapestry belong to natives of Am-paro's home town. Secondary characters are well drawn and believable, even when they are eccentric. They include Olimpia Moret, the brilliant nobleman's daughter and closeted lesbian whose passion for Amparo was not reciprocated;

Manuela Roca, the sensitive woman from a distinguished family who was briefly married late in life and who dies in a solitary car accident; Agustín Sánchez del Olmo, Manuela's idealistic and possibly gay ex-husband, who was put through medical school thanks to Amparo's generosity (he was the son of Amparo's mother's shop assistant); and Agustín's sister Társila or Tarsi del Olmo, who never married and owns a successful beauty salon. Although Amparo knows these people, she does not reconnect with them, even when they coincide. She trespasses into Olimpia's garden, eavesdropping as her long-ago friend reads Shakespearean verses before an open balcony. When she goes to Társila's salon for a massage, Amparo pretends that she is a foreign tourist, going so far as to feign a bad Spanish accent and speak condescendingly about how inexpensive everything is in Spain. Amparo is invited to use the bathroom in the salon owner's adjoining residence and while there she discovers a meaningful object from her past: the heavy mirrored armoire that she used to talk to when she was growing up. (Amparo and her mother Ramona had given their furniture to Ramona's assistant, Társila's mother, when they left the country.) The piece of furniture seems like an old friend; she talks with it once again, moved to tears.

Amparo does connect with some residents she did not know in her youth, most of whom are women from younger generations (Amparo's thirtysomething daughter María and her eight-year-old granddaughter Caroline also make brief appearances in New York). The youthful contingent in the Spanish city includes Valeria Roca, Manuela's niece who has a thought-provoking radio program and edits a highly regarded poetry magazine, and Rita Bores (Abel's daughter), the owner of an inviting antique shop located in the house where Amparo grew up. This street is no longer called Calle del Olvido, though it looks much the same; as with many sites it was renamed during Spain's transition to democracy (usually to erase the name of a Francoist official). Others with whom Amparo interacts include Marcelo Ponte, a handsome lighting technician and budding *zarzuela* [Spanish operetta] actor whom she meets on the train into town, and Ricardo, an aspiring writer who works as a waiter at Amparo's hotel. One last category in the cast of individual characters includes townspeople whose orbits do not intersect with that of Amparo: Alicia, a young member of the Roca family who is recovering from anorexia, and a series of housekeepers and assistants.

There is also an important collective character in the novel: a group of ladies who savor aperitifs and gossip in the salon of Amparo's hotel, the Excelsior. These women represent what barman Ricardo, a consummate observer, accurately labels "un coro griego" [a Greek chorus] (201). Chapter 2 entirely comprises dialogue among these characters (extending for twelve pages), and another dialogue constitutes the last part of chapter 28 (covering six pages). In addition to commenting on the action, the traditional function of a Greek chorus, these women communicate popular opinions: the all-important "¿Qué dirán?" [What will people say?] of provincial life, a phrase that recurs several times in the novel.

Sometimes these judgments convey information, such as the fact that Amparo speaks four languages thanks to scholarships and intensive study in her youth. In other instances they supply commentaries that are both accurate and sardonic, as when one character laments that only second-rate theater companies (specifically, *zarzuela* groups) come to the provinces. The conversation can be poignant, especially when these middle-aged women lament the changes that time has wrought and the opportunities that have passed them by. Each speaker in the chorus has a distinct voice which, when preceded and followed by others, creates a cascade of comments. Martín Gaite enjoyed reading these dialogues aloud for others, playing different characters with intonations and emphasis appropriate to each one. Audiences can still see and hear her on YouTube, where there is a three-minute clip of her reading some of the lines in chapter 2 (pp. 44–46) and singing two snippets of *zarzuela* verses (p. 45), posted by fan Roberto Salas years later. This fragment was taken from a full reading of the chapter that she delivered in Madrid in November 1998, at a presentation of the Círculo de Lectores version of *Irse de casa*.[6]

Resolution of characters' stories resembles the plot of a romance novel, or *novela rosa*, as in her 1976 novel *Fragmentos de interior* about a dysfunctional Madrid family and its servants. This was a genre for which Martín Gaite had great affection, despite her repudiation of its cultural premises—a subject addressed in *El cuarto de atrás*. Soon after that novel's publication, when asked about her influences, she confessed to Ana Puértolas and Rafael Chirbes that "los que me han influido de verdad, y nunca lo digo delante de un micrófano, porque me da vergüenza, son los folletines" [The ones that truly influenced me—and I never say this in front of a microphone because it's embarrassing—are serialized romance novels]. Almost all the stories in *Irse de casa* eventuate in happy endings, starting with that of the protagonist. By the conclusion of the novel Amparo has not only found her roots, she has determined that she will strengthen her ties with her children, realizing that it is never too late to correct past mistakes. Secondary characters also prevail over life's challenges. They are empowered by the multiplicity of options now available to them, even as they are faced with a bewildering array of choices (and, for women over fifty, too little preparation for change). Except for Manuela Roca, they all begin to find fulfillment by the end of the novel, and even Manuela (who had studied to be a lawyer) was on a path to self-actualization before her untimely death. Usually characters overcome their trials with help from one another, demonstrating that interpersonal relationships are the best, if not the only, source of individual salvation. Whether it be by rekindling a childhood relationship thanks to the generosity of an old friend, vanquishing an eating disorder or a drug addiction with the aid of a concerned physician, accepting the departure of an abusive boyfriend thanks to a friend's support, or beginning a new life after divorce with assistance from a sibling, characters enable one another to conquer adversity.

Postmodern Salamanca and the Archeology of Memory

The provincial city in *Irse de casa* is never named, just as the town name was omitted from *Entre visillos*. Nevertheless it has been widely recognized as Salamanca.[7] Because the author was such a faithful chronicler of the world around her, changes in her native city over time can be traced in her literature, as critics have shown.[8] The Salamanca to which Amparo returns after four decades is still a typical provincial burg. As another visitor (the *zarzuela* actor Marcelo Ponce) observes, "en las ciudades pequeñas la vida marcha a otro ritmo, como entre un pasado que no gusta y un porvenir sin dibujar" [in small cities life moves at a different pace, suspended between a distasteful past and an unknowable future] (110). Yet provincial life also has changed, as the author acknowledged to interviewer Amaia Uriz in 1998: "Las ciudades de provincias tienen algo parecido, estable, muy invariable, como es el chismorreo. Eso sigue. Pero en cambio, ha variado muchísimo la vida, la mentalidad de la gente joven" [Provincial cities have something in common, something that doesn't change, like gossiping. That still goes on. But on the other hand, life there has changed a lot, and so has the mentality of young people]. Late-twentieth-century Salamanca is only vaguely reminiscent of the restrictive, conservative town that Amparo experienced in the 1940s and 1950s, an era recalled by the ladies of the Greek chorus. Instead, the city is postmodern. In Spain the freedoms of the postmodern era are associated with throwing off the yoke of the Franco dictatorship (1939–1975) as much as with skepticism and relativism, since his totalitarian reign was the antithesis of postmodern uncertainties. *Irse de casa* is set in 1997—three years before the millennium, as one member of the chorus intones for emphasis. Fragmentation, the rejection of grand explanatory narratives, and a mistrust of hierarchies—fundamental characteristics of postmodernism—are now hallmarks of Spanish culture, even in the provinces.

In such a fluid environment, it is natural to turn inward to find meaning, and memory becomes a primary tool in the search for self-knowledge. One of the most lyrical lines in the novel is Amparo's declaration that "La geografía de la memoria está surcado por caminos de memoria y grutas del olvido" [The geography of memory is interlaced with paths to remembering and caves of forgetting] (301). She later describes her childhood as having been hidden away in a cave beyond the reach of memory (330). José Jurado Morales has singled out *Irse de casa* as one of the author's most important memory novels because it continually evokes the interplay of remembering and forgetting (*Trayectoria* 404). As Amparo muses on her first day there, everything in the city that exists now might well be resting on the ashes of what was there before (53–54), ashes being a fitting metaphor for memories. Amparo experiences a disconnect between the tall, flat buildings she now sees and her own retained "geografía interior" [inner geography] (54). If the old city she remembers is submerged below the existing one, she decides, then only an archeologist could recover it. As in *Lo raro es vivir*, this idea of unearthing the past coincides with what Henri Lefebvre defined as "architectonics," a field devoted to elucidating the cultural endurance of preexisting structures (229). But this is not the mission that Amparo came for. As she admonishes herself: "Sabes muy bien que la ciudad es otra, que han pasado más de cuarenta años, ¿y qué?, hay que afrontar los cambios, si no ya me dirás qué haces tú aquí ni qué sentido tiene tu viaje." [You know full well that this is a different city, that forty years have gone by, and so what? You have to face the changes. If not, then tell me what you're doing here and how your trip makes any sense] (55). Amparo has always been ahead of her time (a characteristic ratified by one of the ladies in the Greek chorus), and this means that for her, curiosity supersedes nostalgia. She has returned to Spain with a single purpose: to clarify her own identity through reexamination of her origins.

The End of Old Taboos

By the end of the twentieth century, the taboos that shaped Amparo's generation—raised under the dominion of Franco's *nacionalcatolicismo* [National Catholicism]—have receded into the past. Change is especially evident in the areas of social stratification, women's rights, and sexual mores. The dedication of Martín Gaite's cultural study *Usos amorosos de la postguerra española* is equally apt for *Irse de casa*: "Para todas las mujeres españolas, entre cincuenta y sesenta años, que no entienden a sus hijos. Y para sus hijos, que no las entienden a ellas" (9) ["For all Spanish women between 50 and 60, who don't understand their children. And for their children, who don't understand them" 9]. As a young woman tells Jeremy in the opening chapter, all mothers have secrets and keep things to themselves, so that "sabemos muy poco de nuestras madres" [we know very little about our mothers] (15). The same can be said for sons and daughters. Amparo knew little about her own mother's inner life, except as it related to her. Her mother Ramona was overbearing, but this was because she wanted Amparo to hold her head high and be spared the suffering that she herself had experienced (308). Amparo did not learn her father's identity until she was eleven years old, though he was aware of his daughter and provided for her. His social class was superior to theirs and he was already married (in an era when divorce was illegal). These circumstances curtailed most possibilities for Amparo's mother, who never saw him again. She did not want the same repressive social norms to affect her only child.

Class consciousness in *Irse de casa* is explored through the interactions of upper- and middle-class characters with the servants who facilitate their lives, primarily in Spain (where even middle-class citizens have housekeepers) but also in Amparo's luxury residence in New York. As in other Martín Gaite novels of the nineties, especially *Nubosidad variable* and *Lo raro es vivir*, servants in *Irse de casa* have agency, integrity, and intelligence. Their perspicacity and decisiveness can exceed those of their employers. For example, when Manuela Roca tries to clean out the closet of her ex-husband Agustín, she is paralyzed by indecision, and her maid Rufina takes control of the situation. In one of the novel's exquisitely constructed sequences (and its many references to plays and films), this episode is recounted as if it were a scene in a play. Manuela knows that she suffers in comparison to the dramatic heroines of Spanish Golden Age (roughly mid-sixteenth to mid-seventeenth century) masters such as Lope de Vega, Tirso de Molina, Agustín Moreto, and Cervantes:

> Ellas nunca lloraban, inventaban tretas para esquivar la vigilancia paterna o marital, escribían cartas, burlaban a varios enamorados, se disfrazaban de hombre, y si llegaba el turno de las lágrimas fingidas, en cuanto el amante despechado hacía mutis, eran sustituidas por una risa triunfal, compartida al unísono por la criada encubridora. ¡Qué envidia sentía de repente por aquellas Cristinicas, Dianas y Fenisas, tan atrevidas, tan ágiles! (81)

> [They never cried, they invented ruses to escape paternal or marital supervision, they wrote letters, they tricked various lovers, they disguised themselves as men. When the time came to cry fake tears, as soon as the scorned lover made his exit, those tears turned into triumphant laughter, shared in unison with the complicit maid. How she suddenly envied those Cristinicas, Dianas, and Fenisas—so daring, so adept!]

Weak and indecisive, Manuela loses her role as leading lady, ceding it to her wise and efficacious maid Rufina. Manuela feels "literally upstaged," as O'Leary and Ribeiro de Menezes have observed (181). Before the curtain comes down, Rufina tells Manuela that she should see to herself, not her ex-husband (whom she divorced), and laments the transient nature of everything today: "la vida es así hoy en día, usar y tirar, quemar etapas, en amores y en todo" [life is like that today, using and discarding, skipping ahead—in love affairs and in everything] (83). Rufina helps her employer see that the disposition of unwanted clothing is a trivial task that is easy to execute. While Manuela feels embarrassed by what has happened, Rufina is left thinking "Qué vidas más raras las de los ricos" [What strange lives rich people lead] (81).

Clear divisions between social classes still exist in the provincial city (Manuela feels diminished by having confided in a servant) but the boundaries are becoming less rigid. One of the middle-aged ladies in the Excelsior salon notes that in her day it would have been unthinkable to have a romance with someone from a lower social class—something that caused great suffering in her own life. Another laments that maids are now engaging in self-improvement by taking online courses to learn English. "¿Y qué pasa?" [And what's wrong with that?] (42) counters a more forward-looking member of the group, adding that the times are different now. Amparo's lingering hurt over the humiliation that she and her mother suffered when she was a girl derives from social prejudice that has diminished greatly, as she is the first to acknowledge. In this provincial city it is possible, though not common, to move to a higher social class than the one into which one is born. Agustín, son of Amparo's mother's shop assistant, achieved social mobility through education and marriage, and his "ascenso de categoría social" [rise in social rank] (259) extended to his sister, Társila. By the end of the novel, Amparo elevates the waiter Ricardo to the role of assistant on her son's film, changing his status and allowing him a privilege that she had to emigrate in order to obtain: self-invention.

Gender is an area that, like social class, has evolved since the proscribed roles of the postwar era, with rights and freedoms in both public and private spheres. Restrictions that shaped the lives of generations of Spanish women have been eliminated. Married women and many others were forbidden from working outside the home during the Franco years, when their legal standing was the same as that of children. In *Irse de casa* women not only work, they are entrepreneurs. Following in the footsteps of Amparo's mother, Ramona, whose sewing shop supported herself and her daughter, women in the novel develop successful businesses of which they are sole proprietors, from Amparo's fashion house to Társila's beauty salon to Rita's antique shop. As they pursue their career ambitions, women are also free to express their sexuality. Of all of Martín Gaite's novels, this one has the most explicit depictions of characters' sex lives. Amparo recalls that she learned to pleasure herself from a young age, even though this was supposedly a sin; her best friend Olimpia encouraged her, pointing out that "los chicos también lo hacen" [the boys do it too] (30). After several days in Spain Amparo wonders if she is sad because she misses Ralph in bed, where he satisfied her without much fanfare ("Quizá echa algo de menos a Ralph, que en la cama cumplía, aunque sin grandes alardes" 243). When her arrogant, two-timing boyfriend Pedro leaves town, Agustín asks Alicia (the anorexic young adult who is his patient) if she cared for him a lot. She replies with frankness: "Hombre, quererle no, pero tenía un buen polvo" [Hey, I wasn't in love with him, but he was great in bed] (225). In addition to sexual practices, the novel deals with sexual fantasies. Társila, the perennial observer of life, has erotic fantasies about her brother Agustín and his then wife Manuela, excitedly imagining what they might be doing in bed. This unusual fetish is depicted with kindness and humor. Ashamed of her obsession, Társila feels the need to confess, but this does not stop the behavior; as a result, she has to go farther and farther outside her neighborhood to attend confession with priests who do not know her.

Problems of the Younger Generation

Contemporary problems have reached the provinces along with new freedoms. In *Irse de casa* there are glimpses of a generation with no prospects and no direction, just as there were in *La Reina de las Nieves* and *Lo raro es vivir*. The novel captures what cultural critic Luigi Landeira called "esa sensación de resaca perpetua y deriva existencial inherente a la juventud posmoderna" [that sensation of perpetual hangover and existential drift that characterizes postmodern young people]. Traditional family support has been diminished by dysfunction, leaving young adults to cope with the assistance of someone to whom they are not related, from physician to friend. Describing her generation's aimlessness, Alicia says "estamos jugando al tenis sin pelota" [we're playing tennis without a ball] (222). This generational malaise happens in the United States as well; Amparo wonders why her children lack motivation, noting that even though she makes everything easy for them, they don't strive to achieve things on their own ("Se lo facilito todo, ¿por qué no se espabilan ellos para conseguir las cosas por sus propios medios?" 144). With persistently high unemployment and limited career opportunities in Spain, young adults there are stymied even when they have ambition; the most successful among them create their own opportunities with their own projects, as do Rita Bores and Valeria Roca.

Apathetic young adults in *Irse de casa* find themselves ending each night at the Bar Oriente, "un bar de mala fama" [a bar with a bad reputation] (77). The author's description of these young men and women is sharply critical. Most of the bar patrons in ripped jeans and T-shirts with logos are either unemployed or piecing together menial jobs to make a living. They have not been able to leave home, even when they scorn their families. They enjoy loud music and abjure politics. These young men and women are both united and separated by their own perceived specialness, all wanting to be artists, looking for a way to feel superior. The hidden truth is that they also long for fixed employment, even as they are ambivalent about what that entails:

> También querrían tener un puesto fijo de trabajo, para poder irse de casa o pagarse ese implante dental que les devolvería una sonrisa sin agujeros, aunque eso no lo confiesen, porque sigue vigente la sospecha de que ese camino de la independencia económica está lleno de trampas y claudicaciones. (221)

> [They also would like a steady job, so that they could leave home or pay for that dental implant that would restore a smile without gaps. But they don't confess this, because there is still a widespread suspicion that the route to economic independence involves being duped and giving in.]

As in *La Reina de las Nieves*, the basement of this bar is the site of drug use. While their elders drink upstairs, unaware that that the establishment has a lower level, young people go downstairs to snort cocaine.

Heroin also makes an appearance, though in a more sinister setting. Of all the stories in the tapestry of *Irse de casa*, this one hits closest to home, since it obliquely references the fate of Martín Gaite's daughter, Marta. While Marta

perished from using heroin and contracting AIDS, a young man in the novel is
saved from perdition thanks to the intervention of a kind physician. Marcelo
Ponte strikes up an acquaintance with Agustín soon after the young man's arrival
with a visiting *zarzuela* troupe, and they take a walk together. When Marcelo
points out the shooting gallery called "La Antesala" [The Anteroom] where
addicts go to inject heroin, Agustín perceptively asks his acquaintance when he
stopped doing so. The answer is that he was clean for a few months but has
recently relapsed. Marcelo gives a rapturous description of heroin's effects, comparing the high to "una hoguera donde todo se funde y el tiempo deja que
existir" [a bonfire where everything comes together and time ceases to exist]
(278). Yet he admits that he did terrible things to his kind employer—everything
from making him cry to robbing him—because of his need for "la maldita droga"
[that damned drug] (280). Agustín pointedly asks Marcelo if he has been tested
for hepatitis B and AIDS. When Marcelo replies that he tested negative for both
illnesses, Agustín is relieved and elated. He urges Marcelo to quit once and for
all while he has the chance: "Acuérdate, por favor, de la gente que ya no lo puede
contar. Estás vivo y sano, eres inteligente, tienes veintidós años. Vive tu juventud, con todo lo difícil que sea . . ." [Please think about the people who are no
longer here to speak for themselves. You're alive and healthy, you're intelligent,
you're twenty-two years old. Live your life, with all its challenges . . .] (281). While
many of the stories in *Irse de casa* can be called "historias de redención" [redemp-
tion stories] (Cruz-Cámara *Laberinto* 196), Marcelo's is especially meaningful.
The importance of the doctor's efforts is recognized and memorialized by his
late ex-wife Manuela. She wills her considerable fortune to the creation of a char-
itable foundation and drug-addiction treatment center, with Agustín as resident director.

Made in the USA: Success and Longing

As noted earlier, *Irse de casa* begins and ends in New York City; another chapter
(chapter 20) is set there while Amparo is in Spain. New York is associated with
the American dream of self-invention—a dream with which the author identified (Brown "Los años americanos" 83). The city also functioned as a symbol of
self-realization in Martín Gaite's later novels: what Alison Ribeiro de Menezes
has called a conduit to "self-understanding" ("New York"). The author's fascination with the United States began long before she ever set foot on U.S. soil.
For Martín Gaite and her generation, the United States loomed large. As she
explained in 1997, attitudes toward the economic engine of the United States were
ambivalent during the lean years after the Spanish Civil War, evincing "[una]
mezcla de fascinación y rechazo" [a mixture of fascination and repudiation]
(*Desde la ventana* 28). She herself was captivated by the depictions of American
culture she saw in films—which, though censored and dubbed, were not pro-

hibited by the Franco regime. Young Martín Gaite admired film stars like Deanna Durbin, whom she imagined being as mischievous, ingenious, and indomitable as the characters she played (*Cuarto* 62). To some extent she identified with American culture, or at least with the version that was projected in popular media. Characters in her early works viewed America as magical: "A mí América me parece un país de mentira" [America seems to me to be an imaginary country], says Laura to her younger sister in the author's 1959 play *La hermana pequeña* [The little sister] (59).[9] This was the decade in which Amparo and her mother would have embarked on their journey to the land of opportunity.

Being an émigré to the United States is the defining factor in Amparo Miranda's life, as Jurado Morales has observed (*Trayectoria* 398). Amparo illustrates the author's maxim that travel enables transformation—a message inscribed in her 1985 children's book *El pastel del diablo*: "Hay que viajar para cambiar de ser" [It is necessary to travel in order to change who you are] (Martín Gaite "Reflexiones" 264). The protagonist's trajectory in her adopted country is one of triumphant self-invention, facilitated by money. While Amparo's financial success was accomplished via traditional means, through marriage and its ascribed status, her professional achievements—both at the United Nations and in her fashion house—were earned. In the United States, Amparo Miranda transformed into Miranda Drake: a beautiful woman who appears to be a decade younger than her age. Her good looks are due partly to healthy habits—she is fit from going to the gym—and partly to the kinds of surgical interventions that are available to affluent women (facelifts and liposuction are both acknowledged). In Salamanca, everyone she encounters assumes that this stunning visitor must be a foreigner, a fiction that Amparo encourages in order to remain anonymous. In many ways Amparo is a foreigner in Spain: she often thinks in English, and there are thirty-three instances in the novel where she uses English phrases or sentences, including when she is speaking to herself. Many of these English interjections include Martín Gaite's own favorite term of endearment, "honey." Even in Spain the soundtrack of her life is in English, with the Beatles song "Yesterday" playing during her dinner with Abel Bores.

Although she was able to reinvent herself in New York in a way that would never have been possible in Spain, Amparo Miranda feels very patriotic toward her country of birth. Comparisons between the United States and Spain demonstrate the wonders of the latter, not the former. When she goes to Társila's beauty salon, she notices that she is treated with much more warmth and directness than would be customary in New York City. In a play on the country's name, Amparo comments that Americans are "tan unidos y tan lejos unos de otros que nadie sabe a ciencia cierta dónde tiene su raíz familiar" [so united and so far from one another that no one knows for certain where their family comes from] (325). A building manager echoes the idea that Americans have very little history, adding that that Spanish young people value the historic area of their city more than their elders because they are "más patriotas" [more patriotic] (156). This is borne out by some of the secondary characters. Rita Bores demonstrates a commitment to the past through her rehabilitation and sale of antiques in the old part of town. Marcelo Ponte observes: "qué mania tenemos con viajar al extranjero sin conocer antes España, que la vienen a ver todos los extranjeros, con los sitios tan fabulosos que tiene" [What an obsession we have with traveling abroad without first seeing Spain, the country that all the foreigners come to see, with its amazing places] (112). And Valeria Roca is so loyal to her birthplace that she feels as though she is in a marriage: "Se abrazó a sus raíces provincianas con una efusión tan dolorida que casi se le saltaron las lágrimas, en la salud y en la enfermedad hasta que la muerte nos separe" [She embraced her provincial roots with an intensity so painful that it almost brought tears to her eyes; in sickness and in health until death do us part] (169). Such devotion to place is not shared by the denizens of New York—even the fortunate ones.

Skyscrapers are emblematic of the impersonal nature of life in New York City. When the author first came to live for a semester in Manhattan, she described her solitary apartment and her "condición de extranjera entre rascacielos" [state of being a foreigner among skyscrapers] (*Desde la ventana* 27). What Lefebvre termed "the arrogant verticality" of these buildings, inserting a "phallocratic element into the visual realm," cows spectators by conveying power and authority (98). In *Irse de casa* Amparo's mother Ramona longs for the country she left, having been too old to adapt to her new homeland in the ways that her daughter did. She was the person who told stories about Spain to her grandchildren as she showered them with love, to the point that two-year-old María thought her grandmother's name was "España" (308). After she dies, her twelve-year-old grandson Jeremy surmises that her life ended because "la abuela no pudo resistir los rascacielos" [Grandmother could no longer endure skyscrapers] (185). Other characters also use the skyscraper to symbolize American culture; the building manager acidly remarks that "el que prefiera los rascacielos que se largue a Nueva York, que para eso están los aviones" [anyone who prefers skyscrapers should just leave and go to New York, that's what planes are for] (156). While the first chapter invokes skyscrapers as points of entry, the last chapter calls for other portals.

Amparo is critical of how disconnected people are in the United States, a reproach that was bluntly stated in the caption of one of Martín Gaite's New York collages, written in capital letters: "AMERICAN PEOPLE ARE LONELY" (*Visión de Nueva York* 21). When Jeremy visits his niece in a hospital for rich people (unmistakably modeled on Manhattan's Lenox Hill Hospital), he muses about how hard illness is for the loneliest group of all, the disenfranchised: "peor todavía sería la enfermedad de los *homeless*, de los emigrantes que no tienen permiso de residencia, de los perseguidos por la policía" [how much worse illness must be for the homeless, for immigrants without green cards, for those who are hunted by the police] (251). Amparo laments that she never had time to put flowers on her mother's grave because in New York no one has time for acts of remembrance: "en Nueva York siempre se hace tarde, no hay tiempo para ceremonias y el olvido corroe como un óxido" [in New York everyone is always running late, there is no time for ceremonies and forgetting is as corrosive as rust] (186). Even more harshly, she declares that "en América se piensa poco" [in the United States people don't think very much] (324). Perhaps for that reason, she observes, "en América todo me resbalaba" [in the United States it was hard for me to get my bearings] (287). Even the food is better in Spain, not to mention the wine. Savoring the first bottle of wine with dinner in the company of Abel Bores, she affirms that it is excellent, noting that this label is unavailable in the United States—one of many things that the United States is missing.

Cultural observations by Amparo about her adopted country are not always correct. Martín Gaite made a few mistakes in her descriptions of the United States—small errors that no Spanish editor has caught but that leap out at an American reader. The luxurious car that Amparo's future husband was driving when they met could never have been a Ford; what she meant was a Lincoln— the luxury brand that was and is owned by the Ford Motor Company but is far removed from a plebeian Ford. The waterfront summer home of the Drake clan would not be on Cape Code (which does not exist) but rather Cape Cod. People in New York referred and still refer to the "Rainbow Room" on the sixty-fifth floor of 30 Rockefeller Plaza, never shortening the name to "The Rainbow" (which would not be understood). Although it would be comprehensible, the Waldorf Astoria Hotel has always been referred to as "The Waldorf" instead of using the entire name, and while food was available there (usually at ceremonial banquets) it was not anyone's idea of a dining destination. Amparo's return flight could not have been on a carrier called "Airlines" because that is not a full name: American Airlines is the most likely choice for the correct name of an airline with regular flights between Madrid and New York. Finally, in 1997 it would be highly unlikely that a group of boys in the Bronx could get away with building a bonfire in front of a building on a main thoroughfare in broad daylight. Such a fire may have been a possibility in 1980, when Martín Gaite lived in a financially distressed city where police and other public services had been curtailed, but much had changed in the intervening years.

THE AUTOBIOGRAPHICAL QUESTION

Some critics have seized on this novel as Martín Gaite's third autobiography, building on my essay "One Autobiography, Twice Told: *Entre visillos* and *El cuarto de atrás*," which outlined autobiographical continuities in those novels (Cruz-Cámara *Laberinto*; Parker). *Irse de casa* is autobiographical in the broadest sense of "autobiografía ambiental" [autobiographical setting]. The author grew up in Salamanca and returned a number of times over the years, usually when she received an honor such as the key to the city. The novel is not autobiographical in the sense of "autobiografía argumental" [autobiographical plot]. (Martín Gaite was the source of these two terms, which are cited in "One Autobiography" [Interview with Brown, November 1984].) Despite the fact that Carmen Martín Gaite was from Salamanca, her experiences were quite different from those of the seamstress's daughter. Martín Gaite's family was patrician. As the child of a happy marriage whose father was a member of the professional elite, the author never experienced the hardships that motivated Amparo's mother to start a new life in the United States. The United States was a catalyst for Martín Gaite's career, hastening her transformation into a literary luminary while providing significant income, and she was grateful for these rewards. Twisting the cliché of Spain's discovery of America, she used to laughingly say that America discovered her.

Nevertheless, she never had any desire to move to America. Instead, she preferred to work abroad and repatriate her financial rewards, in the longstanding Spanish tradition of the *indiano* or Spanish adventurer who returns wealthy from the New World (Brown, "Los años americanos"). Not only did Martín Gaite choose to remain in her native Spain, she never left the Madrid home that was a wedding present from her father in 1953. For the author, moving did not seem to be an effective solution to personal problems, despite its being in vogue: "No sé por qué, pero hay un momento en que la gente cree que cambiando de casa cambiará de vida," she commented in the year the novel was published [I don't know why, but there's a point when people think that changing homes will change their lives] (Moret, "Novela"). The secondary character Olimpia notes the ubiquity of this misconception when she exclaims to her niece, "¡qué mania tenéis todos con irse de casa!" [What a fixation you all have with leaving home!] (316). In the novel it is Amparo who reflects the author's experience: "Supo que a partir de cierto momento, imposible de localizar, el aliciente de irse de casa ha perdido definitivamente su espejismo cabrilleante de vida nueva" [She knew that from a certain moment, one that was impossible to pinpoint, the lure of leaving home was no longer associated with the shimmering mirage of a new life] (243).

Although they could speak in the same voice, Carmen Martín Gaite differed from her avatar in *Irse de casa* in important ways. The author was not as superficial as her fictional creation. Unlike Amparo Miranda, she was focused on intellectual pursuits. Martín Gaite did not care at all about material things; for example, friends learned not to voice admiration for any bauble she was wearing, as she would promptly remove the item and insist that the friend accept it as a gift. She never redecorated her home (unlike her sister Anita who constantly undertook renovation projects) and she never submitted to drastic physical interventions in the name of beauty (as did some of her contemporaries on both sides of the Atlantic). Even her hair color was natural—more accurately colors, as her hair evolved from brown to salt-and-pepper to gray to white. She used the same paper hair curlers that she described in *El cuarto de atrás* throughout her life, resulting in a cascade of curls beneath the berets that she favored. Martín Gaite's apartment, also described in *El cuarto de atrás*, was charming and bohemian with its burgundy wallpaper, series of connected rooms, and large open terrace—none of which remained after her sister inherited and redid the apartment. As for a facelift, the author never displayed Amparo's telltale post-surgical look, frankly described in the novel as "un poco rara pero guapa" [a bit strange but pretty] (22). Photographs attest to the fact that Martín Gaite was a radiant and naturally beautiful woman, throughout every stage of her life.

———

Irse de casa combines a Cinderella story with an episode of the American television series *Finding Your Roots*, in which celebrities discover their ancestry. In her last completed novel Martín Gaite takes the reader on a journey of discovery. Instead of leaving home, Amparo Miranda goes home. She returns after forty years to the provincial Salamanca of her youth and chronicles its evolution into a postmodern metropolis. Like the author herself, Amparo Miranda has reinvented herself and achieved international success. The novel chronicles a late-life reassessment and last-chance renewal, as Amparo takes stock and contemplates change. She is willing to take risks and begin anew: starting a career as a film producer, forging closer bonds with her children, and reconnecting with the man who was her true love. By the end of the novel, the heroine's problems have receded or been resolved, as have those of the many characters from which this narrative tapestry is woven. *Irse de casa* is a triumphant work. At the age of seventy-three Martín Gaite published a novel that makes peace with the past, captures the present, and looks to the future.

CHAPTER 7

Los parentescos

FRACTURED FAMILIES IN THE TWENTY-FIRST CENTURY

Martín Gaite's last novel *Los parentescos* [Family relations] (2001) tells the story of an exceptional young man who tries to decipher the chaotic world around him, starting with his own family. Unlike her other novels, *Los parentescos* does not supply its dates of composition on the last page. There is no final chapter because she did not live to finish the book. Nevertheless, it is possible to reconstruct its development with confidence. She began a short story entitled "El niño cúbico" [The cubic boy] during the summer of 1992, according to her daily planner (qtd. in Teruel "Notas" 1532), and the story would eventually grow into *Los parentescos*. By 1998 she had begun working on the novel in earnest, mentioning it to me and to others. This timeline indicates that most likely she would have completed the novel by the spring of 2001—undoubtedly delivering what she called "paquetes bombas" [package bombs] of chapters to the publisher so that the book would be out in time for the Madrid Book Fair at the end of May (mentioned in an article on Anagrama by Iker Seisdedos).[1] As she revealed to interviewer Amaia Uriz in July of 1998, she needed a minimum of two years to write a novel, though the process need not be linear:

> Necesito, al menos, dos años para terminar una novela. Además no tengo por qué escribirla de corrido. Tomo notas en mis cuadernos sobre un personaje, sobre la sensación que me produce una cosa, un acontecimiento y tal vez esas notas con el tiempo se conviertan en trama.

> [I need at least two years to finish a novel. And there's no reason to write it all at once. I take notes in my notebooks about a character, about the feeling that something evokes, about an event, and in time might these notes might transform into a plot.]

Martín Gaite went on to distinguish between a novel and a story or a poem, which owe much to spontaneous inspiration and have a much shorter period of gestation (Uriz).

This interview was given in Soria, though she had planned to be in France. She and her sister Anita had accepted my mother's invitation to visit our family in Provence, at a rented château that could accommodate many guests. After a hectic year, this would be a respite and reunion, one that was especially comfortable thanks to the Martín Gaite sisters' fluency in French. As the author wrote in May 1998, "tanto Anita como yo estamos muy ilusionadas con la idea de iros a ver a Barbentane" [both Anita and I are excited about going to see all of you in Barbentane] adding that her new novel *Irse de casa* was coming out in two weeks and she would send it (Letter to Brown, Madrid, 5 May 1998). A card from Anita the following month confirmed that they were looking forward to this vacation: "Estoy dispuesta a pasarlo muy bien con vosotros y a hacer todo tipo de excursión y planes veraniegos. La región es preciosa . . . Carmiña muy contenta con su excelente nuevo libro. Ya hablaremos despacio." [I'm ready to have a good time with all of you and for any kind of day trips and summer activities. The region is lovely . . . Carmiña very pleased with her excellent new book. Soon we'll have lots of time to talk] (Letter to Brown, Madrid, 4 June 1998). Those were our first plans to fall through because of illness—in this case because a member of my family was diagnosed with cancer. What none of us could predict was that the disease would claim the life of Carmen Martín Gaite in two years' time.

She did not slow down until the year she died. Not much had changed in her personal life between 1998 and the winter of 2000. Her assistant was still taking care of the minutiae of daily life. Spain was also on the same path. The incumbent conservatives in the Partido Popular under José María Aznar won reelection in March of 2000, consolidating their power by achieving an absolute majority in parliament. Martín Gaite continued to distance herself from politics, preferring literature. In early 1999 her three-act play *La hermana pequeña* had its debut in the Centro Cultural de la Villa [Cultural Center of the City] of Madrid; it was published a few weeks later. This drama had a curious history: it was written in 1959 and shared only with friends in the intervening decades (my photocopy of the typescript is from the 1970s). The story line is pertinent to Martín Gaite's final novel, as it also involves twisted family ties: the protagonists are two half-sisters who have different expectations about their relationship. Also in 1999 the author recorded poems for the CD and accompanying volume *Carmen Martín Gaite recita sus poemas* [Carmen Martín Gaite recites her poetry] (1999). Her last completed books, both published in 2000, were translations. One was a critical edition of the French *Cartas de amor de la monja portuguesa Mariana Alcoforado* [Love letters of the Portuguese nun Mariana Alcoforado], first published in 1669 as *Lettres Portugueses* [The Portuguese letters]; these letters are now known to have been penned by a man, Gabriel de Lavergne, vicomte de Guilleragues.[2] The other translation is most relevant to *Los parentescos*: a Spanish version of Charlotte Brontë's *Jane Eyre* (1847). The English tale of an orphan in search of love and family resonates in the characters, plot, and themes of the novel that the author was composing simultaneously.

Martín Gaite had already made what would be her last trip to the United States, but she traveled within Europe during this time. She went to Milan in 1999 to see a version of *Caperucita en Manhattan* performed with marionettes, which she enjoyed very much (as she told me when she returned) and which echoes in some of the characters and the plot of *Los parentescos*. She also went to Paris for the launch of the French translation of *Lo raro es vivir*. Within Spain she gave talks in several cities in 1999 and 2000, including Madrid and Barcelona, on subjects ranging from the value of stories to a work by Portuguese realist master Eça de Queiroz on the centenary of his death. *La hermana pequeña* was presented in Salamanca in 1999, and she traveled to her birthplace for the last time. She performed poems from her new book and CD in Tarragona and at Madrid's Círculo de Lectores (where she was an honorary member) in early 2000, but could not continue with the more extensive tour that she and her editor had planned.[3] In the spring she was named an Honorary Member of the Círculo de Lectores in Barcelona and was feted with the Premio Pluma de Plata del Club de la Escritura [Silver Pen Prize of the Writing Club] at the Madrid Book Fair. Martín Gaite's last award, and also her last public appearance, was on 8 June, 2000, when Madrid's mayor presented her with La Medalla de Oro del Ayuntamiento de Madrid, the municipality's Gold Medal.

Already in poor health in June of 2000, she went back to the sisters' country house in El Boalo to recuperate. Anita had a spacious new master bath and sitting area with a view of the mountains installed in her downstairs home to facilitate her sister's care. (They had long ago divided their parents' country house into two separate apartments, with the author upstairs.) I would not see my friend again. My planned visit was postponed several times, as she urged me to wait until she felt better; although her voice sounded weak over the phone, I had no idea that she was so ill. Letters between us had all but ceased, replaced by long-distance phone calls that were no longer a costly luxury. The last time we spoke our conversation was interrupted by a doctor's house call, and I could sense that she was not getting better. She died on 23 July 2000, without ever knowing that she had cancer; Anita decided that it was best not to tell her. Anita had her sister moved to a private hospital in Madrid (the Clínica Ruber) shortly before she died. There she spent her last days clutching a notebook to her chest, preparing for a talk that she would never give. After her sister's death, Anita assumed the role of executor of her estate, a position to which she would devote herself until her own death on 27 May 2019.

At first Anita did not know what to do with the manuscript of *Los parentescos*. She said that when she picked it up she felt as though it were burning her hands. Her sister had read her some parts of the novel and Anita knew how much she wanted to finish it. As Anita said to interviewer Trinidad de León-Sotelo the year it was published, "Necesitaba liberarme del peso de aquella angustia" [I had to free myself from the weight of that anguish]. She dispatched the manuscript to her friend Jorge Herralde, who was still at the helm of the publisher Anagrama; he found the pages so compelling that he believed the novel should be published. *Los parentescos* appeared in February 2001, with a sixteen-page prologue in seven parts by novelist Belén Gopegui, whom Martín Gaite had mentored. Years later, after Herralde retired, Anita moved the novel to the Siruela publishing house. In 2018 Siruela published an unchanged version of *Los parentescos* with a different, four-page prologue by José Teruel. Each prologue features speculation about how Martín Gaite would have ended the novel, with spoilers that will diminish the reader's experience. For this reason both preliminary texts should be skipped over, either entirely or until finishing the last lines of Martín Gaite's text. Belén Gopegui suggests this strategy in her prologue, advising readers to stop after the first section and to return after reading the novel—preferably a few days later, after they have had time to formulate their thoughts.

A METALITERARY BILDUNGSROMAN

Los parentescos is a bildungsroman or novel of personal development. The protagonist is a brilliant, endearing, thoughtful, and imaginative young man who hooks the reader from his startling opening line: "Cuando mis padres se casaron, yo tenia ocho años para nueve" [When my parents got married I was eight going on nine] (25). The novel is narrated in metaliterary fashion, with the narrator commenting on the construction of his story as he writes it. The book is structured in a way that will be familiar to readers of the author's other novels of the 1990s. Its 225 pages are divided into two parts with multiple sections: seventeen short chapters in the first part and four completed chapters plus the beginning of a fifth in the unfinished second part. Chapters once again have titles (absent from the preceding novel, *Irse de casa*). These are pithy and evocative, from the enigmatic "La boda de mis padres" [My parents' wedding] of the opening chapter to the transcendent "La raya invisible" [The invisible line] of what would be the final chapter. The narrator is named Baltasar (nicknamed Baltita or Balti) and he lives in Madrid in the present day. As he reaches his eighteenth birthday he looks back at his life, and especially his formative years in the nearby historic city of Segovia, where his family resided until he was eight years old. His parents' wedding is a fulcrum for the story, with a "before" and "after" that organize its development.

Baltasar is the fourth child of a beautiful and kind but unpredictable and unknowable mother, whose mystery is enhanced by the fact that she is never named. She is a free spirit who is not impressed by status symbols; when Baltasar asks her what it means to be a duke, she explains the label by comparing it to the alligator on his polo shirts. She can be nurturing but also difficult: "mamá pocas veces cumplía sus promesas. Era voluble y estaba siempre algo pirada" [Mother rarely kept her promises. She was mercurial and always seemed a bit crazy] (120), the young narrator explains. Baltasar is the only child of Damián Almazán, a wealthy financial consultant and heir to a dukedom. The couple's chaotic household in a rambling Segovia house is dubbed the "casa zurriburri" [madhouse] by their longtime housekeeper. It includes Baltasar's three older half-siblings, his mother's children from a previous relationship. Damián dislikes the house and is only an intermittent presence there. He often stays at the grand home of his widowed mother, la Duquesa de Almazán [the Duchess of Almazán], whose given name is Baltasara. He divides his time to the point that in their Segovia house they refer to Damián's ancestral home as "la otra casa" [the other house] (97). Like Sofía and Eduardo in Martín Gaite's 1992 *Nubosidad variable*, Damián and Baltasar's mother have mismatched interests. Baltasar's free-spirited mother has a part-time job at the local cultural center but her greatest joys involve imaginative activities: reading novels and creating costumes for marionettes. Damián is a conventional man whose business dealings consume his energy. Complicating matters is the fact that the duchess does not approve of Baltasar's mother and wants nothing to do with their blended family. The couple does not formalize their relationship through marriage until after the duchess's death, whereupon Damián inherits her wealth.

Baltasar situates his family at the center of his story. In addition to being a self-conscious narrator, he is a mesmerizing one: his metaliterary commentary not only undergirds the story, it involves the reader in its creation. At times he seems to address the reader directly, remarking that he has already gone over a certain part of the story or using a locution that conveys immediacy, such as "luego . . . ya ni te cuento" [I can't even begin to tell you about what happened later] (64). The retrospective narrative focuses on Baltasar's development in the context of his enigmatic family, with the narrator's thoughts interspersed among vivid, cinematic scenes. As José Jurado Morales has observed, this is a "novela de aprendizaje y de búsqueda . . . con el propósito último del narrador-protagonista de encontrar su sitio, de saber qué lugar ocupa en la madeja social y familiar" [novel of apprenticeship and searching . . . with the narrator-protagonist's ultimate goal of finding his place, of knowing what role he occupies in the social and familial network] (*Juego* 217). Biruté Ciplijauskaité has characterized *Los parentescos* as a bildungsroman focused on the inner self, in which "la formación va por dentro, es un crecimiento interior, un proceso de concienciación, una lucha por conservar el *yo* primario mientras va adquiriendo sabiduría mundana" [personal development happens internally; this is an inner growth, a process of awareness, a struggle to sustain the ego while acquiring worldly knowledge] (131). At various junctures Baltasar questions whether it is worthwhile for him to continue telling his story. He considers ending it at the point where it would constitute a novella (the author's original intent) but decides that this would be unsatisfactory. Still, he has doubts about his project. Baltasar wonders whether it is worthwhile to "seguirles la pista a aquellos personajes de Segovia" [follow the trail of those characters in Segovia] (81). He goes on to ask: "tengo diecisiete años, ¿de qué me sirve retroceder a cuando tenía cuatro, y luego ocho y luego quince?" [I'm seventeen years old; what use is it to go back to when I was four, then eight and later fifteen?] (81). Fortunately for the reader, his tenacity leads him to proceed with the fascinating story of his life.

Baltasar's narrative is a compendium of asynchronous reminiscences about episodes when he was four, eight, fourteen, seventeen, and eighteen years old. These epochs roughly correspond to the cognitive phases proposed by psychologist Jean Piaget, according to which development is "a process which occurs due to biological maturation and interactions with the environment" as summarized by Saul McLeod. The novel begins with the hero having passed the preverbal "sensorimotor" stage (birth to two years). When the reader meets him, Baltasar is in the "preoperational" stage (two to seven years). In this stage children are primarily egocentric and tend to think in concrete terms; they are just beginning to acquire the ability to think symbolically. Language development is a hallmark of the preoperational stage, a characteristic that is explored through the protagonist's fascination with words and their meanings. Baltasar soon moves to the "concrete operational" stage (seven to eleven years), during which logical thinking and inductive logic are developed—marking the beginning of what Piaget termed "operational thought." Baltasar then progresses to the final "formal operational" stage (age eleven and above), in which adolescents use deductive reasoning to delve into abstract social, ethical, and philosophical questions (stages detailed by McLeod). It is during this epoch that Baltasar examines his values and those of the surrounding society.

Distinct periods in Baltasar's life are reconstructed from memory and from contemporaneous notebooks—the same techniques on which his creator relied for her narrative inventions. Although they cut back and forth in time, clear designations enable the reader to follow along and mentally file scenes in their proper order. Baltasar's narrative is cinematic in that it comprises a series of flashbacks (analepses) and flash-forwards (prolepses). Tension is heightened by foreshadowing, such as when he recalls that a certain scene was the last happy time he remembered in the Segovia house, "antes de que las cosas empezaran a hundirse sin remedio en la casa zurriburri" [before things started to go irretrievably downhill in the madhouse] (124). Baltasar's metaliterary commentary includes musings on the use of flashbacks in film. He notes that the device can become tiresome but that its use should come as no surprise, given that it is taken from real life ("En fin, el truco del flashback puede aburrir, pero extrañar no extraña. Está tomado de la vida" 99). Critics have likened the novel's structure to a collage (Ciplijauskaité 131) or a "warp and weave of . . . intersecting narratives" in the words of Catherine O'Leary and Alison Ribeiro de Menezes (261); the latter description evokes a tapestry. Both the collage and the tapestry metaphors are apt and both highlight the author's ability to surprise and delight her readers as they assimilate the novel's parts.

Recalling fragments of the past, Baltasar uses stories to interpret his experiences—especially the tropes of stories for children. For example, when he learns from a schoolmate that the old woman with a cane whom he has glimpsed outside—the duchess—is actually his grandmother, he understands the concept in literary terms: "Dentro de los parentescos, el [papel] de abuela era el más fácil de entender, en todos los cuentos salía una, o un abuelo, los padres de los padres del niño" [In family relations the grandmother's role was the easiest to understand, there's one in every story—or else a grandfather—the parents of the child's parents] (101). He takes in so many stories that eventually he becomes overwhelmed by them, comparing his condition to that of an overstuffed suitcase. Near the end of his time in Segovia, Baltasar explains: "simplemente no me cabían más historias, ni de verdad ni de mentira, añadidas a las que ya día y noche me pisoteaban la cabeza." [I simply could not fit any more stories in my head, either real or invented, in addition to the ones that were already tormenting my brain around the clock] (219). Some of Baltasar's stories come from people, but many come from books. He is fascinated by reading, observing that between the ages of four and seven books were for him "como una ventana que se abre para que entre un aire menos contaminado" [like a window that you open to bring in purer air] (115).

He also delights in what he learns in school and devotes entire passages to relaying his discoveries—stories about the world—in fields that range from phonetics to cell biology. Like Martín Gaite's two previous novelistic male protagonists, David Fuente of *Ritmo lento* and Leonardo Villalba of *La Reina de las Nieves*, Baltasar is an independent thinker trying to understand his circumstances. His deliberations closely resemble those of a minor character in *Irse de casa*: young Caroline, the protagonist's granddaughter who makes story-drawings (her term is "dibujo-cuentos," 250) to explain the world around her. For Ester Bautista Botello, this device is a key to Martín Gaite's poetics, revealing "the intrinsic relationship between drawing and storytelling" in her later novels (183). In *Irse de casa* the hospital-room scene between Jeremy (Amparo Miranda's son) and Caroline (his injured niece), in which Caroline explains the story told by her drawing of a castle, prefigures the author's depiction of Baltasar at age eight in *Los parentescos*. Both children are just beginning to think in symbolic terms, and their insights can astound. Baltasar studies, reads, listens, and formulates conclusions that are rational and original. For Martín Gaite, the roots of storytelling are located in childhood. She explained in her 1983 volume of literary theory *El cuento de nunca acabar*:

> Desde la infancia nos vamos configurando al mismo tiempo como emisores y como receptores de historias, y ambas funciones son estrechamente interdependientes, hasta tal punto que nunca un buen narrador creo que deje de tener sus cimientos en un niño curioso, ávido de recoger y de interpretar las historias escuchadas y entrevistas, de completar lo que en ellas hubiera podido quedar confuso, abonándolo con la cosecha de su personal participación. (91)

> [From childhood we develop simultaneously as producers and receivers of stories. Both functions are closely intertwined, to the point where I believe that a good narrator is always grounded in his or her beginnings as a curious child—eager to collect and interpret stories seen and heard, to fill in any confusing parts and to enhance them with the fruits of personal experience.]

As the author told me many years ago when we discussed her young protagonists, children are instructive. They can deliver valuable insights to receptive adults: "Te enseña mucho más de lo que tú le puedes enseñar la persona [el niño] que tú piensas controlar" [The person (the child) whom you think you control can teach you much more than you can teach him or her] (Interview with Brown 1978).[4]

Saga of the Cubic Boy

Baltasar did not utter a word until he was four years old, but this was not because he was slow. His sister Lola describes Baltasar as the smartest one in the household, and this is patently clear to the reader: his wordplay, associations, and inventions show a highly intelligent, original mind at work. As one of his brothers explains, young Balti likes to decipher things—much as the reader does with his narrative. With language as with other skills, Baltasar's development naturally trails that of his three half-siblings, who are much older than he is. His independent and headstrong half-sister Lola—with whom Baltasar is closest—is sixteen when he is nearly nine. The middle brother Máximo, a handsome and dashing young man whom Baltasar nicknames "Max-flash," is three years older than Lola. The oldest brother Pedro—who unlike the others is unattractive and stodgy—is three years older than Max, or twenty-two on the day the novel opens (the day of their mother's wedding). Baltasar's three older siblings have the same father: Gabriel. Handsome and creative, Gabriel is the son of Bruno and Elsa, two principals of a marionette theater who live in an apartment that connects to the family home in Segovia, behind a door hidden by a tapestry. Gabriel now lives in Milan but sends his parents scripts for their marionette shows: Bruno calls him the soul of their troupe. When Gabriel left Madrid and Baltasar's mother for good, Damián came to put the puppeteers' finances in order; he consoled the bereft young mother, and the two fell in love. Gabriel is also the father of Baltasar's fascinating cousin Olalla, the forceful and original young woman who becomes Baltasar's love interest from the day she attends his parents' wedding. Olalla has a different mother, so she and Baltasar are not related—a fact that he works out (with his sister's help) as he assembles the puzzle pieces of his family tree. It is Olalla who first calls Baltasar "el niño cúbico," literally "the cubic boy." Bruno later explains that this is an invented name for someone who resembles a vivid cubist painting: "raro, diferente. Que sale por donde no te esperas" [odd, different; coming from an unexpected place] (145).

Baltasar recalls his first words, which were not transcendent (he said that Lola went to the movies) but which symbolize the end of his preverbal silence. Delayed language has symbolic importance, as Andrew Bush has elucidated: "thus postponed, language acquisition is thematized in the novel as the route to transcendence" (173). Also at age four Baltasar reconstructs his transformative experience at a marionette play entitled *La libélula bondadosa* [The kindhearted dragonfly]— reminiscent of the author's description of her magical experience of the theater as a child in her novel *El cuarto de atrás*. In the play a magical dragonfly is able to bring about a reconciliation between an ogre and a princess. The dragonfly does this by entering the ogre's body, burrowing into a pocket on his back; from this internal vantage point he changes the ogre's behavior by altering his soul. Baltasar further remembers his visit with the upstairs neighbors who staged the show, where he glimpsed the dragonfly puppet whose clothing his mother had sewn. There he also saw a portrait of the puppeteers' handsome son Gabriel, who looked like a younger version of Baltasar's half-brother Max. Bruno suggests to his wife that Baltasar might have supernatural abilities: "¿Te has fijado en los ojos de ese niño, Elsa? Tiene poderes seguro." [Did you notice that boy's eyes, Elsa? He surely has powers] (76).

Though the novel never vaults its protagonist into the realm of the fantastic (the boy's one enduring "power" is that he can guess what people are talking about from a distance), Baltasar does discover a special talent. At age eight he realizes that in school soccer matches he can stop all goals attempted by the opposing team, a skill that transforms him from a misfit into a respected member of his class. With this newfound confidence he makes a friend, Isidoro, an independent and studious boy four years older than Baltasar, who lives above his family's bookstore and whose sister is a friend of Max's. Isidoro initiates Baltasar into the pleasures of adventure stories with Daniel Defoe's classic *Robinson Crusoe*, duplicating the experience of the protagonist whose friend encouraged her to read the book in *El cuarto de atrás*. Isidoro also invites Baltasar to experience the pleasures and horrors of two Robert Louis Stevenson novels: *Treasure Island* and *The Strange Case of Dr. Jekyll and Mr. Hyde*. The latter novel shapes their understanding of Isidoro's late father—a frustrated writer who turned into an abusive monster when he drank, expressing his "diablos ocultos" [hidden demons] (192). This concept of "desdoblamiento" or split personalities—of the individual whose reflection in the mirror symbolizes a different person from the one inside—is the aspect of *Los parentescos* that has received the most critical attention to date.[5]

Stevenson's novel about Dr. Jekyll and Mr. Hyde also helps Baltasar comprehend the shattering episode that he experienced when he was eight, involving his beloved housekeeper, Fuencisla. She was the woman who provided stability and comfort to their Segovia home; she also initiated Baltasar into the pleasures of literature, telling him life-and-death stories from her village as he sat with her in the kitchen. Fuencisla is arrested for the murder of her boyfriend, a widowed butcher whom she adored and pursued (and who allowed her to cook and clean for him free of charge). Fuencisla, who had been drinking, stabbed the butcher when she found him having sex behind the counter with a young Colombian assistant—who survived and called the police. Fuencisla is led away from Baltasar's home by two civil guards, never to return; her family later comes to Segovia to claim her belongings and insult her former employers. After the housekeeper's departure a badly shaken Baltasar is sent to a summer camp in Galicia, a restorative time that he hardly remembers but that he reconstructs from his notebooks. Baltasar is summoned back to Segovia by his father a week before camp ends. Damián asks Baltasar to help him deal with the death of his own mother (the duchess), who sadly died without achieving what she most wanted: meeting her grandson. When he returns from camp, Baltasar meets Fuencisla's provisional replacement. She is a disturbed young woman who takes a liking to Baltasar and comes close to molesting him, stopped only when he removes her hand from his body and reminds her that he is eight years old. Soon after, the family moves to Madrid.

In the present day, when Baltasar turns eighteen, the saga of life within his fractured family continues. The family has lived in Madrid for a decade, moving to progressively better neighborhoods. They first lived in a rented house (where his parents had their wedding) for two years, then in a temporary home that they owned for three years, and finally in the permanent home where they have resided for five years. After they married, Baltasar's parents' relationship deteriorated. From a young age Baltasar intuited that his parents needed help (he wondered if a magical dragonfly might solve their problems) because "solos uno con otro se las arreglaban mal" [they could not fix things by themselves] (73). An inflection point came when Damián struck his wife in front of his son, ostensibly to calm her during a bout of hysterical crying. By the time they moved into their present Madrid home—a luxurious abode on Calle de Velázquez in the Salamanca district—they had separate bedrooms. On Baltasar's eighteenth birthday his parents are in the midst of one of their trial separations, some of which have lasted as long as a month, during which it is Damián who suffers most. Baltasar was never close with his father, who was frightened by the way that young Baltasar sometimes looked at him and who inexplicably got along better with his stepchildren than with his own son. But as a young adult Baltasar comes to understand his father. Baltasar sees that Damián is someone who needs love and has no idea how to ask for it. He notices that his father is falling apart, comparing this revelation to spying someone with disheveled makeup or a tell-tale facelift scar ("yo sé que mi padre está hecho polvo, desamparado, se lo noto en la cara. Es como si se le hubiera corrido el maquillaje o se le viera la cicatriz de algún lifting" 105). It is possible that the story that Fuencisla told him as a boy was really true: that the duchess put a spell on her son, ensuring that he would be handsome, smart, and successful but never free.

By the time he turns eighteen his beloved sister Lola, who had wanted to be an actress, has been part of a successful television series. But things are not going well for her now. She lives alone in an attic apartment and has started drinking, much like Águeda (before meeting Tomás) in *Irse de casa*. The dashing Max has left for unknown adventures, while oldest half-brother Pedro and his wife (formerly girlfriend) Beatriz live with their five-year-old son in the affluent residential district of La Moraleja. Baltasar himself has gone through several phases since moving to Madrid. When he fell in with his peers (known for being the Spanish version of preppies, "pijos") in the wealthy Salamanca neighborhood he became focused on preparing for a lucrative career. Fortunately he caught himself and returned to his true values. "Ahora me aburre acordarme de aquel joven . . . totalmente volcado en los saberes de tipo práctico . . . incapaz de inventar un disparate lingüístico" [Now it bores me to think back on that young man . . . totally committed to acquiring practical knowledge . . . incapable of wordplay], he recalls (241). In the present Baltasar has just earned a very high score on the Spanish university entrance exam, and is deciding how to proceed. He is dating a bright young woman who is interested in him but his heart is not in the relationship; he still pines for his cousin Olalla.

How or even if the dangling threads of these characters' lives would have been tied off, the reader cannot know, but it is possible to hazard a guess. Based on the hopeful endings of the author's other novels of this decade, it is likely that Baltasar would have found love and fulfillment, probably with the object of his affection, Olalla. Absent for most of the story, she is invoked in the first chapter of the novel's second part, entitled "Datos sobre Olalla" [Facts about Olalla]. The final completed chapter (chapter 5 of part two) reproduces a letter to Olalla that Baltasar wrote after meeting her, but never sent. The author planted a clue that may prefigure the eventual transformation of Olalla's feelings, which were not reciprocal: the dragonfly puppet. Bruno gave it to Baltasar as parting gift. The puppeteer assured him that, just as in the play, Baltasar can use it to "renovar el alma de alguien" [change someone's soul] (145) at the appropriate time. O'Leary and Ribeiro de Menezes have compared Bruno to Miss Lunatic in *Caperucita en Manhattan*, noting that in this novel as in that one, "someone who is not biologically connected to the protagonist will convey the most important message of his life" (264). They identify this message as his mantra "Fu, fu, fu, fu, mucha calma. El secreto está en el alma" [Foo, foo, foo, foo, stay calm and collected. The secret resides in your soul] (145). Bruno also predicted that "para llegar al milagro tienes que haber pasado mucho tiempo no entendiendo nada" [to reach the miracle you have to have gone through a long period of not understanding anything] (146). This prophecy has already come to pass: Baltasar has matured into a perceptive and astute young man who can conquer a woman's affection. Would the cubic boy and the girl who lays down imaginary lines find happiness together? The wisdom that Baltasar dispenses to his mother and his teacher, who want to know the ending to a story he wrote, can also be applied to *Los parentescos*: "queda mejor con misterio" [it's better if it remains a mystery] (123).[6]

FAMILY SECRETS AND FAMILY DYNAMICS

In *Los parentescos* the author's enduring theme of family relations is explored in new configurations at the start of the twenty-first century. Binding ties of traditional Spanish society have dissolved during Spain's quarter-century of constitutional government. Legal discrimination against women under the Franco dictatorship, symbolized by the marital "law of the father" or *patria potestad*, whereby men had sole jurisdiction over women and children, has long since been abolished.[7] Contraceptives were legalized in 1978, divorce became legal in 1981, and abortion was made lawful (within specific limitations) in 1985. With women's freedom, patriarchal decrees have given way to individual choices, and family ties have become tangled. In the present day Baltasar notes that many of his father's counterparts—executives in Madrid's tall office buildings—are "seguramente divorciados con niños de distintos apellidos a su cargo" [surely divorced and responsible for children with different last names] (103). Bush has observed that the fact that Baltasar was born out of wedlock (something his parents and siblings conspire to keep from him) makes him "the embodiment of a permissiveness, an affirmation in defiance of social controls, represented here by the No of the mother" (179). Baltasar tries to unravel his family ties in his quest for self-knowledge, declaring that "las asignaturas más difíciles eran los parentescos" [family relations were the most difficult subject of all] (25). His operative question is the common denominator in deciphering a family tree: What is this person to me?

As in all novels of development, the protagonist serves as a mediator of the world around him. In this case it is a fragmented, postmodern environment that Jurado Morales has compared to a "vorágine" or maelstrom, where the macrocosm of society's deterioration is mirrored in the microcosm of the family unit

("Mundo" 209). The postmodern environment is difficult to decipher, since all-encompassing explanatory narratives (such as religion) no longer hold sway, and this makes Baltasar's search for answers all the more difficult. Fuencisla explains to him that some things that happen in real life resemble stories: "son secretos de familia" [they are family secrets] (110). Baltasar tries to bring these stories into the light, even though his sister advises against it: "Las cosas de familia, y más si es una familia como la nuestra, mejor que cada uno se las guarde como las entendió" [For family affairs, and especially if it's a family like ours, it's best for each person to stick with their own interpretation] (82). In Lola's view, rummaging around in family business can only generate bad vibes ("lo veo un mal rollo" 82).

Lola could have been trying to protect her brother from the dark side of family secrets. Nevertheless, Baltasar discovers them. He observes that "el agujero negro de los parentescos podía convertirse en un nido de víboras" [the black hole of family relations could turn into a nest of vipers] (113). Peering into this black hole, Baltasar finds incompatible parents who were not married for the first half of his life; three half-siblings from an older generation whose father abandoned them; a titled grandmother whom he will never meet; an elderly couple of pup-peteers, grandparents of his half-siblings, who lived in a hidden apartment; and a cousin who is their grandchild and half-sister of Baltasar's siblings.[8] None of these relationships is explained to the young boy, a fact that leaves him feeling insignificant. After his parents depart for their honeymoon (when he is eight), he badgers his sister into answering his questions, beginning with the identity of Olalla. Lola explains that her reluctance to share information with him is a response to the fact that he is hypersensitive: "¡a ti te ponen tan nervioso los asuntos de los parientes!" [anything involving relatives stresses you out], she exclaims (212). Proving her point, Baltasar becomes outraged when Lola tells him that Olalla is her sister. He demands to know what she means by that, calming down only after she agrees to answer all his questions—and when he learns that Olalla is not his blood relative.

The principle that Baltasar discovers early on is that people are intercon-nected: "De la infancia lo que se queda pegado a la piel es que hay que contar con los demás: que no somos islas" [From childhood what sticks with you is that you have to depend on others: that we are not islands] (107). He poetically describes each person's family as his or her picture frame: "ellos son el marco del cuadro" (107). For Baltasar, this frame comprises all the members of his household. With little parental intervention, the influence of his siblings and his mother-surrogate, Fuencisla, takes on greater importance. According to devel-opmental models of family dynamics, siblings play a central role in a child's evo-lution: "siblings' extensive contact and companionship during childhood and adolescence—increasingly outside the direct supervision of parents or other adults—provides ample opportunity for them to shape one another's behavior and socioemotional development and adjustment," in the words of Susan McHale and colleagues. This is evidently the case for Baltasar. His brother Max initiates him into the magic of theater by taking him to a marionette show (a life-changing event) and also serves as a role model. His brother Pedro helps him move into his own room (an important marker of independence) by assembling a necessary bookshelf, and shares words of wisdom. Lola serves as his mirror—Baltasar's word—as well as his mediator with the adult world. Nevertheless Baltasar's siblings, like his parents, are often unavailable. The one consistent household member is Fuencisla, whose job involves her presence on a daily basis. For the first seven years of Baltasar's life, Fuencisla is a vitally important maternal substitute. When she is taken away, Baltasar and Lola cry together over what has been lost. Lola expresses the sentiment they share: "Casa, lo que se dice casa, desde que se fue Fuencisla no volveremos a tener ninguna. Nunca jamás." [We will never have a home, a real home, since Fuencisla left. Never again] (214).

HOUSES AND HOMES

Homes are associated with mothers and nurturing in Martín Gaite's fiction. In *El cuarto de atrás* the family home was a place of refuge during the Civil War. That home and the Segovia home of *Los parentescos* were laid out with front and rear spaces, whose symbolism has been analyzed by Bush. Both homes have back rooms: while in *Cuarto* the back playroom of the work's title was commandeered for storage, in *Los parentescos* the back storeroom is converted into Baltasar's first room of his own. Also in *Cuarto* the back room represents a link between parent and child; the narrator asks her mother to draw and discuss her own childhood home—which similarly had a back room—a project that is mutually rewarding. In addition to being shaped by their layout, homes are formed by the relationships within their walls. Disintegrating relationships that shatter a home constitute a recurring theme in the author's fiction. From the dissolved couple in *Retahílas* to the damaged family in *Fragmentos de interior* to the divorced parents in *Lo raro es vivir*, and including the author's personal situation implicit in *El cuarto de atrás*, marriages do not last. In *Los parentescos*, Max characterizes their family situation before they move from Segovia—a time when they had stopped all meaningful communication—as the fall of the House of Usher (a misprint substitutes the homonym "Husserl").[9] Lola counters: "Es la diaspora . . . no nos engañemos" [It's the Diaspora . . . let's not kid ourselves] (220). In Martín Gaite's novels of family dissolution the mother keeps the home (an exception being Augustina Sousa in *Fragmentos de interior*, who commits suicide). Baltasar's Segovia home, replete with dark passageways and a secret apartment, belongs to his mother—a fact that emerges when she asserts her independence in an argument with her husband-to-be. As in most of her later novels—*Nubosidad variable, La Reina de las Nieves, Lo raro es vivir*, and *Irse de casa*—in *Los parentescos* maternal protection extends to home ownership. This was the case in real life for the author and her daughter, Marta, who lived in the Madrid apartment that had been a gift from Martín Gaite's father when she married Rafael Sánchez Ferlosio.

Homes in the author's novels also reveal symbolic character traits. As Elide Pitarello has noted, in *Los parentescos* "una vez más el espacio doméstico habla de los personajes que lo habitan y viceversa" [once again domestic space speaks volumes about the characters who inhabit it, and vice versa] (42). Baltasar's mother is happy with the bohemian arrangement in the Segovia "casa zurriburri." Damián disapproves of the Segovia house physically just as he disapproves of the way it is run. With its rambling layout and coal-fired stove, the home is too old-fashioned for him. He particularly dislikes that it has great expanses of hallway—a characteristic of the author's own apartment (vividly described in *El cuarto de atrás*). When he becomes very wealthy, Damián indulges in a real estate acquisition that is ostentatious to the point of being ridiculous, similar to the lavish bathroom installation overseen by the supremely materialistic husband Eduardo in *Nubosidad variable*. The home renovation that Damián undertakes is a blatant reflection of his materialism, as he combines two traditional apartments into a single dwelling that boasts six balconies and seven bathrooms: "una pasada" [over the top] (242), in his son's eyes. As Baltasar comments, they have more and more space as the family need for it diminishes; his older siblings rarely spend the night and they never have houseguests.

Baltasar views "la casa de ahora" [the present house] as precarious and endangered. The penultimate chapter of *Los parentescos* is entitled "De terremotos" [About earthquakes]. It involves an extended metaphor comparing the family's current home with Pompeii after the eruption of Mount Vesuvius in 79 A.D. Mindful of the many rapid changes outside his home's walls, Baltasar senses danger within. He imagines that the entire apartment building is constructed on volcanic soil, and that a catastrophe is imminent. He sleeps fearfully, conflating the three Madrid homes he has known and fearing that that the cement that holds them together is defective: "Las tres casas de Madrid bailan una dentro de otra, víctimas de pequeñas sacudidas y a punto de desplome cuanto más quiero afirmar los pies en ella. No hay manera, me vomitan de sí . . ." [The three Madrid houses dance one inside the other, subject to small tremors. The more I want to stand firmly, the closer they come to falling over. There's no solution, they vomit me out . . .] (243). On a date with the young woman who likes him, Baltasar explains that he has become obsessed with Pompeii. He reads her a letter from the fateful eruption's sole survivor, Pliny the Younger. Soon after they are gripped by a real urban danger, when a group of youths "con muy mala pinta" [who look dangerous] (246) approaches their car, one wielding a knife. They escape and she drives him back to where he had parked his motorcycle, disaster averted.

Dangers abound in *Los parentescos*, most of them within the home. When he is young, Fuencisla warns Baltasar to beware: "¡Ay, Dios mio! Nunca se sabe de dónde salen las amenazas. Vive uno pensando que está a salvo, que todo va a acabar bien. Pero no te fíes." [Oh My God! You can never tell where threats will come from. You go along thinking that you're safe, that everything will turn out fine. But don't believe it] (111). Most threats to well-being are emotional, especially for the young boy, who is rarely informed of family members' plans and feels angry when he learns of them (for instance, when he finds out that Max and Lola have gone to Milan without telling him). Sexual abuse looms in the inappropriate actions of the family's temporary housekeeper. Physical harm is also inflicted. For the first time in the author's fiction, domestic violence rears its head. Damián strikes Baltasar's mother, swearing that he has never done it before but thereby changing their relationship forever. Baltasar's friend Isidoro's father gashes his mother's face in a drunken rage, leaving a lifelong scar. The most violent crime in the novel is committed by the figure who represents hearth and home, Fuencisla. It is doubly ironic that the character who unites the family in the kitchen uses a kitchen implement, a butcher's knife, to end her boyfriend's life. This perversion of a maternal figure is both shocking and effective in conveying what the author described from experience as "la esencia precaria, amenazada y efímera de la felicidad" ("Bosquejo" 232) ["the precarious, vulnerable, ephemeral nature of happiness"] ("Sketch" 242).[10]

The Grandchildren's Generation

Baltasar emerges intact from the hazards of his childhood. He starts to comprehend adults as he morphs into one: "A los mayores un niño los entiende mal. Cuando los empieza a entender un poco es porque ya se ha metido en líos que lo sacan a él mismo de ser niño." [A child is incapable of understanding adults. When he begins to understand them it's because he's already gotten himself into the sorts of trouble that distance him from childhood] (121). Baltasar enters the world of adults at a specific moment. He belongs to the first cohort to enter adulthood in the twenty-first century: a Spanish "millennial." Since he turns eighteen in the year 2000, his inferred birth year would be 1982.[11] Trappings of the information age are evident in the novel: Damián is attentive to his cell phone, and the career advice he gives to his son is to master technology and English. Spanish youth culture in the twenty-first century is the backdrop for Baltasar's individual choices. This generation has sometimes been called the "nini" or "ni-ni" [neither-nor] generation because many of them neither work nor study, for reasons that are largely beyond their control. Damián criticizes his son for having too many interests, a hallmark of his generation. He warns Baltasar that even though he is gifted the world is hypercompetitive now and he has already lost time between secondary school and university.

Los parentescos reflects the limited opportunities available to Spanish millennials. The autocratic nature of university admissions, whereby a score on the

Selectividad [entrance exam] determines an individual's career options (if a student does not attain the cut-off score, he or she must choose a different field), is condemned by a secondary character. In the bar where Baltasar meets Damián to pick up his birthday check when he turns eighteen, an acquaintance of his father's commiserates with Baltasar's indecision regarding a career path:

> El otro dice que eso les pasa también a sus hijos, bueno, a todos los chicos, es la falta de estímulo, tampoco ellos tienen la culpa, la universidad española está atascada, una pura tómbola, ves a gente metida en Arquitectura cuando lo que les tiraba era ser médico, y a licenciados en Historia del Arte poniendo un bar o un tenderete en el Rastro, lo mejor es un máster en Estados Unidos. (104–105)

> [The other man says that the same thing is happening to his children, actually to all young people. The problem is that they're not motivated, but it's not their fault. Spanish universities are jammed up now, they're basically a lottery. You see people studying architecture when they wanted to be a doctor, and people with degrees in art history opening a bar or a stand in (the flea market) El Rastro. The best thing is to get a master's degree in the United States.]

To Baltasar, these words are nothing new: "he oído la canción demasiada veces" [I've heard that song too many times before] (105) he comments as he sips his martini.

Baltasar knows that he is more fortunate than most. Others in his generation face obstacles that seem insurmountable—problems that persist for young people today. As real-life millennial Naomi Merchán Carballo shared in a letter to the editor of the Spanish newspaper *El País*: "¿Estudiaré para no tener trabajo? ¿Trabajaré para no tener pensión? ¿Y si nunca encuentro lo que me motiva? Y, sobre todo, ¿y si no puedo cumplir todas las expectativas puestas en mí?" [Will I study and then not find work? Will I work and then not have a pension? And what if I never find my passion? And, above all, what if I can't fulfill all of the expectations placed on me?]. As a rich man's son, Baltasar's future is more assured. In the novel's last completed chapter (involving seismic eruptions) he comments on his family's predictable future, adding: "El [futuro] mío incierto, claro, como el de todos los hijos de papá de mi edad. . . . Nos enfrentamos al dilema *light* de decidir por dónde se tira y qué opción promete mejor salida económica." [My own (future) is uncertain, obviously, as it is for everyone my age. . . . We're facing the minor dilemma of deciding which direction to take and which option guarantees greater financial rewards] (240). He goes on to lament that his generation is continually overwhelmed by new information. Although sometimes they act rebellious or fed up, in fact they have internalized the values of the surrounding culture. For Baltasar's millennial cohort, staying up-to-date is paramount. Unfortunately, "bajo tanta avalancha de información se va sepultando los sueños" [dreams are buried beneath this avalanche of infomation] (241).

The author wanted nothing more than for young people to hold onto their dreams. For Martín Gaite, Baltasar would be the age of a grandchild, had her daughter's life taken a different turn. The "autobiographical attitude" in Martín Gaite's fiction is well established, as Maria Vittoria Calvi has observed, and her longing for grandchildren was palpable to those who knew her. As a member of her daughter's generation I witnessed her delight in our millennial children: son Alexander Asher (who is Baltasar's age) and daughter Sarah (who lent her name to the protagonist in *Caperucita en Manhattan*). The author referred to herself as their fairy godmother, and behaved like one. She took a sincere interest in their growth: listening to them, playing games with them, and always urging them to follow their dreams. She gave gifts that they would keep forever—often reference books, just as Baltasar inherits his grandmother's set of Espasa-Calpe encyclopedia volumes. (My son still has the big unabridged Larousse French-English dictionary that she brought him—with a lengthy and inspirational inscription on the flyleaf.) Photographs in the Martín Gaite Archive in Valladolid document her talking and playing with the Brown children in the 1990s in El Boalo (as in figures 2.3 and 2.4 in this volume). These images show how she inhabited the role of an older friend, just as Bruno defined his relationship to Baltasar in *Los parentescos*.[12] When asked in 1998 whether she herself had any unfulfilled dreams, Martín Gaite gave a succinct answer: "Tener un nieto. Ese hubiera sido un sueño logrado muy grande." [To have a grandchild. That would have been a very big dream come true] (Uriz).

Martín Gaite was aware that her family line was destined for extinction. In a poignant and intimate letter to her sister she addressed their loss and longing, without referring to Marta by name:

Querida Anita, la única manera de aguantar la realidad es no mirarla a la cara, construirse inventos para vivir en una realidad ficticia. Tanto tú como yo hemos seguido este difícil camino, muchas veces contra viento y marea, y los momentos en que la lucidez nos hace comprender que ese camino se cierra, sentimos el vértigo del abismo, de la traca final. . . . Nos podemos inventar todo menos un heredero que recoja el fruto de nuestros afanes y la antorcha que a nosotros nos iluminó. . . . ¿Para quién somos depositarias de las joyas y muebles que a ella le gustaban, de los campos donde jugó? La lucidez de mirar a la cara de esta realidad terrible, de enfrentarnos a esta pregunta sin respuesta no puede ser más que pasajera, porque no se resiste. Y sin embargo, como decía Machado "vale más ver negro que no ver." . . . Lo que pasa es que no sé cómo consolarte ni cómo consolarme a mí misma. Lo único que pienso es que a ella no le gustaría vernos así. (Qtd. in Teruel, "Introducción" 49)

[Dear Anita, the only way to withstand reality is to not look it in the eye, to create fantasies so as to live in an imaginary world. Both you and I have followed this difficult path, often against all odds. In clear-eyed moments when we realize that this path is closing in on us, we can sense the vertigo of the abyss, of the end. . . . We can invent everything except an heir to inherit the fruits of our efforts and the torch that lit our way. . . . For whom are we the keepers of the jewels and possessions that she liked, of the fields where she played? We can't bear to face this reality for long; this question without an answer can only be considered briefly, because it is crushing. And yet, as Machado used to say, "It is better to see darkness than to not see." . . . The problem is that I don't know how to console you or how to console myself. The only thing I can think of is that she would not like to see us like this.]

Martín Gaite also knew that her daughter would have wanted her to keep writing. In *Los parentescos* she once again constructs a beautifully told, gripping story that seems taken from real life. As with all of her later novels, the transformation of life into literature brought consolation. The author herself expressed it best to interviewer Rosa Mora: "La realidad es muchas veces insoportable y algunos tenemos la suerte de poderla transformar" [Reality is often unbearable and some of us are lucky enough to be able to transform it].

Los parentescos is a satisfying novel despite its lack of an ending. Even without the final chapters, it feels substantial; it is slightly longer than two other Martín Gaite novels of the nineties, *Caperucita en Manhattan* and *Lo raro es vivir*. In *Los parentescos* the verbally gifted protagonist captures and holds the reader's interest, aided by dramatic plot developments that include murder. This novel reflects the disintegration of traditional familial norms in contemporary Spain—norms that are purely historical to millennials such as Baltasar, born after Spain's transition to democracy. Twenty-first-century anxieties are vividly depicted, especially as they affect what for Martín Gaite would have been her grandchildren's generation. The breakdown of the social contract, whereby Spanish young people could pursue the career of their choice, first in university studies and subsequently in the job market, is a defining reality for Baltasar's generation and those that follow. Martín Gaite prided herself on finishing what she started, and she dearly wanted to conclude *Los parentescos*. Death forced her to relinquish Baltasar's story before it could come to an end.

Conclusion

THE LATER NOVELS AND MARTÍN GAITE'S LEGACY

Martín Gaite's last six novels are an essential part of her legacy. Not only do they comprise over half of her novelistic production, they also demonstrate the mature prowess of a superbly gifted author. Martín Gaite's skills as a novelist and social critic make these books required reading for anyone interested in contemporary Spain and its literature. Unfettered by censorship in the democratic era and enriched by her new knowledge of the United States, these books reflect Martín Gaite's expertise as a cultural historian. All of them engage with the world around her on the cusp of the twenty-first century. They pull back the curtain on the realities of Spain in the post-Franco era from the Transition (1975–1982) through the long Socialist regime (1982–1996) to the return to conservative rule under the Partido Popular that began in 1996 and was in full force at the turn of the century. Two novels set fully or partially in the United States also illuminate life in New York City. Martín Gaite's last novels focus presciently on concerns that have become even more urgent today. Among them are the self-actualization of women of diverse ages and social classes, the recovery of historical truths that have been hidden or suppressed, the corrosive effects of money and power in a time of globalization, and the vicissitudes of family and society in the postmodern era. As with their predecessors, the later novels show rather than tell. Characters come to life as they inhabit worlds that are recognizable and believable even to those who have not experienced them.

Martín Gaite's last novels have charted new territory in both content and structure. *Caperucita en Manhattan* introduced the genre of young adult fiction to Spain. This novel about a brave young American girl and her marvelous mentor—the author's last foray into the genre of the fantastic—became her most translated, inspiring readers around the world. *Caperucita* also paved the way for the novels to come, as it enabled a return to fiction writing after an absence that threatened to go on indefinitely. *Nubosidad variable*, the second-most-studied work in the Martín Gaite novel canon, renovated the epistolary form. This novel evinced tenets of third-wave feminism through portraits of two fascinating middle-aged Spanish women during the country's frenetic post-Transition era. *La Reina de las Nieves* combined a collage structure with a fairy-tale hypotext and tropes of detective fiction to explore Spain's "lost generation," victims of heroin and AIDS during the hedonistic years of the transition to democracy. *Lo raro es vivir* delivered a Proustian memoir of a mother-daughter love, loss and reconciliation from beyond the grave; at the same time, it explored existential doubts in a time of political unease, as fascism resurfaced in Spain at the end of the twentieth century. *Irse de casa* offered a tapestry of interrelated stories united by a triumphant professional woman's return to the provincial Spanish town of her youth—the same provincial city that was the backdrop for the author's first novel, set in the 1950s. Lastly, *Los parentescos* offered a gripping story of the development of a gifted young man, a Spanish millennial, who tries to uncover the secrets of his fractured family.

In all of Martín Gaite's novels of the 1990s, characters work through issues of present-day identity by sorting through memories of the past. As she wrote in an essay at the beginning of the decade, memory was for her the fundamental basis of art:

> No en vano los griegos consideraban a la memoria, Mnemósyne, como madre de todas las musas y opinaban, con razón, que nada puede aflorar al exterior en forma de obra de arte si no ha sido trabajado e hilado cuidadosamente en el interior caótico del individuo.

> [Not in vain did the Greeks regard memory, Mnemosyne, as the mother of all the muses. They rightly believed that nothing can flourish externally, in the form of a work of art, unless it has been reworked and carefully stitched together internally, within the individual's chaotic psyche.] ("Memoria y memorias" [Memory and memories] 291)

In an interview with Margarita Rivière published near the end of her career, Martín Gaite further explained that "el hilo de todo lo que he escrito es la memoria, el deseo de encontrar cada cual su propia coherencia de memoria y olvido: entender cada uno donde está. Eso es muy difícil." [The unifying thread in everything I have written is memory—the desire of each person to find a balance between memory and forgetting, to understand where he or she is now. That is very difficult] (qtd. in Rivière 191). The reconciliation of memory with identity had personal resonance for Martín Gaite in the 1990s. It helped salve the greatest trauma of her life: the loss of her daughter Marta Sánchez Martín in 1985, a victim of the scourges that decimated her generation. All of Martín Gaite's later novels are rooted in her own experience, and five of the six address her country's past and present. Together, these novels vanquish ghosts from the past using the tools of memory, language, and writing, as José Colmeiro observed for *El cuarto de atrás* (69). They do so in order to advance confidently into the future.

The preoccupation with memory and identity that weaves through the later novels was not unique to Martín Gaite, though she executed it in singular ways. This concern situated her in the mainstream of Spanish literature, and especially literature by women. Carmen de Urioste's study of female authors in Spain who came to prominence in the 1990s found that memory and/or identity are central to their works:

> The works of most of the women writers of the 1990s possess two intertwined characteristics: memory as a driving force and the search for a new identity. Moreover, the act of writing, whether in the form of letter or diaries, plays an indispensable role in many of these novels as a way of providing a coherent explanation of the protagonists' world. (286–287)

Evidence for this conclusion comes from an analysis of twenty-three novels and several short story collections by Spanish women authors in the 1990s, with tables summarizing key elements.[1] Under the heading "Narration Categories," Urioste demonstrated that fourteen of the twenty-three novels analyzed feature memory, identity, or both (295). Although there is no similarly comprehensive comparative study, many novels by Spanish male authors at the end of the twentieth century also were fixated on memory and identity. This preoccupation illustrates that in the 1990s, as before, Martín Gaite was connected to the cultural zeitgeist even as she helped shape it.

Martín Gaite's later novels were embraced by huge numbers of readers when they appeared, beginning with her novel for all ages, *Caperucita* (published by Siruela). Recalling the success of her last completed novels for adult readers, all published by his firm Anagrama, Jorge Herralde revealed that they achieved a level of readership that would be unimaginable today: "Cuando empezamos a publicar a Carmen Martín Gaite, de sus cuatro últimas novelas vendimos más de 100.000 ejemplares, una cifra que hoy puede obtener *Las sombras de Gray*, pero no busques algo parecido en buena literatura" [When we began to publish Carmen Martín Gaite, we published more than 100,000 copies of her last four novels, a figure that today might be achieved by *Fifty Shades of Gray*, but don't look for anything similar in the realm of good literature] (qtd. by Alejandro Luque). As José Jurado Morales has noted, is difficult to say with certainty why Martín Gaite's novels would be read by so many people, including after her death. Nevertheless, he and I agree that this can be explained by the enjoyment they bring: "el placer estético que proporciona la lectura de sus obras" [the aesthetic pleasure afforded by reading her works] (*Trayectoria* 453). Such reading pleasure

reflects the author's own joy in writing, a vocation which for her was insepara-
ble from living. The final line of a book dedication written at the start of her most
prolific era encapsulates Martín Gaite's sense of the unity of life and literature.[2]
Signed with a "C" for Calila in May 1990, these words are a fitting ending to this
study of the novels of the last decade of her life: "Mientras siga la vida, sigamos
con el cuento" [As long as life goes on, we'll go on with the story].

Notes

INTRODUCTION

1. The gift of intimacy associated with the name Calila—which her daughter bestowed when she was learning to talk—was a milestone for those who cared for her. It always followed a period of using "Carmen" or, more familiarly, "Carmiña" (the Galician diminutive used by family members, childhood friends, and close acquaintances). A year after we met she still signed her letters "Carmen," even though they contained warm sentiments: "A veces me he acordado de ti. De la rapidez con que nos hicimos amigas. Y siempre con enorme simpatía." [At times I've thought about you. About and how quickly we became friends. And always with great affection] (Letter to Brown, Madrid, 29 August 1977). Not until the summer of 1978, following a wonderful visit, did she end a letter: "Te echo mucho de menos. Un abrazo, Calila" [I miss you a lot. Sending a hug, Calila] (Letter to Brown, Madrid, 29 August 1978). The author's published letters to friend and author Juan Benet trace a similar, though much faster, trajectory. She signed her first three letters to him as Carmiña, not introducing the name Calila until the fourth one (*Correspondencia* 31–44). Fittingly, in her personal notebooks she always referred to herself as Calila, as in "Ánimo, Calila" [You can do it, Calila] (*Cuadernos* 496).

2. Earlier versions of portions of chapter 2 were published as "Carmen Martín Gaite's *Caperucita en Manhattan*: Rescuing Red Riding Hood," *Hispania*, vol. 100, no. 2, 2017, pp. 202–212. Parts of an earlier version of chapter 3 appeared as "*Nubosidad variable*: Postmodern Feminism in Post-Transition Spain," *Hispanófila*, vol. 183, 2018, pp. 301–316.

CHAPTER 1 — BACKSTORY

1. Biographical information in this chapter comes from published and unpublished sources. The only formal autobiography that Martín Gaite produced was the "Bosquejo autobiográfico," or "Autobiographical Sketch," that she wrote for my first book, *Secrets from the Back Room: The Fiction of Carmen Martín Gaite* (1987), republished with a new English translation in my edited volume *Approaches to Teaching the Works of Carmen Martín Gaite* (2013). Martín Gaite wrote a generational memoir entitled *Esperando el porvenir* [Waiting for the future], published in 1994, in which she discussed her development

as a young writer in Franco's Spain. She also conveyed autobiographical information in her posthumously published notebook excerpts (*Cuadernos de todo*), in some of her essays, and in interviews. As of this writing there is no comprehensive biography of Carmen Martín Gaite, but a number of introductory book chapters present fundamental information. One such chapter is José Teruel's opening essay ("Introducción" [Introduction]) in the first volume of Martín Gaite's *Obras completas* [Complete works], which traces her development. The MLA volume *Approaches* also begins with a biographical introduction to the author in the context of contemporary Spanish history (Brown "Introduction"), as does my chapter on Martín Gaite in *Women Writers of Contemporary Spain* ("Reaffirming"). A schematic biography by Teruel appears on the website of the Carmen Martín Gaite Archive under the heading "Biografía" [Biography].

Unpublished information that informs this chapter includes the many conversations we had over the years. It also includes a recently rediscovered biographical interview conducted in Madrid on 6 August 1978. This was the interview that I had planned to use as the basis for the first chapter of *Secrets*, which instead became an English version of Martín Gaite's "Autobiographical Sketch" (the original Spanish appeared as an appendix). All references to "Interview" here refer to this one.

2. Although her house was demolished in the 1970s, that address and the building next door now house one of the locations of the Centro Documental de la Memoria Histórica [Documentary Museum of Historical Memory] created in 2007. A large statue of the author graces the park on the Plaza de los Bandos where she played as a girl.

3. Martín Gaite viewed these two summer experiences as so decisive that she began taking notes for a book entitled *Coimbra, Cannes y lo que creció en medio* [Coimbra, Cannes and what sprouted in their midst] (Interview). When she went to Coimbra, she said, "yo fui más inguenua" [I was more innocent], whereas by the time she went to Cannes "me consideraba más adulta" [I saw myself as more grown up] (Interview).

4. This group also became known as "la generación de los cincuenta" [the fifties generation]. The 1950s are when most of the "niños de la guerra" or "children of the war" began to publish, having been born in the mid-1920s.

5. In an essay on the relationship between literature and politics novelist Juan Goytisolo—who formed part of the Barcelona contingent (and later the exiled contingent) of resistant writers—observed that censorship under Franco resulted in a type of testimonial literature not found elsewhere:

> La censura ha actuado de modo involuntario como catalizador. Mientras los novelistas franceses, pongamos por caso, escriben sus libros independientemente de la panorámica social en que les ha tocado vivir . . . los novelistas españoles—por el hecho de que su público no dispone de medios de información veraces respecto a los problemas con que se enfrenta el país—responden a esta carencia de sus lectores trazando un cuadro lo más justo y equitativo posible de la realidad que contemplan. De este modo la novela cumple en España una función testimonial que en Francia y los demás países de Europa corresponde a la prensa . . .

> [Censorship has unintentionally served as a catalyst. While French novelists, to give one example, write their books independent from the surrounding social landscape in which they find themselves . . . Spanish novelists—because their readers do not have accurate sources of information about the problems facing their country—respond to their readers' privation by painting the most truthful and objective portraits possible

of the reality they see. In this way the novel in Spain fulfills a testimonial role that in France and other European countries is carried out by the press . . .] ("La literatura perseguida por la política" [Literature pursued by politics], *El furgón de cola* [The caboose] 68-69)

6. There were only six issues of *Revista española*; the first was published in 1953 and the last one came out in 1954. José Jurado Morales's magisterial study of the journal, *Las razones éticas del realismo: Revista Española (1953-1954) en la literatura del medio siglo* [The ethical basis of realism: *Spanish Journal* (1953-1954) and midcentury literature] (2012), explains its genesis and demonstrates how it shaped Spanish realism at midcentury.

7. As Janet Winecoff Díaz explained in her 1968 essay "Luis Martín-Santos and the Contemporary Spanish Novel," *Tiempo de silencio* had the good fortune to be translated soon after its publication. Appearing to rapturous reviews in 1964 in France and Holland, it subsequently achieved fame in Spain—beyond the small group of writers and intellectuals who had appreciated it when it first appeared. Martín Gaite was among that group. Martín-Santos also appreciated *Ritmo lento*: "creo que es la persona que más encendidamente me ha hablado nunca de ella" [I think that he is the person who spoke more enthusiastically about the novel than anyone else before or since], the author recalled in a 1975 note to the third edition of this novel ("Nota a la tercera edición" [Note to the third edition]). So similar did the two think their novels that they jokingly conflated the titles:

Dimos en llamarlas de broma "Ritmo de silencio" y "Tiempo lento", porque él les atribuía ciertas afinidades y les auguraba una significación y una suerte paralelas, cosa en la que—como es patente—se equivocó. Pero ahora, al cabo de los años, creo que en aquellas afinidades que creyó descubrir no andaba tan descaminado. Prescindiendo de todo juicio valorativo, nuestras novelas del año 62 supusieron las primeras reacciones contra el "realismo" imperante en la novela española de postguerra, dos intentos aislados por volver a centrar el relato en el análisis psicológico de un personaje, yo influida por Svevo, él por Joyce.

[We jokingly took to calling them "Rhythm of Silence" and "A Slower Time," because he attributed certain similarities to them and predicted that they would have the same significance and fate—something about which he obviously was wrong. But now, after all these years, I think that he was not mistaken about the resemblances he saw. Putting aside any type of value judgment, our 1962 novels represented the first reactions against the "realism" that dominated the Spanish postwar novel. They were two isolated attempts to refocus the story on the psychological analysis of a character, my influence being Svevo and his, Joyce.] ("Nota a la tercera edición" [Note to the third edition])

8. In a speech launching the publication of *Retahílas* in May 1974 she described how the novel made its way into her historical notebooks as she worked in various archives, forcing her to draw a line under her research notes to insert the "irrupciones inesperadas" [unexpected eruptions] of this other project. The posthumously published version of this talk, which is not identical to the manuscript given to me by the author and cited in *Secrets*, includes this description ("Para la publicación de *Retahílas*" [For the publication of *Retahílas*] 1061).

9. Dozens of these book reviews have been reprinted in the final volume of the author's *Obras completas* (vol. 7, 2019), under the heading "Artículos [Articles] (1949-2000)." *Diario*

16 was a liberal-centrist daily newspaper published in Madrid from 1976 to 2001. It was relaunched as a digital publication in December 2016 (diario16.com).

CHAPTER 2 — *CAPERUCITA EN MANHATTAN*

1. The first time she left off fiction writing was in 1962, after the publication of her novel *Ritmo lento*; her next novel, *Retahílas*, was published in 1974.

2. As part of her preparation for the Yale conference Martín Gaite worked to bring her spoken English up to the level of her written skills, which were already proficient (her Spanish translation of Virginia Woolf's *To the Lighthouse* had been published by Edhasa in 1978). She wrote in November of 1978 that English classes helped cheer her up, as she had just lost her father (in October) and her mother was very ill (she would pass away in December):

> Me he puesto a dar clase alterna con una profesora para refrescar mi inglés que—sobre todo en lo que a conversación ser refiere—lo tengo muy verde. No quiero hacer mal papel entre tus paisanos. Y además, este pretexto de estudiar inglés me ha sacado de mi actual desánimo. Es lo único que hago con un poco de gana.

> [I've started reciprocal lessons with a (female) teacher to refresh my English which, especially when it comes to conversation, is pretty rusty. I don't want to do a bad job of it with your American colleagues. And also, this excuse to practice English has taken me out of my current malaise. It's the only thing I look forward to doing.] (Letter to Brown, Madrid, 6 November 1978)

3. The main character of the 1499 dialogue-drama *Tragicomedia de Calixto y Melibea* [Tragicomedy of Calisto and Melibea] by Fernando de Rojas, universally known as *La Celestina*, is a "trotaconventos" or "procuress" and brothel owner. She is also something of a sorceress who makes and sells potions. In the play Celestina acts as a go-between for the nobleman Calisto (or Calixto in old Spanish) and his love object Melibea. The epigraph for the second part of *Caperucita* is a quote from the play: "A quien dices tu secreto, das tu libertad" [To whomever you tell your secret, you give your freedom]. In chapter 10 of part two, Miss Lunatic tells Sara the same thing, stressing "nunca lo olvides" [Don't ever forget it] (151). As Isabel Roger has pointed out, the association between Celestina and Miss Lunatic does not extend to their philosophies: "La experiencia de Miss Lunatic no está dominada por la astucia y la codicia que mueven a la acción en *La Celestina*, sino precisamente por todo lo contrario" [Miss Lunatic's experience is not shaped by the cunning and greed that animate the plot in *La Celstina*, but rather by precisely the opposite] (329–330).

4. Nearly half of these studies focus on the novel's revision of Perrault's fairy tale, notably those of Beckett, Jurado Morales in *Trayectoria*, and Soliño. New York City is the only other topic that has elicited more than a single critical response, with especially insightful analyses by Jurado Morales in *Trayectoria*, Ribeiro de Menezes, and Elisabetta Sarmatti.

5. The major exception to the dearth of prizes for young adult fiction is the pioneering Premio Edebé de Literatura Juvenil [Edebé Prize for Young Adult Literature], launched in 1993 with Carlos Ruiz Zafón's *El Príncipe de la Niebla* [*The Prince of Mist* 2010].

6. These included prizes that now detached young adult fiction from children's books, as well as new prizes for YA fiction. An example of a literary prize that began to distinguish between children and young adults is the Premio Juvenil Everest [Everest Prize

for Young Adult Fiction]. It was established in 2009, thirteen years after it was created for combined "literatura infantil y juvenil" [literature for children and young adults]. An example of a literary prize established for young adult fiction is the Premio "La Caixa" / Plataforma Novela Juvenil ["La Caixa" / Plataforma Prize for the Young Adult Novel], inaugurated in 2010.

7. Most of the bestsellers for young adults in Spain today are translations of already successful English-language YA books. The most heralded Spanish YA author uses an English pseudonym, Blue Jeans (*Libros más vendidos*). Other successful contemporary Spanish YA writers include Maite Carranza, Laura Gallego, David Lozano Garbala, Fernando Marías, Chris Pueyo, Esther Sanz, and Carlos Ruiz Zafón, along with so-called Youtubers who parlay their Internet presence into books, such as the one who uses the name Dallas Review (*El cultural*).

8. Of the three works, *Caperucita en Manhattan* is the only one that has given rise to a published linguistic analysis: a study by Ángela Arce Castillo of the modalities that serve to express subjectivity and involve the reader as an active participant.

9. Martín Gaite explained in a speech on 20 June 1978 at the Barcelona publication party for *El cuarto de atrás*: "Siempre he pensado que el que no se divierte escribiendo difícilmente conseguirá divertir a los demás" [I've always thought that if you don't take pleasure in writing, you will be hard pressed to bring pleasure to others] (Untitled).

10. Morales Ladrón carried out a comparative study of Martín Gaite's rendering of the Red Riding Hood story with that of Angela Carter ("The Company of Wolves") in *The Bloody Chamber and Other Stories*. She concluded that only Martín Gaite's version of Red Riding Hood challenges patriarchal values. Referring to *Caperucita*, she observed: "Esta nueva versión incorpora ideologías más acordes con la sociedad moderna y promueve la libertad y el individualismo" [This new version incorporates ideologies that are more in keeping with modern society while promoting freedom and individualism] (169).

11. As he and Sara exit the park hand-in-hand, Edgar Woolf muses: "Tenía razón Greg Monroe: por culpa del negocio, se había negado a sí mismo muchas satisfacciones. Tener un nieto debía ser una cosa muy bonita." [Greg Monroe was right when he said that his obsession with business had cost him many of life's greatest joys. It must be very lovely to have a grandchild] (169).

12. For instance, she recommends Italo Calvino's 1959 allegorical fantasy *Il cavaliere inesistente* (published in Spanish in 1961 as *El caballero inexistente* [*The Nonexistent Knight* 1962])—about a suit of armor with no knight inside—to a police commissioner, as a remedy for fear. This novella was much admired by the author. In a book review, she singled it out as the best of the three comprising *I nostri antenati* (1952–1959) that were published together in Spanish in 1977 as *Nuestros antepasados* [*Our Ancestors* 1962]. (*El caballero inexistente* subsequently was published separately by Siruela in 1998.) Martín Gaite's description of Calvino's achievement applies equally well to *Caperucita*:

La mayor innovación de Calvino reside en su capacidad de narrar lo peregrino sin afectación, ponerlo delante de nuestros ojos con la misma naturalidad y detalle con que nos transmitiría la historia de un matrimonio burgués, sin cargar nunca de reticencias simbólicas su relato, sino aligerándolo por medio del humor. Nos creemos todas las extrañas peripecias que van aconteciendo, por lindando que estén con lo irreal.

[Calvino's greatest innovation lies in his ability to narrate strange things matter-of-factly, presenting them with the same naturalness and detail as he would use to describe a bourgeois married couple. He never weighs down the story with overt criticism, but rather lightens it through humor. We accept all of the strange incidents as they happen, no matter how close they come to being unbelievable.] ("Los confines" 141)

13. Spelling errors in English have been corrected in the version that appears in the second volume of the *Obras completas*; for example, "Lexinghton Avenue" has been changed to "Lexington." The errors discussed here remain.

14. Kahlo's painting *El suicidio de Dorothy Hale* [The suicide of Dorothy Hale] immortalized the 1938 demise of the society woman who jumped to her death from a high floor.

15. One occasion when the author actually played the role of *hada* or magical fairy godmother was a Halloween party in the United States. She dressed as a bad witch with stars on her hat who, with the removal of outer garments, transformed into a good witch holding a wand. Each guest at the party had to read a fragment of poetry or prose, and she invented her own amusing poem which she described as "algo 'esproncediano'" [somewhat in the style of (nineteenth-century Spanish Romantic poet José de) Espronceda]. The final verses of the poem, which she copied into a letter in progress, presage Miss Lunatic's philosophy in *Caperucita*:

Salga la luna y la tormenta ruja
y vuelvan la alegría y la alborada
y cese ya el vaivén que nos empuja
a acatar una vida programada
donde jamás la bruja
podrá atreverse a convertirse en hada.

[Let the moon come out and the storm pour down
bringing the return of joy and a new dawn,
ending the uncertainties that push us
to conform to a preprogrammed life
where the witch would never
dare transform into a fairy godmother.]
(Letter to Brown, Charlottesville, 30 October 1982)

CHAPTER 3 — *NUBOSIDAD VARIABLE*

1. The English translation omits the collage (signed "CMG 91") but features an original full-page pen-and-ink drawing by the author, signed "CMG 97." This sketch depicts a window framed by long curtains, through which the viewer sees clouds, letters and envelopes, the protagonists' names, and the Spanish and English titles of the book: *Nubosidad variable* and *Variable Cloud* (a British weather descriptor that in American English would be rendered as "variably cloudy").

2. For her fiction Martín Gaite always listed the dates of composition on the work's final page, along with the locales where she began and finished it. For her nonfiction she was less consistent, sometimes identifying publication dates individually and sometimes noting the place and date where she finished a book.

3. José Teruel has asserted that the novel's two main characters are both autobiographical, forming a composite of the author herself ("Ficción"), and María-José Blanco has echoed this interpretation, stating that "the two characters gradually merge into one which is Carmen Martín Gaite the writer" (*Life Writing* 135). Each main character does enact some of Martín Gaite's personal experiences, as Teruel observes. Nevertheless, this

interpretation minimizes the art involved in crafting each singular protagonist, while overlooking a key source of inspiration for the character of Mariana (a physician friend of the author's).

4. The notion of someone who maintains another's memory was introduced in an essay discussed here in another context: "Las mujeres liberadas" [Liberated women]. In it Martín Gaite described the fervent desire of women, especially those who are over thirty, to leave a trace of themselves in another person: "El anhelo de perdurar en otro, ese contar con que alguien guarda nuestra imagen con todas sus contradicciones y quebraduras . . . no es, en definitiva, sino un prurito de coherencia y continuidad . . ." [The wish to live on in another person, to know that someone maintains our image with all its contradictions and inconsistencies . . . certainly reflects a yearning for coherence and continuity . . .] ("Las mujeres" in *Búsqueda* 102).

5. The fact that the authors of these novels were attuned to commercial interests, responding to market forces that propelled them to fame and reluctant to critique patriarchal social norms, has led at least one critic, Catherine Bellver, to distinguish novels of the 1990s as a separate phase in the development of the Spanish feminist novel (39).

6. Insertion of real names in her fiction was an occasional practice that dates back to the author's first novel, *Entre visillos*: Natalia or Tali Guilarte was a friend and classmate of Martin Gaite's at the University of Salamanca who hailed from Valladolid; the two girls' families were close and often visited one another. Along with the young heroine of *Caperucita* and the publisher in *Nubosidad variable*, other characters in the later novels who are named after cherished friends include Emilio Williams in *La Reina de las Nieves* and Pablo Sorozábal in *Irse de casa*.

7. As the author shared with Benet, their correspondence spurred her to delve more deeply into ideas that surfaced in her letters, and to explore them in her personal notebooks:

A mí el escribirte me sirve de aliciente para explayar luego a solas las mismas cosas que con motivo de la carta se me han venido someramente a las mientes. Antes de iniciar esta correspondencia había dejado de escribir casi absolutamente en mis «cuadernos de todo» y ahora en cambio, sobre todo los días que siguen a la carta que te escribo, anoto muchas cosas.

[For me, writing to you is an incentive to delve into the same ideas that surfaced in the letter afterwards, when I am alone. Before beginning this correspondence I had almost completely left off writing in my "notebooks about everything" but now I jot down a number of things, especially in the days after writing to you.] (*Correspondencia* 99)

8. *Usos amorosos de la postguerra española* was written between 1984 and 1986, and the essays in *Desde la ventana* that are dated are from 1986 and 1987; both books were published in 1987. As Janet Pérez observed, the cultural information in *Usos amorosos de la postguerra española* complements the protagonists' narratives in *Nubosidad variable*, and the "fruits" of the author's literary investigation in *Desde la ventana* are evident in the novel ("*Nubosidad variable*" 301).

9. The Bustamante interview appeared in the women's section of *Madrid*, a daily newspaper published from 8 April 1939 to 25 November 1971, when Franco's government—dissatisfied with its increasingly independent stance—shut it down. The copy in my possession was given to me by the author.

10. Three of Martín Gaite's eleven novels have male leads. Male characters narrate her third novel, *Ritmo lento* (1963), and her final, unfinished novel, *Los parentescos* (2001); her eighth novel, *La Reina de las Nieves* (1994), has a male protagonist and features extensive excerpts from his journals.

11. Well-known examples of Spanish women writers who refused to be identified as "feminist" include Rosa Chacel (1898–1994), Federica Montseny (1905–1994), and María Zambrano (1904–1991). Roberta Johnson has ventured an explanation that foreshadows Martín Gaite's repudiation of the term: "In many cases one suspects that in rejecting the feminist label women writers wish to avoid the kinds of ridicule leveled at feminists, who were caricatured from the earliest years of the century forward in the popular press and in novels" ("Issues" 247).

12. This special issue of *Triunfo* appeared on 24 April 1971. The magazine was published between 1962 and 1982; issues have now been digitized and made available online by the University of Salamanca. "Las mujeres liberadas" was reprinted in 1972 in Martín Gaite's essay collection *La búsqueda de interlocutor y otras búsquedas*.

13. In "The Feminism of an Anti-Feminist" María-José Blanco extracted the author's comments about feminism over time from personal notebooks excerpted in the posthumously published volume *Cuadernos de todo*. This compilation is useful despite some of the essay's controversial conclusions (such as the assertion that Martín Gaite "extols the virtues of home life and housework for women" [52]).

14. The first text that inspired her was Virginia Woolf's *A Room of One's Own*, which she read avidly in New York in 1980 while she was a visiting professor at Barnard College. This initial interest was further developed at Vassar College in 1985. North American colleagues suggested feminist readings of the day, including Judith Fetterley's *The Resisting Reader*, Sandra Gilbert and Susan Gubar's *The Madwoman in the Attic*, Adrienne Rich's "When We Dead Awaken: Writing as Re-vision," and Elaine Showalter's *Feminist Criticism in the Wilderness* (Martín Gaite, *Desde la ventana* 25–32).

15. Mario Conde was released after ten years for good behavior, but in 2016 he went to prison again for financial malfeasance—released after several months when two officials of the Fundación Francisco Franco [Francisco Franco Foundation] put up a 300,000 euro bond. In 2018 his name surfaced at the top of the government's published list of debtors, with nearly 15 million euros owed.

16. Butler's theory of gender performativity was applied to the female protagonists in four of Martín Gaite's short stories, two from the 1950s and two from the early 1970s, by Ángeles Encinar, who concluded that the stories demonstrate the author's "feminismo anticipado" [anticipatory feminism] ("Cuentos").

CHAPTER 4 — *LA REINA DE LAS NIEVES*

1. In a 1989 interview, Martín Gaite recounted: "Cuando vine de Chicago en diciembre mi hija ya estaba enferma; murió en abril del año 85" [When I came back from Chicago in December my daughter was already sick; she died in April of '85] (Interview with Calvi 171). In 2004 the father of Marta's boyfriend Carlos, a psychiatrist whose son was his namesake, described both of them as well as their heroin use and its consequences—his son died from AIDS-related complications one year later—in the second volume of his memoirs (Castilla del Pino).

2. In 1987 Martín Gaite published *Usos amorosos de la postguerra española* (*Courtship Customs in Postwar Spain*, 2004) and *Desde la ventana: Enfoque femenino de la literatura española.*

3. The mini-series *Celia* aired on La 1 or Channel One of public television; in 2009 all six episodes were made available by RadioTelevisión Española (RTVE) on its website.

4. The Transition began with Franco's demise, ending the dictatorship installed after the Spanish Civil War of 1936–1939. Although different end dates have been proposed, Spain's transition to democracy is generally thought to have concluded when the previously outlawed PSOE came into office following national elections in 1982. Salient political issues of the Transition, rooted in competing ideologies—from communist to fascist—include regional autonomy or nationality versus national unity, amnesty versus justice for war crimes, amnesia versus recovery of historical memory, national insularity versus internationalization, and reformation of existing institutions versus a clean break with the past. Contemporary reexaminations of the Transition include Santos Juliá's comprehensive volume *Transición: Historia de una política española (1937–2017)* [Transition: History of a Spanish policy (1937–2017)], *La Transición contada a nuestros padres: Nocturno de la democracia española* by Juan Carlos Monedero [The Transition as told to our parents: Night of Spanish democracy] and *La Transición sangrienta: Una historia violenta del proceso democrático en España (1975–1983)* [The bloody Transition: A violent history of the democratic process in Spain (1975–1983)] by Mariano Sánchez Soler. Although it is not devoted specifically to the Transition, Paul Preston's *A People Betrayed: A History of Corruption, Political Incompetence and Social Division in Modern Spain* contextualizes the period, reaching back to 1876 and extending to 2018.

5. Depictions of La Movida in all the author's novels are analyzed by Nuria Cruz-Cámara in *El laberinto intertextual* [The intertextual labyrinth]. The movement's presence in *La Reina de las Nieves* is discussed in chapter 5, and chapter 4 explores its treatment in Martín Gaite's next two novels: *Lo raro es vivir* (1996) and *Irse de casa* (1998).

6. This would ultimately be seen as part of the Transition's emphasis on *reforma* [reform] over *ruptura* [rupture] after Franco (detailed by Victoria Prego 215). Adolfo Suárez came to symbolize disenchantment. Widely viewed as incapable of ushering in a different future, he submitted his resignation on 26 January 1981 (Juliá 536–537).

7. One painting in particular, Caspar David Friedrich's nineteenth-century *Wanderer above the Fog*, is described in detail. As Cruz-Cámara has shown, this example of ekphrasis or description of a work of art in literature has special importance in the novel as an emblem of Romanticism ("Re-creación"). Martín Gaite herself referred to Friedrich in a talk about the Romantic hero, delivered in Barcelona in 2000: "Ese hombre, en las pinturas de Friedrich, por ejemplo suele contemplar de espaldas, con ademán desolado y estático aquello que no abarca ni penetra" [This man, for example in Friedrich's paintings, is usually seen from behind, contemplating with quiet desolation that which he can neither encompass nor penetrate] ("Los amores malditos" [Doomed loves] 313). It is likely that Martín Gaite got to know *Wanderer above the Fog* in 1990 when she gave a series of lectures in Germany, spending nearly a month there (Letter to Brown, Madrid, 18 April 1990).

8. Martín Gaite created occasional collages for her own enjoyment, sharing some with friends and publishing two during her lifetime: a small image on the cover of *Nubosidad variable* (1992) and a larger self-portrait on the dust jacket of the essay collection

Agua pasada (1993). Her only published assemblage of collages is the posthumous volume *Visión de Nueva York* (2005), chronicling the semester she spent as visiting professor at Barnard College in the fall of 1980. Her self-portrait collage (figure 3.1) was added to her New York collages to become the first entry in that volume.

9. The translation by Margaret Jull Costa, who also translated *Nubosidad variable* into (British) English, retitles the novel *The Farewell Angel*. This title is a reference to a drawing that is introduced late in the work. The lovely and well-read Mónica sketches the silhouette of an angel reading a book and labels the image (in English) "The farewell angel." Mónica gives the drawing to Leonardo, telling him: "Parece como si cayeras del cielo" (213) ["It's almost as if heaven sent you" 192].

10. The two children's novels are the author's *El castillo de las tres murallas* and *El pastel del diablo*.

11. O'Leary and Ribeiro de Menezes are the sole critics to have recognized that the novel evokes or "recalls" conventions of the detective genre (144). However, they reject this classification because they consider that "*Reina* is not a detective novel in the strict sense of the term" (147), a determination that I believe is refuted by the theorists cited here.

12. The other two categories in Roth's taxonomy are the "hard-boiled detective novel" and the "spy thriller."

13. Marta and I met in 1976. She was my sister's age—I was four years older—and we instantly bonded. She and I were the same size and whenever I visited she insisted on lending me whatever items of clothing I had neglected to bring, starting with a swimsuit for the pool at El Boalo when I first went there. In turn, I helped locate American books for her research, back in the days before online book sales. Marta introduced me to friends who came to the apartment at Calle del Doctor Esquerdo 43 when I was visiting, always offering to include me in their outings. Though we sent regards back and forth, I did not see Marta after she moved out in the spring of 1983. I was aware that Marta had moved back in the spring of 1985 and that she was ill. But I was stunned by the news of her passing. After her death, her mother opened Marta's closet and asked me to take as much as I wanted of her clothing—orphaned objects, like the ones mentioned near the end of *Reina*.

14. In Martín Gaite's 1960 novella *Las ataduras* the young protagonist Alina talks with a wise grandparent—in this case her grandfather—about family ties. "Las verdaderas ataduras son las que uno escoge," he tells her, "las que se busca y se pone uno solo, pudiendo no tenerlas" [The real ties are the ones you choose, the ones you seek out and assume of your own volition, being free not to have them] (117).

15. The dedication reads: "Y en memoria de mi hija, por el entusiasmo con que alentaba semejante colaboración [con Hans Christian Andersen]" (8) ["And in memory of my daughter, for the enthusiasm with which she encouraged that collaboration (with Hans Christian Andersen)" n.p.].

CHAPTER 5 — *LO RARO ES VIVIR*

1. In a journal entry from 1974, Martín Gaite included "Vidal y Villalba y otros cuentos del archivo" [Vidal y Villalba and other stories from the archive] on a list of possible future projects (*Cuadernos* 287). Another journal entry, from 1976, begins: "Tengo que volver al Archivo Histórico Nacional . . ." [I must return to the National Historical Archive . . .], recalling that she has a number of projects dispersed among her notebooks, including one about "un aventurero del XVIII y su criado" [an eighteenth-century adven-

turer and his manservant], concluding that there remains "todo un mundo en el que debería ahondar" [an entire world that I should delve into] (*Cuadernos* 367). In January 1977, while riding on a train, she vividly recalled a scene involving Vidal y Villalba, telling herself that she could write his life as a fantastic tale: "historia abierta, enigmática" [an open, enigmatic story] (*Cuadernos* 401).

2. Martín Gaite knew this concept, and Natalia Ginzburg's oeuvre, very well. She translated two of Ginzburg's novels into Spanish, including her 1963 novel *Lessico Famigliare* [*Family Sayings*]. For Martín Gaite, a family lexicon symbolized cohesion; when this shared language is lost, so are interpersonal connections. In *Nubosidad variable* Martín Gaite cited Ginzburg's expression in the text, with an example shared by Sofía and her husband (18).

3. Proustian elements in Martín Gaite's fiction have been analyzed in two of her works, *Retahílas* and *El cuarto de atrás*, by Claudia Jacobi, with emphasis on the concepts of memory and death in those novels and in Proust's *À la recherche du temps perdu*.

4. Jeannette Pucheu explored homes as palimpsests in several novels by the author, concluding that "the message the Martín Gaite conveys in *Lo raro es vivir* is the fact that one cannot construct a genuine home without a strong foundation of memories" (129).

5. Martín Gaite's pride in autochthonous Spanish culture was especially evident in the area of cuisine. In one of the cultural passages about Spain in our textbook *Conversaciones creadoras*, she wrote: "Algunos jóvenes prefieren comidas al estilo americano en lugares como Burger King y McDonald's. Pero aún predominan los que siguen eligiendo «pinchos», «tapas» o «guisos» de tipo español. Los locales especializados en bocadillos también tienen gran demanda" [Some young people choose to eat American-style meals in places such as Burger King or McDonald's, but the majority still prefer traditional Spanish "skewers," "tapas," or "stews." Places that specialize in *bocadillos* (sandwiches on long loaves of bread) are also very popular] (96).

6. This information was transmitted by the author, who also hummed the saying to my son and daughter when each was young, drawing out the accented syllable in each line so that it sounded soothing: "No te pre-o-CU-pes / que hay un pas-a-DIZ-o" [Don't you WORRY, there's a WAY out].

7. The original title of this book when it appeared in 1970 was *Macanaz, otro paciente de la Inquisición* [Macanaz, another victim of the Inquisition]. In 1988 the book's title was changed to *El proceso de Macanaz: Historia de un empapelamiento* [Macanaz's trial: A convoluted history]. She immersed herself completely in the project, as described in 1978:

Las veces que me he dedicado a la investigación histórica me lo he planteado como una pesquisa novelesca o policíaca. "El proceso de Macanaz" fue una obra que me costó siete años. Estuve todo ese tiempo tratando de enterarme de lo que le había sucedido a aquel viejo y rodando por archivos. . . . De alguna manera alimenté una pasión absolutamente loca. (Qtd. in Pérez Cavero iv)

[Whenever I have devoted myself to historical research, I have approached it as if it were a novelistic or detective quest. "Macanaz's Trial" was a work that took me seven years. I spent all that time trying to learn what had happened to the old man, hanging out in archives. . . . Somehow I managed to sustain this crazy passion.]

8. During one dress fitting to which I accompanied her, Jesús del Pozo observed that he was very pleased that she would be wearing his creation, because in his experience

"los intelectuales sois muy mal vestidos" [you intellectuals dress very badly], which made her laugh. The protracted ritual of having a dress made (memorably described in *El cuarto de atrás*) became therapeutic, in large part because the designer was so charming and amusing.

9. As Cruz-Cámara has elucidated:

Ritmo lento, Retahílas, El cuarto de atrás, Nubosidad variable y *La Reina de las Nieves* nos presentan personajes que no sólo rememoran, sino que a la vez van imponiendo un orden y un sentido a los acontecimientos que narran. . . . Recontándose el pasado, el personaje se descubre a sí mismo, analiza lo que ha sido y por qué ha llegado a ser lo que es. ("Un aspecto" 30)

[*Ritmo lento, Retahílas, El cuarto de atrás, Nubosidad variable*, and *La Reina de las Nieves* show us characters who not only remember the past, but go along imposing order and meaning on the events they narrate. . . . Retelling the past, characters discover themselves, analyzing what has come before and why they have become who they are.]

10. In Martín Gaite's case the lapsed dissertation had different causes, beginning with a successful career as a writer of fiction that interrupted her academic pursuits. She also had an indifferent advisor who contributed to her loss of interest in her original topic. Nevertheless, she finished her doctoral degree from the University of Madrid (begun in 1948) with honors in 1972, publishing her revised thesis that same year as the acclaimed book *Usos amorosos del dieciocho en España* (with a prizewinning English translation by Maria G. Tomsich, *Love Customs in Eighteenth-Century Spain* 1991).

CHAPTER 6 — *IRSE DE CASA*

1. Martín Gaite explained her newly elevated status in Spain to an interviewer in the year that *Irse de casa* was published:

Ahora muchos se refieren a mí "como esa escritora nueva que ha salido." Me gusta eso de que me llamen y me traten como si fuera una escritora nueva. Está bien. Me gusta eso de que en la Feria del Libro se me acerque un chico de 18 años para pedir un autó-grafo, aunque antes no sabía nada mío, pero le habían dicho que era muy *guay*. Es bonito. Es curioso que en la segunda etapa de mi producción, eso de la escritora nueva, la de *Los usos amorosos de la posguerra, Caperucita en Manhattan* o *Nubosidad varia-ble*, me ha hecho pasar de la barrera de ser reconocida a tope en el extranjero a ser leidísima aquí. (Mora)

[Now a lot of people refer to me as "that new writer who's just come out." I like it that they call me a new writer and treat me like one. That's fine. I like how at the Madrid Book Fair an eighteen-year-old boy will come up to ask for my autograph, even though he didn't know any of my work before, because he's heard that I was really cool. That's lovely. It's interesting that in the second stage of my career, that of the new writer, the author of *Los usos amorosos de la postguerra española, Caperucita en Manhattan*, or *Nubosidad variable*, I have crossed over from being constantly recognized abroad to being very widely read here.]

2. Aznar would be evicted from office in 2004, after he and his party accused the Basque separatist organization ETA of carrying out the Madrid train bombings of 11 March—a falsehood that angered the Spanish people. The attacks (ten bombs on commuter trains in and near Madrid killed nearly 200 people and injured almost 2,000) were carried out

by Islamic extremists who objected to Spain's support of the Iraq war. Socialist José Luis Rodríguez Zapatero, who before the train bombings had not been expected to win, became prime minister in 2004 and was reelected in 2008.

3. A moving recollection of Martín Gaite's generosity as a mentor is that of Marcos Giralt Torrente. He met the author when he was a boy because she was a family friend (he is the grandson of author Gonzalo Torrente Ballester). As an adult he was able to forge his own relationship with her:

> Cuando . . . empecé a escribir y a querer convertirme en escritor, me distinguió con el tesoro de su infatigable estímulo. Me recomendó lecturas, leyó y comentó mis manuscritos, me compró ordenadores cuando yo no podía comprarlos y puso su tiempo a mi disposición siempre que lo necesité. ("Prólogo" 9–10)

> [When . . . I began to write and to try to become an author, she honored me with the gift of her tireless encouragement. She recommended readings, read and commented on my manuscripts, bought me computers when I could not afford them, and always made herself available whenever I needed her.]

4. This narrative device, usually involving a prologue or prelude and an epilogue, was first employed in *Ritmo lento* and next appeared in *Retahílas*. In *El cuarto de atrás*, the first and last (seventh) chapters bracket the central portion of the novel.

5. Martín Gaite's cinematic technique originated in her first novel, *Entre visillos* (Brown, *Secrets* 66–70) and was honed over the years. The author's one film screenplay was for a 1976 feature entitled *Emilia . . . parada y fonda*, loosely based on her 1958 short story "Un alto en el camino" [Stopover] (published in the anthology *Las ataduras*). She had more experience authoring scripts and adapting the works of others for stage or television. Her two original plays are the three-act drama *La hermana pequeña*, written in 1959 though not staged until 1999, and the one-act monologue *A palo seco*, written in 1985 and staged in 1987 (published in 1994 in *Cuentos completos y un monólogo*). She wrote the teleplays for three Spanish television miniseries: an eight-episode series on Santa Teresa de Jesús [Saint Teresa of Ávila] in 1982–1983, a made-for-television movie based on her 1976 novel *Fragmentos de interior* in 1984, and a six-episode series on the *Celia* novels of Elena Fortún in 1993. She also wrote the script for and starred in the 1983 documentary *Esta es mi tierra: Salamanca* [This is my land: Salamanca]. In the realm of classic drama, Martín Gaite adapted Gil Vicente's sixteenth-century *Don Duardos* for a 1979 stage production; a critical edition of her version of the play was published in 2018. She also adapted Tirso de Molina's seventeenth-century *El burlador de Sevilla* [The trickster of Seville] for performance at the Almagro festival in 1988, and developed a version of Fernando Pessoa's early twentieth-century *El marinero* [The sailor] that was staged in 1990.

6. Led by publisher Constantino Bártulo, this event, entitled "Veladas Literarias" [Literary vigils], was taped in its entirety; my copy of the video was given to me by a mutual friend. Instead of delivering a speech, Martín Gaite read chapter 2 of *Irse de casa* to a rapt audience. During a subsequent question-and-answer session, she was asked if her novelistic dialogues reflected exactly how people spoke. She answered no, that it wasn't exactly what you would hear but rather an artistic distortion of actual speech.

7. As Cruz-Cámara has observed, the city's identity is easily recognized in both of the author's novels that are set there, separated by forty years: *Entre visillos* and *Irse de casa*. In *Irse de casa*, "la misma ciudad provinciana se evoca claramente mediante dos de sus puntos de referencia emblemáticos, la Catedral y los bailes del Casino" [the same provincial

city is clearly evoked through two of its emblematic points of reference, the cathedral and dances at the Casino] ("Salamanca posmoderna" 32). Martín Gaite told me long ago that the city in her first novel was indeed Salamanca (Brown, "Nonconformist" 166).

8. Critics have succinctly outlined the progression of Martín Gaite's depictions of Salamanca in a collection of short-form essays entitled "Recuerdos de Salamanca: La ciudad en la literatura de Carmen Martín Gaite" (ed. Brown), published in the journal *Hispania*. These include Jurado Morales, "Salamanca de los años cuarenta"; Guardiola, "Salamanca censurada"; Brown, "Secretos de Salamanca"; and Cruz-Cámara, "Salamanca posmoderna."

9. For the author, as for many Spaniards at that time, the term "America" encompassed both North and South America. In another Martín Gaite work written in 1959, the novella *Las ataduras*, the protagonist Alina has a friend, Eloy, who tells her that he is going to go to America. From what he says soon after, it is clear that for him "América" means South America and specifically Buenos Aires. Later Alina expresses the same sense of wonder described by Laura in *La hermana pequeña*: "Aunque decía muchas veces la palabra 'América' y se acordaba de los dibujos del libro de Geografía, no lo podía, en realidad, comprender" [Even though I said the word "America" many times, and I recalled the illustrations in our Geography book, I could not really comprehend it] (42).

CHAPTER 7 — *LOS PARENTESCOS*

1. Martín Gaite referred this way to her series of deliveries in a letter she wrote to her friend and Anagrama publishing head Jorge Herralde in April of 1994, as she was finishing *La Reina de las Nieves*. Using a fountain pen on flower-edged stationery from Philadelphia, she wrote: "Querido Jorge, ya se ha iniciado la época de los 'paquetes bombas', que tanta marcha nos da a ti y a mí. En el de hoy te mando los capítulos XV y XVI . . ." [Dear Jorge, the time has come for the 'package bombs' that get both of us moving. In this one I'm sending chapters XV and XVI . . .] (rpt. by Seisdedos)

2. This gender façade was a common ploy at the time. As epistolary fiction became increasingly popular in the seventeenth and eighteenth centuries, the genre—associated with women writers as well as with women readers—was successfully practiced by male authors who adopted a female voice. The best-known example of this technique is Pierre Ambroise François Choderlos de Laclos's 1792 *Les liaisons dangereuses* [*Dangerous Liaisons*], the then scandalous account of a young girl's seduction by two charming but abominable aristocrats. Models for Laclos's epistolary novel in a female voice included Samuel Richardson's *Clarissa* (1748) and Jean-Jacques Rousseau's *Julie, ou La nouvelle Héloïse* [Julie, or the new Heloise] (1761) (observed by P.W.K. Stone 11).

3. Recordings of these presentations were not released. Years later, singer-songwriter and friend Amancio Prada allowed a video of Martín Gaite reciting a poem at one of his concerts at Madrid's Círculo de Bellas Artes in 1998 to be uploaded to YouTube (EdicionesCaseras). From memory, she delivers a moving rendition of her poem "No te mueras todavía" [Please don't die so soon]. Her sister would read this same poem at her funeral on 24 July 2000, as she was laid to rest in the El Boalo cemetery alongside her daughter and her parents.

4. She and I discussed young characters in her fiction as I was preparing a conference paper entitled "Neurotic Children in a Crazy World: Young Characters in the Fiction of Carmen Martín Gaite." The paper analyzed the social criticism conveyed by idealistic young nonconformists in the short stories "Tendrá que volver" [He has to come back]

and "La chica de abajo" [The girl from downstairs], as well as the novels *Entre visillos* and *Ritmo lento*. In those works, as in *Los parentescos*, children shed light on issues in the adult world.

5. Jurado Morales has singled out Stevenson's *Dr. Jekyll and Mr. Hyde* as the key intertextual referent in *Los parentescos*: "Aunque la doble personalidad queda aplicada en principio a Jacinto [el padre de Isidoro], la verdad es que todos los personajes de *Los parentescos* son en buena medida Jekyll y Hyde" [Although the concept of a split personality is originally applied to Jacinto (Isidoro's father), the truth is that all the characters in *Los parentescos* are, to a large extent, versions of Jekyll and Hyde] ("Mundo" 222). Ciplijauskaité has concurred, though without mentioning the housekeeper, Fuencisla: "Uno de los grandes temas de *Los parentescos* es la índole doble de cada ser: la abuela [112], la madre [135], el padre del amigo [186]. Baltita mismo contiene varias facetas . . ." [One of the major themes of *Los parentescos* is the dual nature of each individual: the grandmother (112), the mother (135), the friend's father (186). Baltita himself is multifaceted . . .] (135). For O'Leary and Ribeiro de Menezes, the abundance of characters "wearing various masks" points to "the message of the novel," which "would seem to be to actively seek out one's destiny and so be true to oneself—the secret of one's soul—rather than be pushed around by events and circumstances" (264).

6. The novel's lack of an ending has been deployed to great advantage as a pedagogical tool, similar to the intentionally unfinished dialogue-stories that Martín Gaite wrote for our textbook *Conversaciones creadoras* [Creative conversations]. In "Analyzing *Los parentescos* and Preparing Students for Creative Writing," Isabel Estrada explains how she uses the novel in advanced university Spanish courses to introduce students to contemporary Spanish literature as well as to the intricacies of narrative technique. Students ultimately work in groups to complete the last chapter and through it, end the novel. In this way students actualize Wolfgang Iser's theory of the reader as active participant, with the professor's guidance (179).

7. Reform of the Spanish Civil Code in May of 1975 brought new freedoms, allowing women to open a bank account, get a passport, enter into a legal contract, spend an inheritance, buy and sell merchandise not intended for household use, and hold a job—all without written permission from a father or husband. Article 62 of the Civil Code allowed women a say in where they lived, eliminating their obligation to follow their husband if he decided to relocate. Article 57 changed the legal language for marital responsibility altogether. It replaced the mandate for a man to protect and a woman to obey with the egalitarian directive: "El marido y la mujer se deben respeto y protección recíprocos, y actuarán siempre en interés de la familia" [Husband and wife owe each other mutual respect and protection, and they will always act in the best interest of the family] (qtd. by Charo Nogueira in an article on the liberation of Spanish women).

8. A helpful chart to illustrate the novel's family relationships was devised by Jurado Morales. The original version of the chart ("Mundo" 218) contained minor errors that were corrected in the authoritative version (*Juego* 220).

9. Besides indicating that Martín Gaite's editors were unfamiliar with the reference, the error whereby "Usher" is rendered as "Husserl" is evidently rooted in the fact that the Spanish pronunciation of both names sounds the same (220). This mistake in the original novel was not addressed or corrected in the version that appears in the *Obras completes* (*Novelas II*, 1499) nor in the reissued version published by Siruela (173). Edgar Allen Poe's 1839 short story "The Fall of the House of Usher" (known in Spanish as "La caída

de la Casa Usher" and also as "El hundimiento de la Casa Usher") is directly relevant to the comment made by Baltasar's brother Max about the family's now awful Segovia home (after the murder committed by their housekeeper). In Poe's horror story an unnamed narrator arrives at the mansion of his childhood friend Roderick Usher, who is ill. The narrator's twin sister Madeleine is also ill (she suffers from seizures) and apparently dies; the two men bury her in the family vault. A week later the narrator discovers that Madeleine was buried alive when she reappears in her blood-stained shroud. Madeleine and Roderick fall to the ground in each other's arms and die in agony. As the narrator rushes out, the house splits apart and sinks into a dark pool of water. In his book on fantastic literature—a book that the author knew well, as evidenced by its role in *El cuarto de atrás*—Todorov summarizes "The Fall of the House of Usher" and uses it as an example of "the uncanny bordering on the fantastic" (*Fantastic* 47). In real life, Martín Gaite used this reference in conversations with friends, including Emilio Williams and myself. She used to joke that after she and her sister died, what would ensue would be "la caída de la Casa Usher" [the fall of the House of Usher].

Edmund Husserl (1859–1938) was a German philosopher and founding father of phenomenology, an evidence-based philosophy of knowledge predicated on the ideas of Immanuel Kant (1724–1804). The fact that Husserl was a real figure may have kept Spanish editors from recognizing this error.

10. Martín Gaite wrote this description regarding what she learned from the death of her first child with Rafael Sánchez Ferlosio. Their son Miguel died of meningitis in 1955, when he was eight months old ("Bosquejo" 232; "Sketch" 242).

11. In Spain, as in the United States, the millennial generation includes those born between 1981 and 1993—children whose parents were part of the "baby boom," born between 1949 and 1968 (summarized by Edurne Concejo in her feature on generations in Spain).

12. When Baltasar asks Bruno, "¿Eres algo mío?" [Are you anything to me?], the older man replies: "Tu amigo mayor" [Your older friend], adding "Es importante tener un amigo mayor. Yo ahora no tengo ninguno porque se me murieron." [It's important to have an older friend. I don't have any now because they all died on me] (95).

CONCLUSION

1. Martín Gaite was mentioned in Urioste's study because she contributed a short story to an anthology of the period (Laura Freixas's *Madres e hijas* [Mothers and daughters] 1996), but her novels of the 1990s were excluded because she did not publish her first work during that decade. The authors of novels included in Urioste's study were Mercedes Abad, Enriqueta Antolín, Nuria Barrios, Lola Beccaria, Graciela Bustelo, Luisa Castro, Dulce Chacón, Lucía Extebarria, Susana Fortes, Espido Freire, Milagros Frías, Belén Gopegui, Almudena Grandes, Begoña Huertas, Ángela Labordeta, Rosa Pereda, Blanca Riestra, Ana Rodríguez Fischer, Fanny Rubio, Juana Salabert, Clara Sánchez, Clara Usón, and Pilar Zapata Bosch.

2. The dedication was written on the flyleaf of a new edition of her 1974 novel *Retahílas*. The book featured a cover by Remedios Varo, the Spanish-Mexican surrealist painter whom we had discovered thanks to an exhibit in Madrid. It reads in full:

Con la novedad de una portada de Remedios Varo, esa amiga nueva para ti y para mí, que nos presentaron Natacha y Amalia [Martínez Gamero], todo unido por un hilo de horas muertas, de naturalezas muertas resucitando, de retahíla, en suma. Mientras siga la vida, sigamos con el cuento.

[With the novelty of a cover by Remedios Varo, that new friend for you and for me, introduced to us by Natacha and Amalia (Martínez Gamero), all united by the thread of idle time, of still lifes coming back to life—in sum, of a yarn. As long as life goes on, we'll go on with the story.]

Works Cited

Letters and notes from Carmen Martín Gaite and her sister Ana María (Anita) Martín Gaite, as well as book dedications from and interviews with the author, are in the possession of Joan L. Brown.

Adichie, Chimamanda Ngozi. *Dear Ijeawele, or A Feminist Manifesto in Fifteen Suggestions.* Knopf, 2017.

———. *We Should All Be Feminists.* Anchor/Random House, 2014.

Alaska. "Hicimos divertida la España de los 70 y 80." Interview with Juan Cruz, *El País,* 27 March 2016, elpais.com/cultura/2016/03/23/actualidad/1458733323_500399.html. Accessed 20 August 2020.

Aldecoa, Josefina Rodríguez de. "Notas biográficas." Ignacio Aldecoa, *Cuentos,* edited by Josefina Rodríguez de Aldecoa, Cátedra, 1977, pp. 11–23.

Allinson, Mark. "The Construction of Youth in Spain in the 1980s and 1990s." *Contemporary Spanish Cultural Studies,* edited by Barry Jordan and Rikki Morgan-Tamosunas, Oxford UP, 2000, pp. 265–273.

Almeida, Lélia. "As amigas en *Nubosdad variable* de Carmen Martín Gaite." *Espéculo: Revista de Estudios Literarios,* vol. 23, March–June 2003, webs.ucm.es/info/especulo /numero23/index.html. Accessed 20 August 2020.

Arce Castillo, Ángela. "Los conectores pragmáticos como índice de modalidad en español actual." *Estudios de Lingüística: Universidad de Alicante,* vol. 12, 1998, pp. 9–23.

Archivo Carmen Martín Gaite. Biblioteca de Castilla y León, bibliotecadigital.jcyl.es /archivo_gaite/es/micrositios/inicio.cmd. Accessed 20 August 2020.

Barnhill, Kelly. "Children's Books: Fairy Tales." *New York Times Book Review,* 19 May 2019, p. 26.

Base de datos de libros editados en España. www.mecd.gob.es/cultura-mecd/areas-cultura /libro/bases-de-datos-del-isbn/base-de-datos-de-libros.html. Accessed 20 August 2020.

Bautista Botello, Ester. *Carmen Martín Gaite: Poetics, Visual Elements and Space.* U of Wales P, 2019.

Beckett, Sandra L. *Recycling Red Riding Hood.* Routledge, 2002.

Bellver, Catherine. "Las ambigüedades de la novela feminista española." *Letras Feme-ninas*, vol. 31, no. 1, 2005, pp. 35–41.

Blanco, María-José. "The Feminism of an Antifeminist in Carmen Martín Gaite's *Cua-dernos de todo*." *Journal of Romance Studies*, vol. 9, no. 2, 2009, pp. 47–57.

———. *Life-Writing in Carmen Martín Gaite's* Cuadernos de todo *and Her Novels of the 1990s*. Tamesis, 2013.

Bravo, María Elena. "Literature as Mother and Lover: Some Reflections on Carmen Mar-tín Gaite's *La Reina de las Nieves*." *Estudios en honor a Janet Pérez: El sujeto femenino en escritoras hispánicas*, edited by Susana Cavallo, Luis A. Jiménez, and Oralia Preble-Nemi, Scripta Humanistica, 1998, pp. 215–230.

Brown, Joan L. "Carmen Martín Gaite: Los años americanos." *Un lugar llamado Carmen Martín Gaite*, edited by José Teruel and Carmen Valcárcel, Siruela, 2014, pp. 82–93.

———. "Carmen Martín Gaite: Reaffirming the Pact between Reader and Writer." *Women Writers of Contemporary Spain: Exiles in the Homeland*, edited by Joan L. Brown, U of Delaware P, 1991, pp. 72–92.

———. "Carmen Martín Gaite's *Caperucita en Manhattan*: Rescuing Red Riding Hood." *Hispania*, vol. 100, no. 2, 2017, pp. 202–212.

———. *Confronting Our Canons: Spanish and Latin American Studies in the 21st Century*. Bucknell UP, 2010.

———. "Constructing Our Pedagogical Canons." *Pedagogy*, vol. 10, no. 3, 2010, pp. 535–553.

———. "A Fantastic Memoir: Technique and History in *El cuarto de atrás*." *Anales de la literatura española contemporánea*, vol. 6, 1981, pp. 13–20.

———. Introduction. *Approaches to Teaching the Works of Carmen Martín Gaite*, edited by Joan L. Brown, Modern Language Association, 2013, pp. 3–10.

———. "The Nonconformist Character as Social Critic in the Novels of Carmen Martín Gaite." *Kentucky Romance Quarterly*, vol. 28, no. 2, 1981, pp. 165–176.

———. "*Nubosidad variable*: Postmodern Feminism in Post-Transition Spain." *His-panófila*, vol. 183, 2018, pp. 301–316.

———. "One Autobiography, Twice Told: Martín Gaite's *Entre visillos* and *El cuarto de atrás*." *Hispanic Journal*, vol. 7, no. 2, 1986, pp. 37–47.

———. "Recuerdos de Salamanca: La ciudad en la literatura de Carmen Martín Gaite." *Hispania*, vol. 102, no. 1, 2019, pp. 21–22.

———. "Rescuing Red Riding Hood: Carmen Martín Gaite's *Caperucita en Manhattan*." *Hispania*, vol. 100, no. 2, 2017, pp. 202–212.

———. "Secretos de Salamanca en *El cuarto de atrás*." *Hispania*, vol. 102, no. 1, 2019, pp. 29–31.

———. *Secrets from the Back Room: The Fiction of Carmen Martín Gaite*. Romance Monographs, 1987.

———. "*Tiempo de silencio* and *Ritmo lento*: Pioneers of the New Social Novel in Spain." *Hispanic Review*, vol. 50, no. 1, 1982, pp. 61–73.

Bush, Andrew. "Dwelling on Two Stories (Carmen Martín Gaite, María Zambrano)." *Revista de Estudios Hispánicos*, vol. 36, 2002, pp. 159–89.

Bustamante, Juby. "Bachillera Carmen Martín Gaite: 'El ser mujer nunca me ha impe-dido hacer lo que me gustaba: mirar y pensar.'" *Madrid*, 20 February 1971, pp. 8–9.

Butler, Judith. *Gender Trouble*. 1990. Routledge, 1999.

Cadden, Mike. "Genre as Nexus: The Novel for Children and Young Adults." *Handbook of Research on Children's and Young Adult Literatures*, edited by Shelly Anne Wolf, Karen Coats, Patricia Enciso, and Cristine A. Jenkins, Routledge, 2011, pp. 302–313.

Calvi, Maria Vittoria. "Poética del lugar y actitud autobiográfica de Carmen Martín Gaite." *Un lugar llamado Carmen Martín Gaite*, edited by José Teruel and Carmen Valcárcel, Siruela, 2014, pp. 124–137.

Carandell, Asunción, and Carme Riera. "Carmen Martín Gaite y su relación con los Goytisolo-Carandell." *Un lugar llamado Carmen Martín Gaite*, edited by José Teruel and Carmen Valcárcel, Siruela, 2014, pp. 36–50.

Carter, Angela. "The Company of Wolves." *The Bloody Chamber and Other Stories*, Penguin, 1993, pp. 110–118.

Castilla del Pino, Carlos. *Casa del olivo: Autobiografía, 1949–2003*. Tusquets, 2004.

Ceberio Belaza, Mónica. "El final de ETA: El dolor por 854 muertos y miles de amenazados y heridos." *El País*, 4 May 2018, elpais.com/politica/2018/05/03/actualidad/1525374369 _414522.html. Accessed 20 August 2020.

Chisholm, Kimberly. "Maternal-Filial Mirroring and Subjectivity in Carmen Martín Gaite's *Lo raro es vivir*." *Carmen Martín Gaite: Cuento de nunca acabar / Never-Ending Story*, edited by Kathleen M. Glenn and Lissette Rolón Collazo, Society of Spanish and Spanish-American Studies, 2003, pp. 109–127.

Chodorow, Nancy. *The Reproduction of Mothering: Psychoanalysis and the Sociology of Gender*. 1978. U of California P, 1999.

Ciplijauskaité, Biruté. "En busca del redondel de luz." *Carmen Martín Gaite: Cuento de nunca acabar / Never-Ending Story*, edited by Kathleen M. Glenn and Lissette Rolón Collazo, Society of Spanish and Spanish-American Studies, 2003, pp. 129–140.

Coats, Karen. "Young Adult Literature: Growing Up in Theory." *Handbook of Research on Children's and Young Adult Literatures*, edited by Shelly Anne Wolf, Coats, Patricia Enciso, and Cristine A. Jenkins, Routledge, 2011, pp. 315–330.

Colmeiro, José F. "Conjurando los fantasmas del pasado en *El cuarto de atrás*." *Carmen Martín Gaite: Cuento de nunca acabar / Never-Ending Story*, edited by Kathleen M. Glenn and Lissette Rolón Collazo, Society of Spanish and Spanish-American Studies, 2003, pp. 69–88.

———. *La novela policiaca española: Teoría e historia crítica*. Anthropos, 1994.

Concejo, Edurne. "Descubre a qué generación perteneces según tu fecha de nacimiento." *La Vanguardia*, 15 July 2018, www.lavanguardia.com/vivo/20180408/442342457884 /descubre-que-generacion-perteneces.html#galeria-foto-o. Accessed 20 August 2020.

Cruz, Jacqueline. "De *El cuarto de atrás* a *Nubosidad variable*: La conquista de la autoridad escrituraria en la obra de Carmen Martín Gaite." *La nueva mujer en la escritura de autoras hispánicas: Ensayos críticos*, edited by Juana A. Arancibia and Yolanda Rosas, Instituto Literario y Cultural Hispánico, 1995, pp. 125–142.

Cruz, Juan. "Volver a Carmiña." *El País*, Babelia, 28 June 2008, elpais.com/diario/2008 /06/28/babelia/1214610615_850215.html. Accessed 20 August 2020.

Cruz-Cámara, Nuria. "Un aspecto de la metaficción en Carmen Martín Gaite: Funciones de la *mise en abysme* en *Lo raro es vivir*." *Explicación de textos literarios*, vol. 26, no. 1, 1997, pp. 30–40.

———. *El laberinto intertextual de Carmen Martín Gaite: Un estudio de sus novelas de los noventa*. Juan de la Cuesta/Hispanic Monographs, 2008.

———. "*Nubosidad variable*: Escritura, evasión y ruptura." *Hispanófila*, vol. 126, 1999, pp. 15–24.

———. "La re-creación del romanticismo en *La Reina de las Nieves* de Carmen Martín Gaite." *Symposium*, vol. 57, no. 2, 2003, pp. 81–91.

———. "La Salamanca posmoderna de la última novela completa de Carmen Martín Gaite: *Irse de casa.*" *Hispania*, vol. 102, no. 1, 2019, pp. 32–34.

———. ¿Se movió la mujer tras la movida?" *La mujer en la España actual: ¿Evolución o involución?*, edited by Jacqueline Cruz and Barbara Zecchi, Icaria, 2004, pp. 268–294.

———. "Utopía y crítica social: Los espacios del *Romance* en *La Reina de las Nieves* de Carmen Martín Gaite." *Revista Hispánica Moderna*, vol. 58, no. 1–2, 2005, pp. 119–133.

El cultural. Libros más vendidos/Infantil, elcultural.com/libros-mas-vendidos#infantil. Accessed 20 August 2020.

Cuñado, Isabel. "Despertar tras la amnesia: Guerra civil y postmemoria en la novela española del siglo XXI." *Dissidences: Hispanic Journal of Theory and Criticism*, vol. 2, no. 2, 2012, article 8, digitalcommons.bowdoin.edu/cgi/viewcontent.cgi?article=1058&context =dissidences. Accessed 20 August 2020.

Delibes, Miguel. *USA y yo*. 2nd ed., 1970. Reprinted in *Obra completa*, vol. 4, Destino, 1975, pp. 307–514.

Díaz, Janet Winecoff. "Luis Martín-Santos and the Contemporary Spanish Novel." *Hispania*, vol. 51, no. 1, May 1968, pp. 232–238.

Echevarría, Ignacio. "Rafael Sánchez Ferlosio: La ostentación de la *españolez* me provoca náuseas (Entrevista)." *El cultural*, 27 March 2015, www.elcultural.com/revista/letras /Rafael-Sanchez-Ferlosio-La-ostentacion-de-la-espanolez-me-provoca-nauseas /36168. Accessed 20 August 2020.

EdicionesCasera. "Carmen Martin Gaite recita 'No te mueras todavía' en un concierto de Amancio Prada en el Círculo de Bellas Artes de Madrid. Una gentileza de Amancio Prada." *YouTube*, uploaded 22 May 2008, www.youtube.com/watch?v=V9fKz9b1-K8. Accessed 20 August 2020.

Encarnación, Omar G. *Democracy without Justice in Spain: The Politics of Forgetting*. U of Pennsylvania P, 2014.

Encinar, Ángeles. "'Cuentos de mujeres': El feminismo anticipado de Carmen Martín Gaite." *Carmen Martín Gaite: Cuento de nunca acabar / Never-Ending Story*, edited by Kathleen M. Glenn and Lissette Rolón Collazo, Society of Spanish and Spanish-American Studies, 2003, pp. 17–32.

Esteban del Campo, Ángel. "La obra pedagógica de Martín Gaite y José Martí." *Estudios de literatura española de los siglos XIX y XX: Homenaje a Juan María Díez Taboada*, edited by José Carlos de Torres Martínez and Cecilia García, Consejo Superior de Investigaciones Científicas, 1998, pp. 853–859.

Estrada, Isabel. "Analyzing *Los parentescos* and Preparing Students for Creative Writing." *Approaches to Teaching the Works of Carmen Martín Gaite*, edited by Joan L. Brown, Modern Language Association, 2013, pp. 173–180.

Faber, Sebastiaan. *Memory Battles of the Spanish Civil War: History, Fiction, Photography*. Vanderbilt UP, 2018.

Fernández, María Antonia. "Mujer." *Diccionario político y social del siglo XX español*, edited by Javier Fernández Sebastián and Juan Francisco Fuentes, Alianza, 2008, pp. 828–838.

Ferrán, Ofelia. "French Feminism(s) and *Écriture Féminine*: Teaching *Nubosidad variable* in a Graduate Seminar." *Approaches to Teaching the Works of Carmen Martín Gaite*, edited by Joan L. Brown, Modern Language Association, 2013, pp. 154–164.

Ferriol-Montano, Antonia. "Identificación, intercambio y libertad en la amistad femenina: La creación del 'nosotras' en *Nubosidad variable* de Carmen Martín Gaite." *Letras Femeninas*, vol. 23, no. 2, 2002, pp. 95–114.

Fuentes, Juan Francisco. "Transición." *Diccionario político y social del siglo XX español*, edited by Javier Fernández Sebastián and Juan Francisco Fuentes, Alianza, 2008, pp. 1173–1183.

Gamalla, Juan F. "Heroína en España 1977–1996: Balance de una crisis de drogas." *Researchgate.net*, 2020, www.researchgate.net/publication/242485727_Heroina_en _Espana_1977-1996_Balance_de_una_crisis_de_drogas. Accessed 20 August 2020.

García Jaén, Braulio. "Martín Gaite y Valente: Vidas hiladas." *Público*, 20 July 2010, www .publico.es/culturas/martin-gaite-y-valente-vidas.html. Accessed 20 August 2020.

Gautier, Marie-Lise Gazarian. "Conversación con Carmen Martín Gaite en Nueva York." *From Fiction to Metafiction: Essays in Honor of Carmen Martín Gaite*, edited by Mirella Servodidio and Marcia L. Welles, Society of Spanish and Spanish-American Studies, 1983, pp. 25–33.

Genette, Gérard. *Figures of Literary Discourse*. Translated by Alan Sheridan, Columbia UP, 1982.

Genevie, Louis, and Eva Margolies. *The Motherhood Report: How Women Feel About Being Mothers*. Macmillan, 1987.

Genillo, Elena. "Los Franco anuncian acciones legales si se lleva a cabo la exhumación." *La Razón*, 29 June 2018, p. 18.

Gil, Andrés. "La anomalía de España con el fascismo: Cuatro décadas de homenajes a la dictadura de Franco." *El diario*, 11 November 2018, www.eldiario.es/politica/anomalia -Espana-homenajes-dictadura-Franco_0_837466932.html. Accessed 20 August 2020.

Gillis, Stacy, Gillian Howie, and Rebecca Munford. Introduction. *Third Wave Feminism: A Critical Exploration*, edited by Gillis, Howie, and Munford, Palgrave Macmillan, 2004, pp. 1–6.

Giralt Torrente, Marcos. "Prólogo: Una novela de hoy." *Ritmo lento* by Carmen Martín Gaite. Siruela, 2010, pp. 9–13.

Gómez González, Gloria. "La novela póstuma de Martín Gaite se publicará antes de la primavera." *Cultura, La semana que vivimos*, no. 194, 5–11 February 2001, www .lasemana.es/archivo/antiguos/194/cultura/culo1.html. Accessed 20 August 2020.

Goytisolo, Juan. "La literatura perseguida por la política." *El furgón de cola*, Seix Barral, 2001, pp. 63–74.

Gracia, Jordi. "Prólogo: Expuesta al extravío." Carmen Martín Gaite, *Obras completas*, vol. 5, *Ensayos literarios*, edited by José Teruel, Espasa / Círculo de Lectores, 2016, pp. 9–29.

Gracia, Jordi, and Domingo Ródenas de Moya. *Historia de la literatura española*, vol. 7, *Derrota y restitución de la modernidad, 1939–2010*. Crítica, 2011.

Grande, Ofelia. "Caperucita en El Boalo." *Turia: Revista Cultural*, no. 83, 2007, pp. 264–266.

Guardiola, María Luisa. "*Nubosidad variable* de Carmen Martín Gaite: Renovación de la novela epistolar." *Hispania*, vol. 98, no. 4, 2015, pp. 672–673.

———. "*Lo raro es vivir*: Novelización de una historia particular/colectiva." *Letras Peninsulares* vol. 17, Fall/Winter 2004–2005, pp. 321–34.

———. "*Lo raro es vivir*: Propuesta vitalista de Carmen Martín Gaite a finales del siglo XX." *Género y géneros: Escritura y escritoras iberoamericanas*, edited by Ángeles Encinar, Eva Löfquist, and Carmen Valcárcel Rivera, Universidad Autónoma de Madrid, 2006, pp. 133–142.

———. "La Salamanca censurada de la novela *Entre visillos*." *Hispania*, vol. 102, no. 1, 2019, pp. 26–28.

Hedgecoe, Guy. "Spanish Elections: How the Far-Right Vox Party Found Its Footing." *BBC News*, 11 November 2019, www.bbc.com/news/world-europe-46422036. Accessed 20 August 2020.

Herzberger, David. *Narrating the Past: Fiction and Historiography in Postwar Spain*. Duke UP, 1995.

Heywood, Leslie, and Jennifer Drake. "'It's All about the Benjamins': Economic Determinants of Third Wave Feminism in the United States." *Third Wave Feminism: A Critical Exploration*, edited by Stacy Gillis, Gillian Howie, and Rebecca Munford, Palgrave Macmillan, 2004, pp. 13–23.

Howie, Gillian. *Between Feminism and Materialism: A Question of Method*. Palgrave Macmillan, 2010.

Ireton, Sean. *An Ontological Study of Death: From Hegel to Heidegger*. Duquesne UP, 2007.

Jacobi, Claudia. "Carmen Martín Gaite, lectrice de Marcel Proust: Variations sur la mémoire et la mort dans *Retahílas* (1974) et *El cuarto de atrás* (1978)." *Revue d'Études Proustiennes*, vol. 1, no. 7, 2018, pp. 153–174.

Johnson, Roberta. "Issues and Arguments in Twentieth-Century Spanish Feminist Theory." *Anales de la Literatura Española Contemporánea*, vol. 30, no. 1/2, 2005, pp. 243–272.

———. "Teaching Martín Gaite as a Feminist Thinker." *Approaches to Teaching the Works of Carmen Martín Gaite*, edited by Joan L. Brown, Modern Language Association, 2013, pp. 208–223.

Juliá, Santos. *Transición: Historia de una política española (1937–2017)*. Galaxia Gutenberg, 2017.

Jurado Morales, José. *Carmen Martín Gaite: El juego de la vida y la literatura*. Visor, 2018.

———. "Mundo interior versus sociedad posmoderna o una lectura de *Los parentescos* de Carmen Martín Gaite." *Revista de Estudios Hispánicos*, vol. 35, no. 1, 2002, pp. 209–225.

———. *Las razones éticas del realismo: Revista española (1953–1954) en la literatura del medio siglo*. Renacimiento, 2012.

———. "La Salamanca de los años cuarenta en los poemas de primera juventud de Carmen Martín Gaite." *Hispania*, vol. 102, no. 1, 2019, pp. 23–25.

———. *La trayectoria narrativa de Carmen Martín Gaite (1925–2000)*. Gredos, 2003.

Knight, Stephen. 2010. *Crime Fiction since 1800: Detection, Death, Diversity*. 2nd ed., Palgrave Macmillan, 2010.

Kronik, John W. "A Splice of Life: Carmen Martín Gaite's *Entre visillos*." *From Fiction to Metafiction: Essays in Honor of Carmen Martín Gaite*, edited by Mirella Servodidio and Marcia L. Welles, Society of Spanish and Spanish-American Studies, 1983, pp. 49–60.

Kübler-Ross, Elisabeth. *On Death and Dying*. Scribner's, 1969.

Labanyi, Jo. "Narrative in Culture, 1975–1996." *The Cambridge Companion to Modern Spanish Culture*, edited by David T. Gies, Cambridge UP, 1999, pp. 147–162.

Laffey, Lee-Ann. "Frente al espejo: Escritura epistolar y creación de un nuevo 'yo' en *Nubosidad variable*." *Cincinnati Romance Review*, vol. 15, 1996, pp. 90–96.

Landeira, Luigi. "'Chica de ayer': La historia de un plagio que Antonio Vega se llevó a la tumba." *El País*, 7 May 2019, elpais.com/elpais/2019/05/07/icon/1557236664_019021.html. Accessed 20 August 2020.

Lechado, José Manuel. *La Movida: Una crónica de los 80*. Algaba, 2005.

Lefebvre, Henri. *The Production of Space*. Translated by Donald Nicholson-Smith, Blackwell, 1991.

Lemon, Lee T., and Marion J. Reis. *Russian Formalist Criticism: Four Essays*. 2nd ed., U of Nebraska P, 2012.

León-Sotelo, Trinidad de. "A punto de ver la luz la novela inacabada en la que Martín Gaite trabajó hasta su muerte." ABC, Cultura, 6 February 2001, www.abc.es/cultura /abci-punto-novela-inacabada-martin-gaite-trabajo-hasta-muerte-200102060300 -10675_noticia.html. Accessed 20 August 2020.

Lewis, C. S. *A Grief Observed*. Harper Collins, 1961.

Libros más vendidos. "Libros juveniles más vendidos." www.libros-mas-vendidos.com /category/libros-juveniles-mas-vendidos/. Accessed 20 August 2020.

Luque, Alejandro. "Jorge Herralde: 'La vanidad literaria es imprescindible.'" *M'Sur*, 31 March 2016, msur.es/2016/03/31/jorge-herralde/. Accessed 20 August 2020.

Mallon, Thomas. *Yours Ever: People and Their Letters*. Vintage, 2010.

Martinell Gifre, Emma. "Ampliación de las noticias sobre Carmen Martín Gaite incluidas en el libro *Al encuentro de Carmen Martín Gaite*, Universidad de Barcelona, 1996." *Espéculo: Revista de Estudios Literarios*, 14 December 2000, webs.ucm.es/info/especulo /cmgaite/962000.html. Accessed 20 August 2020.

Martín Gaite, Ana María. "La vida se impuso a la pérdida." A La Carta, RadioTelevisión Española, 13 May 2016, www.rtve.es/alacarta/audios/24-horas/24-horas-ana-maria -martin-gaite-vida-se-impuso-perdida-13-05-16/3607713/. Accessed 20 August 2020.

Martín Gaite, Carmen. "Los amores malditos." *Pido la palabra*, Anagrama, 2002, pp. 312–324.

———. "Artículos (1949–2000)." *Obras completas*, vol. 6, *Ensayos III: Artículos, conferencias y ensayos breves*, edited by José Teruel, Espasa / Círculo de Lectores, 2017, pp. 49–547.

———. "Las ataduras." *Cuentos completos*, Alianza, 1984, pp. 89–135.

———. *The Back Room*. Translated by Helen Lane, City Lights, 2000 [translation of *El cuarto de atrás*].

———. *Behind the Curtains*. Translated by Frances M. López-Morillas, Columbia UP, 1990 [translation of *Entre visillos*].

———. "Un bosquejo autobiográfico" / "An Autobiographical Sketch," translated by Joan L. Brown. *Approaches to Teaching the Works of Carmen Martín Gaite*, edited by Brown, Modern Language Association, 2013, pp. 225–246.

———. "La búsqueda de interlocutor." *La búsqueda de interlocutor*, Anagrama, 2000, pp. 23–32.

———. *Caperucita en Manhattan*. Siruela, 1990. 55th ed., 2015.

———. "Carmen Martín Gaite: Contemplar la vida con una pluma en la mano." *Semblanzas entrevistas: Carmen Martín Gaite, Narciso Yepes, Manuel Gutiérrez Mellado*, edited by Juan Cantavella, PPC, 1995, pp. 12–90.

———. "Carta a Joan L. Brown, Madrid: 9 de enero de 1978." [Letter to Joan L. Brown, Madrid, 9 January 1978.] *Obras completas*, vol. 7, *Miscelánea*, edited by José Teruel, Espasa / Círculo de Lectores, 2019, pp. 1152–1153.

———. *El castillo de las tres murallas*. Lumen, 1981.

———. "Los confines de lo irreal. *Nuestros antepasados*, de Italo Calvino." (*Diario 16*, 7 de noviembre de 1977). *Tirando del hilo (artículos 1949–2000)*, edited by José Teruel, Siruela, 2006, pp. 140–141.

———. *Courtship Customs in Postwar Spain*. Translated by Margaret E. W. Jones, Bucknell UP, 2004 [translation of *Usos amorosos de la postguerra española*].

———. *Cuadernos de todo*. Barcelona: Areté / Random House Mondadori, 2002.

———. *El cuarto de atrás*. Siruela, 2009.

———. *El cuento de nunca acabar*. Siruela, 2009.

———. *Cuentos completos y un monólogo*. Anagrama, 1994.

———. *Desde la ventana: Enfoque femenino de la literatura española*. Espasa-Calpe, 1987.

———. *Dos cuentos maravillosos*. Círculo de Lectores, 1983.

———. *Dos relatos fantásticos*. Lumen, 1986.

———. *Esperando el porvenir: Homenaje a Ignacio Aldecoa*. Siruela, 1994.

———. *The Farewell Angel*. Translated by Margaret Jull Costa, Harvill, 1998 [translation of *La Reina de las Nieves*].

———. *La hermana pequeña*. Anagrama, 2001.

———. Interview with Maria Vittoria Calvi. *Dialogo e conversazione nella narrativa di Carmen Martín Gaite*, by Calvi, Arcipelago, 1990, pp. 165–172.

———. *Irse de casa*. Anagrama, 1998.

———. "La libertad como símbolo." *Pido la palabra*, Anagrama, 2002, pp. 138–153.

———. *Living's the Strange Thing*. Translated by Anne McClean, Harvill, 2004 [Translation of *Lo raro es vivir*].

———. *Love Customs in Eighteenth-Century Spain*. Translated by Maria G. Tomsich, U of California P, 1991 [translation of *Usos amorosos del dieciocho en España*].

———. "La memoria." [Interview]. *El mundo según las mujeres*, by Margarita Rivière Aguilar, 2000, pp. 191–193.

———. "La memoria y las memorias." *Agua pasada*. Anagrama, 1993, pp. 291–293; rpt. from *El Sol*, 11 November 1990.

———. "Las mujeres liberadas." *Triunfo*, vol. 26, no. 464, "Extra: El matrimonio," 24 April 1971, pp. 32–33. www.triunfodigital.com/mostradorn.php?a%F10=XXVI&num=464&imagen=32&fecha=1971-04-24. Accessed 20 August 2020. Reprinted in *La búsqueda de interlocutor*, pp. 96–102.

———. "Nota a la tercera edición." *Ritmo lento*, Barcelona, 1975, p. 6.

———. *Nubosidad variable*. Anagrama, 2002.

———. "Reflexiones sobre mi obra." *Pido la palabra*, Anagrama, 2002, pp. 247–265.

———. *La Reina de las Nieves*. Anagrama, 1994.

———. "Retahíla con nieve en Nueva York." *From Fiction to Metafiction: Essays in Honor of Carmen Martín Gaite*, edited by Mirella Servodidio and Marcia L. Welles, Society of Spanish and Spanish-American Studies, 1983, pp. 19–24.

———. *Ritmo lento*. Siruela, 2010.

———. *Obras completas*, vol. 1, *Novelas II (1979–2000)*. Edited by José Teruel, Galaxia Gutenberg / Círculo de Lectores, 2009.

———. "Para la publicación de *Retahílas*." *Obras completas*, vol. 6, *Ensayos III: Artículos, conferencias y ensayos breves*, edited by José Teruel, Espasa / Círculo de Lectores, 2017, pp. 1058–1064.

———. *El pastel del diablo*. Lumen, 1983.

———. Untitled speech delivered at publication party for *El cuarto de atrás*, 20 June 1978, Editorial Destino, Barcelona. Not published.

———. *Usos amorosos de la postguerra española*. Anagrama, 1987.

———. *Usos amorosos del dieciocho en España*. 1972; Anagrama, 1988.

———. *Variable Cloud*. Translated by Margaret Jull Costa, Harvill, 1995 [translation of *Nubosidad variable*].

———. "The Virtues of Reading." Translated by Marcia L. Welles, *PMLA*, vol. 10, no. 3, 1989, pp. 348–353.

———. *Visión de Nueva York*. Siruela / Círculo de Lectores, 2005.

Martín Gaite, Carmen, and Juan Benet. *Correspondencia*. Edited by José Teruel, Galaxia-Gutenberg / Círculo de Lectores, 2011.

Martín Gaite, Carmen, and Joan L. Brown. *Conversaciones creadoras: Mastering Spanish Conversation*. 4th ed., Cengage, 2016.

McCleod, Saul. "Jean Piaget's Theory of Cognitive Development." *Simply Psychology*, updated 2018, www.simplypsychology.org/piaget.html. Accessed 20 August 2020.

McHale, Susan M., Kimberly Updegraff, and Shawn D. Whiteman. "Sibling Relationships and Influences in Childhood and Adolescence." *Journal of Marriage and the Family*, vol. 74, no. 5, 2012, pp. 913–930, www.ncbi.nlm.nih.gov/pmc/articles/PMC3956653/. Accessed 20 August 2020.

Medina, Alberto. "Over a Young Dead Body: The Spanish Transition as *Bildungsroman*." *MLN*, vol. 130, no. 2, 2015, Hispanic issue, pp. 298–315.

Meisler, Stanley. "Franco's Dark Legacy Hovers over Madrid's New Regime." *Los Angeles Times*, 21 July 1996, www.latimes.com/archives/la-xpm-1996-07-21-op-26437-story.html. Accessed 20 August 2020.

Merchán Carballo, Naomi. "La generación perdida." *El País*, 21 October 2018, elpais.com/elpais/2018/10/20/opinion/1540057840_544170.html. Accessed 6 April 2020.

MLA International Bibliography. Modern Language Association, 2020, www.mla.org/Publications/MLA-International-Bibliography. Accessed 20 August 2020.

Monedero, Juan Carlos. *La Transición contada a nuestros padres: Nocturno de la democracia española*. Catarata, 2017.

Mora, Rosa. "Carmen Martín Gaite: 'Me gusta que la gente me trate como si todavía fuera una escritora nueva.'" *El País*, 21 December 1997, elpais.com/diario/1997/12/21/cultura/882658805_850215.html?id. Accessed 20 August 2020.

Morales Ladrón, Marisol. "Caperucita reescrita: *The Bloody Chamber*, de Angela Carter, y *Caperucita en Manhattan*, de Carmen Martín Gaite." *Revista canaria de estudios ingleses*, vol. 45, November 2002, pp. 169–183.

Moret, Xavier. "Carmen Martín Gaite presenta su última novela, 'Lo raro es vivir.'" *El País*, 30 May 1996, elpais.com/diario/1996/05/30/cultura/833407206_850215.html. Accessed 20 August 2020.

———. "Martín Gaite novela el deseo de la gente de 'cambiar de casas para cambiar de vida.'" *El País*, 23 May 1998, elpais.com/diario/1998/05/23/cultura/895874412_850215.html. Accessed 20 August 2020.

Navarro-Daniels, Vilma. "Carmen Martín Gaite's *Irse de casa* or the Metafictional Creation of Self." *Women in the Spanish Novel Today: Essays on the Reflection of Self in the Works of Three Generations*, edited by Kyra A. Kietrys and Montserrat Linares, McFarland, 2009, pp. 9–20.

———. "La invención interminable de la historia deseada en *Lo raro es vivir*, de Carmen Martín Gaite." *Leading Ladies: Mujeres en la literatura hispana y en las artes*, edited by Yvonne Fuentes and Margaret R. Parker, Louisiana State UP, 2006, pp. 60–69.

———. "Teaching *La Reina de las Nieves*: Metafiction, History and Student Writing." *Approaches to Teaching the Works of Carmen Martín Gaite*, edited by Joan L. Brown, Modern Language Association, 2013, pp. 165–172.

Nogueira, Charo. "La liberación de las españolas." *El País*, 5 March 2018, elpais.com /politica/2018/03/05/actualidad/1520255765_087307.html. Accessed 20 August 2020.

Odartey-Wellington, Dorothy. "De las madres perversas y las hadas buenas: Una visión sobre la imagen esencial de la mujer en las novelas de Carmen Martín Gaite y Esther Tusquets." *Anales de la Literatura Española Contemporánea*, vol. 25, no. 2, 2000, pp. 529–555.

———. "Martín Gaite y el triunfo de la imaginación en *La Reina de las Nieves*." *Hispanic Journal*, vol. 18, no. 1, 1997, pp. 79–87.

O'Leary, Catherine, and Alison Ribeiro de Menezes. *A Companion to Carmen Martín Gaite*. Tamesis, 2008.

Ordóñez, Elizabeth. "The Decoding and Encoding of Sex Roles in Carmen Martín Gaite's *Retahílas*." *Kentucky Romance Quarterly*, vol. 27, 1980, pp. 237–244.

Ordóñez, Esteban. "Heroína y Transición: ¿Narcóticos de Estado o síntoma de una sociedad rota?" *CTXT Revista Contexto y Acción*, no. 152, 17 January 2018, ctxt.es/es/20180117 /Politica/17297/Esteban-Ordo%C3%B1ez-heroina-estado-espa%C3%B1a-arriola-droga .htm. Accessed 20 August 2020.

Oropesa, Salvador. "*Nubosidad variable* de Carmen Martín Gaite: Una alternativa ética a la cultura del pelotazo." *Letras Peninsulares*, vol. 8, no. 1, 1995, pp. 55–72.

Parker, Margaret R. "Revisiting Spain as Liberation from the Past in 'Irse de casa' and 'A Woman Unknown': Voices from a Spanish Life." *South Central Review*, vol. 18, nos. 1–2, Spain Modern and Postmodern at the Millenium (spring–summer 2001), pp. 114–126.

Penna, Rosa E. M. "*La Reina de las Nieves*: De Hans Christian Andersen a Carmen Martín Gaite." *El cuento*, Homenaje a María Teresa Mairoana, 12–15 October 1995, pp. 254–259.

Pérez, Janet. "*Nubosidad variable*: Carmen Martín Gaite and Women's Words." *Inti: Revista de Literatura Hispánica*, vol. 40–41, 1994–1995, pp. 301–315.

———. "Presencia de la 'quest-romance' en las últimas obras de Carmen Martín Gaite." *Escribir mujer: Narradoras españolas hoy. Actas del XIII Congreso de Literatura Española Contemporánea*, edited by Cristóbal Cuevas García, U of Málaga P, 2000, pp. 89–111.

———. "Structural, Thematic and Symbolic Mirrors in *El cuarto de atrás* and *Nubosidad variable* of Martín Gaite." *South Central Review*, vol. 12, no. 1, 1995, pp. 47–63.

Pérez Cavero, Carlos. "Carmen Martín Gaite, la literatura como sucedáneo." *Diario de Barcelona de la cultura*, 8 March 1978, pp. iv–v.

Pérez-Magallón, Jesús. "Más allá de la metaficción: El placer de la ficción en *Nubosidad variable*." *Hispanic Review*, vol. 63, no. 2, 1995, pp. 179–181.

Pitarello, Elide. "Prólogo: Las últimas novelas de Carmen Martín Gaite." Carmen Martín Gaite, *Obras completas*, vol. 2, *Novelas II (1979–2000)*, edited by José Teruel, Galaxia Gutenberg / Círculo de Lectores, pp. 9–45.

PopulationPyramid.net "Spain, 1985." www.populationpyramid.net/spain/1985/. Accessed 20 August 2020.

Prego, Victoria. *Así se hizo la Transición*. Plaza & Janés, 1995.

Preston, Paul. *A People Betrayed: A History of Corruption, Political Incompetence, and Social Division in Modern Spain*. Liverwright/Norton, 2020.

———. *The Spanish Civil War: Reaction, Revolution and Revenge*. Norton, 2006.

Pucheu, Jeannette. "The Home as Palimpsest: *Nubosidad variable*, *Lo raro es vivir* and *Irse de casa*." *Beyond the Back Room: New Perpsectives on Carmen Martín Gaite*, edited by Marian Womack and Jennifer Wood, Peter Lang, 2011, pp. 109–134.

Puértolas, Ana, and Rafael Chirbes. "Carmen Martín Gaite: Verbo-sujeto-predicado." *La Calle*, vol. 28, 3–9 October 1978.

RTVE. Radiotelevisión Española: "La heroína, el mal que se llevó por delante a la generación de la Movida." Trailer for *Cuéntame cómo pasó*, 9 April 2015, www.rtve.es/television/20150409/heroina-mal-se-llevo-delante-generacion-movida/1125875.shtml. Accessed 20 August 2020.

Ramil, Ana. "La personalidad resistente de los gallegos." *La Opinión A Coruña*, 18 February 2010, www.laopinioncoruna.es/sociedad/2010/02/18/personalidad-resistente-gallegos/359611.html. Accessed 20 August 2020.

Resina, Joan Ramon. "Faltos de memoria: La reclamación del pasado desde la Transición española a la democracia." *Memoria literaria de la Transición española*, edited by Javier Gómez-Montero, Veuvert, 2007, pp. 17–50.

Ribeiro de Menezes, Alison. "New York as 'Portico' in Martín Gaite's Late Work." *Espéculo: Revista de Estudios Literarios*, no. 52, January–June 2014, pp. 48–56.

Riera, Carmen. "Cuando las mujeres tengan papeles predominantes, le aseguro que habrá más mujeres en la RAE." Interview on Sin Claqueta, 3 April 2018, *YouTube*, www.youtube.com/watch?v=LPyjJEMGeHM. Accessed 20 August 2020.

El rincón del vago. "*Caperucito en Manhattan*; Carmen Martín Gaite." html.rincondelvago.com/caperucita-en-manhattan_carmen-martin-gaite_3.html. Accessed 20 August 2020.

Rodríguez, Maria Elena, and M. Douglas Anglin. "The Epidemiology of Illicit Drug Use in Spain." *Bulletin on Narcotics* (United Nations Office on Drugs and Crime, UNODC), vol. 39, no. 2, January 1987, pp. 67–74, www.ncbi.nlm.nih.gov/pubmed/3502392. Accessed 20 August 2020.

Roger, Isabel. "*Caperucita en Manhattan* (Nota)." *Revista Hispánica Moderna*, vol. 45, no. 2, December 1992, pp. 328–331.

Rolón Collazo, Lissette. "Fairy Tales and Rewriting: Teaching *Caperucita en Manhattan*." *Approaches to Teaching the Works of Carmen Martín Gaite*, edited by Joan L. Brown, Modern Language Association, 2013, pp. 139–146.

Roth, Marty. *Foul & Fair Play: Reading Genre in Classic Detective Fiction*. U of Georgia P, 1995.

Rzepka, Charles J. *Detective Fiction*. Polity, 2005.

Salas, Roberto. "Martín Gaite, *Irse de casa*, fragmento." Veladas Literarias, Centro Cultural del Círculo de Lectores, Madrid, November 1998. *YouTube*, posted 21 April 2013, www.youtube.com/watch?v=SX_CngFgC4M. Accessed 20 August 2020.

Sánchez Soler, Mariano. *La Transición sangrienta: Una historia violenta del proceso democrático en España (1975–1983)*. 2nd ed., Ediciones Península, 2018.

Santodomingo Carrasco, Joaquín. "Historia de las adicciones y su abordaje en España." *Historia de las adicciones en la España contemporánea*, edited by Miguel Ángel Torres

Hernández, Gobierno de España, Ministerio de Sanidad y Consumo, 2009, pp. 37–82, www.pnsd.mscbs.gob.es/en/profesionales/publicaciones/catalogo/bibliotecaDigital /publicaciones/pdf/HistoriaAdicciones_EspContem.pdf. Accessed 20 August 2020.

Sarmatti, Elisabetta. "Visiones de Nueva York en *Caperucita en Manhattan* de CMG." *Espéculo: Revista de Estudios Literarios*, no. 52, January–June 2014, pp. 57–70, webs.ucm. es/info/especulo/Carmen_Martin_Gaite_Especulo_52_2014_UCM.pdf. Accessed 20 August 2020.

Saum-Pascual, Alex. "Carmen Martín Gaite: Una provocación desde la cultura digital." *Hispania*, vol. 98, no. 4, December 2015, pp. 674–675.

Schwartz, Alexandra. "Love Is Not a Permanent State of Enthusiasm: An Interview with Esther Perel." *New Yorker*, 9 December 2018, www.newyorker.com/culture/the-new -yorker-interview/love-is-not-a-permanent-state-of-enthusiasm-an-interview-with -esther-perel. Accessed 20 August 2020.

Seco, Manuel. "La lengua coloquial: 'Entre visillos' de Carmen Martín Gaite." *El comentario de textos*, vol. 1, 1973, pp. 361–379.

Seisdedos, Iker. "En la cueva del tesoro de Anagrama." *El Pais*, Babelia, 29 March 2019, elpais.com/cultura/2019/03/29/babelia/1553884343_304731.html. Accessed 20 August 2020.

Snyder, R. Claire. "What Is Third Wave Feminism? A New Directions Essay." *Signs*, vol. 34, no. 1, 2008, pp. 175–196.

Soja, Edward William. *Thirdspace: Journeys to Los Angeles and Other Real-and-Imagined Places*. Basil Blackwell, 1996.

Soliño, María Elena. "Los cuentos de hadas de Carmen Martín Gaite: La voz femenina domina al lobo de la tradición." *Carmen Martín Gaite: Cuento de nunca acabar / Never-Ending Story*, edited by Kathleen M. Glenn and Lissette Rolón Collazo, Society of Spanish and Spanish-American Studies, 2003, pp. 197–213.

Soriano, Juan Carlos. "Ana María Martín Gaite: 'nadie, ni siquiera yo, conoció del todo a Carmiña.'" *Turia*, no. 83, June–October 2007, pp. 267–279.

Stone, P.W.K. Introduction. Choderlos de Laclos, *Les liaisons dangereuses*, translated by Stone, Penguin, 1961, pp. 7–14

Sullivan, Constance A. "The Boundary-Crossing Essays of Carmen Martín Gaite." *The Politics of the Essay: Feminist Perspectives*, edited by Ruth-Ellen Boetcher Joeres and Elizabeth Mittman, Indiana UP, 1993, pp. 41–56.

Teruel, José. "Biografía de Carmen Martín Gaite." Archivo Carmen Martín Gaite, Biblioteca de Castilla y León, www.archivomartingaite.es/#biograf%C3%ADa. Accessed 20 August 2020.

———. "Un contexto biográfico para *Caperucita en Manhattan* de Carmen Martín Gaite." *Género y géneros: Escritura y escritoras iberoamericanas*, vol. 2, edited by Ángeles Encinar, Eva Löfquist, and Carmen Valcárcel, Universidad Autónoma, 2006, pp. 143–151.

———. "Ficción autobiográfica de tres mujeres: *Nubosidad variable*." *Confluencia: Revista Hispánica de Cultura y Literatura*, vol. 13, no. 1, 1997, pp. 64–72.

———. "Introducción: Nombres y tramos para una vida en 'obras.'" Carmen Martín Gaite, *Obras completas*, vol. 1, *Novelas I (1975–1978)*, edited by José Teruel, Galaxia Gutenberg / Círculo de Lectores, 2008, pp. 9–54.

———. "Notas: *Los parentescos*." Carmen Martín Gaite, *Obras completas*, vol. 2, *Novelas II (1979–2000)*, edited by José Teruel, Galaxia Gutenberg / Círculo de Lectores, 2009, pp. 1531–1532.

———. "*Ritmo lento* and Carmen Martín Gaite's Role in the Renewal of the Spanish Novel of the 1960s." *Approaches to Teaching the Works of Carmen Martín Gaite*, edited by Joan L. Brown, Modern Language Association, 2013, pp. 60–70.

Tibbitts, Amy L. "Laying Down the Map: Tracing the Self through the City in Carmen Martín Gaite's *Lo raro es vivir*." *Hispanófila*, vol. 165, May 2012, pp. 67–85.

Thomas, Michael D. "'El callejón sin salida': Images of Confinement and Freedom in *Ritmo lento*." *From Fiction to Metafiction: Essays in Honor of Carmen Martín Gaite*, edited by Mirella Servodidio and Marcia L. Welles, Society of Spanish and Spanish-American Studies, 1983, pp. 61–72.

Todorov, Tzvetan. *The Fantastic: A Structural Approach to a Literary Genre*. Translated by Richard Howard, Cornell UP, 1975.

———. "The Typology of Detective Fiction." *The Poetics of Prose*. Translated by Richard Howard, Cornell UP, 1977, pp. 42–52.

Tolliver, Joyce. "The Geography of Time: Martín Gaite's *Irse de casa*." *Disciplines on the Line: Feminist Research on Spanish, Latin American, and U.S. Latina Women*, edited by Anne J. Cruz, Rosilie Hernández-Pecoraro, and Joyce Tolliver, Juan de la Cuesta, 2003, pp. 257–268.

Turpín, Enrique. "*La Reina de las Nieves*: Carmen Martín Gaite y la lírica aplicada." *Quimera*, vol. 128, 1994, pp. 50–56.

Umbral, Francisco. *La década roja*. Planeta, 1993.

Urioste, Carmen de. "Narrative of Spanish Women Writers of the Nineties: An Overview." *Tulsa Studies in Women's Literature*, vol. 20, no. 2, Autumn 2001, pp. 279–296.

Uriz, Amaia. "Entrevista a Carmen Martín Gaite. Soria, 5 de julio de 1998." *Iguazú: Revista artesanal de literatura y cultura*, 12 March 2007, revistaiguazu.wordpress.com /2007/03/12/entrevista-a-carmen-martin-gaite/. Accessed 20 August 2020.

Uxó González, Carlos. "El interlocutor en *La Reina de las Nieves* de Carmen Martín Gaite." *Journal of Iberian and Latin American Studies*, vol. 5, no. 1, 1999, pp. 59–71, www .tandfonline.com/doi/abs/10.1080/13260219.1999.10429962. Accessed 20 August 2020.

Vilarós, Teresa M. *El mono del desencanto: Una crítica cultural de la transición española (1973–1993)*. Siglo Veintiuno, 1998.

Villán, Javier. "Carmen Martín Gaite: Habitando el tiempo." *La Estafeta Literaria*, vol. 549, 1 October 1974, pp. 21–23.

Welles, Marcia L. "Review of *Nubosidad variable* by Carmen Martín Gaite." *Revista Hispánica Moderna*, vol. 47, no.1, June 1994, pp. 256–259.

Wilson, Caroline. "Restoration of the Maternal Order. A Circle of Infinite? The Mother-Daughter Relationship in Carmen Martín Gaite's *Lo raro es vivir*." *Bulletin of Hispanic Studies*, vol. 89, no. 7, 2012, pp. 712–720.

Wlodarczyk, Justyna. *Ungrateful Daughters: Third Wave Feminist Writings*. Cambridge Scholars Publishing, 2010.

Womack, Marian, and Jennifer Wood, eds. *Beyond the Back Room: New Perspectives on Carmen Martín Gaite*. Peter Lang, 2011.

Woolf, Virginia. *A Room of One's Own*. Harcourt Brace Jovanovich, 1929.

Young Adult Library Services Association, USA. www.ala.org/yalsa/aboutyalsa. Accessed 20 August 2020.

Index

About the Author

Joan L. Brown holds the Elias Ahuja Chair of Spanish at the University of Delaware in Newark, Delaware. She graduated from Vassar College with a degree in Hispanic Studies and earned MA and PhD degrees in Romance languages–Spanish from the University of Pennsylvania. Her publications have explored canon formation, literature by women, the contemporary Spanish novel, and language and literature pedagogy. Previous books include *Secrets from the Back Room: The Fiction of Carmen Martín Gaite*, *Women Writers of Contemporary Spain: Exiles in the Homeland* (editor), *Confronting Our Canons: Spanish and Latin American Literature in the 21st Century*, *Approaches to Teaching the Works of Carmen Martín Gaite* (editor), and, with Carmen Martín Gaite, the textbook *Conversaciones creadoras: Mastering Spanish Conversation*.